CHUTNEFYING ENGLISH

CHUTNEFYING ENGLISH
The Phenomenon of Hinglish

Edited by

RITA KOTHARI
RUPERT SNELL

PENGUIN BOOKS

PENGUIN BOOKS
Published by the Penguin Group
Penguin Books India Pvt. Ltd, 11 Community Centre, Panchsheel Park,
New Delhi 110 017, India
Penguin Group (USA) Inc., 375 Hudson Street, New York, New York 10014, USA
Penguin Group (Canada), 90 Eglinton Avenue East, Suite 700, Toronto,
Ontario, M4P 2Y3, Canada (a division of Pearson Penguin Canada Inc.)
Penguin Books Ltd, 80 Strand, London WC2R 0RL, England
Penguin Ireland, 25 St Stephen's Green, Dublin 2, Ireland
(a division of Penguin Books Ltd)
Penguin Group (Australia), 250 Camberwell Road, Camberwell,
Victoria 3124, Australia (a division of Pearson Australia Group Pty Ltd)
Penguin Group (NZ), 67 Apollo Drive, Rosedale, Auckland 0632,
New Zealand (a division of Pearson New Zealand Ltd)
Penguin Group (South Africa) (Pty) Ltd, 24 Sturdee Avenue, Rosebank,
Johannesburg 2196, South Africa

Penguin Books Ltd, Registered Offices: 80 Strand, London WC2R 0RL, England

First published by Penguin Books India 2011

Foreword copyright © Harish Trivedi 2011
Introduction copyright © Rita Kothari and Rupert Snell 2011
The copyright for the individual pieces vests with the authors

All rights reserved

10 9 8 7 6 5 4 3 2 1

ISBN 9780143416395

Typeset in Cambria by SŪRYA, New Delhi
Printed at Replika Press Pvt. Ltd, Sonepat

CONTENTS

FOREWORD

Harish Trivedi

This conference on Hinglish[1] is doubly innovative. First, it is to the best of my knowledge, and as indeed it claims to be, 'India ka pehla conference' on Hinglish (except that my native-speaker UP instinct tells me that should read 'ki pehli'). It thus focuses in a serious and sustained manner on the coming together of, and the dialogic intercourse between, Hindi and English, the two power languages of India. Second, and no less important, it brings together in terms of participants two distinct and mutually exclusive worlds—that of academic discourse, here represented by the university disciplines of Hindi, English, sociology, anthropology, and perhaps a couple of others, and that of popular and commercial communication, here represented by eminent practitioners of cinema, advertising, and media. This is not to forget, of course, many younger participants currently studying media and communication as a discipline at the institution hosting this conference. One set of participants has descended from ivory towers, the other has emerged from golden palaces, and it is only apt that we should meet here in a five-star hotel in the commercial capital of India. To push the stakes, one could suggest that this conference represents a remarkable conjunction of Saraswati and Lakshmi—believed to be goddesses of such opposite domains that no man or woman can hope to be blessed by both! Regardless of whether or not we at this conference are going to be doubly blessed, it is a double pleasure and privilege for me to be here.

Defining 'Hinglish'

To begin with a basic question: What is Hinglish? It is obviously a mixture of Hindi and English—but is it the use of Hindi words and syntactical elements in English, or the use of English words and syntax in Hindi? The name Hinglish sounds far more like English than like Hindi. In terms of orthography, of its eight letters, it has six in common with English and only two with Hindi. In terms of pronunciation, it is just like English (in which word the initial 'E' is of course pronounced as 'I'), with just the H of Hindi prefixed to it. In fact, I suspect that a vast proportion of the population of England, when asked to enunciate Hinglish will probably produce a sound that most Indians would hear as 'Inglish. Remember the ravishingly lower-class Eliza Doolittle, the eponymous *My Fair Lady*, whom Professor Henry Higgins (or 'Enry 'Iggins as she calls him), assiduously trains to pronounce the initial 'H' with the help of a mnemonic drill: 'In Hartford, Hereford and Hampshire, hurricanes hardly happen.' In fact, in comparison with the comprehensively (h)imitative Hinglish, even an obviously cloned term such as 'Bollywood' begins to look good, for the British at least pronounce their Bs, even though they may sound to us (with our fifty-six letters of the Devanagari alphabet) more like Bhs!

In the interest of transparency, this may be the moment to reveal that long before this conference could begin, the organizers and the invited speakers were already sparring over just what Hinglish means. The plot thickened when it was revealed that the two conference coordinators, my old friends Rita Kothari and Rupert Snell, themselves held somewhat divergent views on the question. It began with Professor Snell (or, as we may say in Hinglish, Mr Rupert) turning out to be the one and only participant to submit his paper by the announced deadline some time before the conference—thus confirming the venerable but also amusing stereotype that the British are pathologically punctual while we Indians live in eternal or, worse, circular time. I promptly read his paper with the vested interest of stealing some ideas from it to kickstart my own paper but found that it was all about English-in-Hindi and not Hindi-in-English! Thus fortified in my own inclinations on the subject, I wrote off to the two coordinators (as well as about a dozen other participants on that mailing list) to ask: 'Is our conference going to be on the incursion of English into Hindi, i.e. Beefing Up Hindi, as your [Snell's] paper suggests, or on the incursion of Hindi into desi English, i.e. "Chutnefying English", as earlier communications and the posh venue suggest?'

A flurry of emails followed within hours. Rupert replied: 'My understanding of our forthcoming debate is that we are to discuss the relationship between two (or more?) contending languages and, if this is correct, it would seem legitimate to pick the matter up and look at it from various different angles before putting it down again . . . If you feel that these "up" and "down" escalators don't belong in the same building then what am I to say? But isn't it rewarding to watch the snakes turning into ladders and vice versa? . . . Regarding "chutnefy" and "Hinglish", I feel that neither term helps our discussions much; they are too hip and journalistic to allow for a cool-headed discussion of these interesting matters. But I always was behind the times.'

Whereupon Dr Rita Kothari came in to give a clear, decisive ruling: 'The debate on Hinglish could be on either end, Hindi mein English or English in Hindi, the two are not mutually exclusive. The idea of naming the conference "Chutnefying" was to suggest a larger framework of hybridization of English worldwide which can provide an overarching context. However this context is not to be viewed without the permeation of English in Indian languages (including Hindi) that takes place at the ground level. Please feel free to make your observations at the conference on any aspect of this language axis, five-star hotel notwithstanding . . . As for Rupert's discomfort with Hinglish, which is both hip and journalistic, I only wish to ask— so? Does that mean it's not worth discussing or not worth naming that way? If it's the latter, this is the forum to contest it, *hai naa*?'

I must confess that now that the conference has got under way, I still have my doubts. Who cares what happens to Hindi except that routinely derided community called the Hindiwallas (and one or two dedicated and stunningly erudite professors of Hindi abroad such as dear Rupert), so this forum here must be all about the state of English. It would have been a very different discourse, it occurs to me, if the host and the venue had been, say, a mofussil university campus in the so-called Hindi belt and we had been seated on creaky chairs under loudly whirring fans, which would have gone off altogether during the frequent power cuts. But let us not anticipate or prejudge, for soon enough, over the next couple of days, we will know which way the tide flows—whether the Ganga flows down to the sea or is made to flow *ulti*, backwards, to the Himalaya.

Basic Issues

Following this preliminary attempt at establishing a semblance of terminological exactitude, it may be best to proceed by asking a set of basic questions about Hinglish.

1. Would the definition of Hinglish and the discourse on it depend on who is asking this question and where the questioner is coming from—as illustrated in the email exchanges cited above?
2. When did Hinglish come into existence? Is it a recent and unprecedented development, quite as exciting and innovative as some of us believe it to be, or can it be seen historically as a part of the larger interaction of languages in modern India?
3. What is the need that Hinglish serves? What are the kinds of effects it produces?
4. Are there several distinct varieties of Hinglish, or is it pretty much the same all over India?
5. In Hinglish, which language has the upper hand? Does not Hinglish constitute a particularly rich site for investigating the state of power relations between our two official languages as they have jostled with each other for public space over the last sixty years?

6. How will the growth of Hinglish impact on the health and future well-being of both Hindi and English in our country, and is it possible to make any projections or predictions in this regard?

7. And finally, the bottom-line question: Is Hinglish a good thing? Where do we stand, each one of us, and for what reasons, on the growth of the phenomenon we have gathered here to expound and debate?

I do not have the time, the competence, or even the ambition to answer all or even most of the questions I have listed here but I can perhaps attempt at least to set the ball rolling. Given that I am an academic by profession, perhaps the last thing that most of the younger members of my audience may wish to be, what I am most inclined to do is to take a long look at Hinglish by (1) historicizing it, (2) locating it geographically, culturally, and in terms of social strata or class, (3) by comparing it with similar hybrid linguistic developments in the past such as Urdu, and finally (4) by projecting into the future to speculate what might happen if Hinglish were to grow to become an Indian lingua franca.

On the first question, even if one accepts for the sake of argument that the term Hinglish denotes equally the introduction of Hindi words into English and vice versa, should not one still try and disambiguate these two distinct, indeed opposite, trends in terms of their scale and scope? In my observation and experience, the Hindi we may find in English is peanuts compared with the English we find in Hindi; in the battle for hybridity, Hindi wins hands down. The enormous influence of English, not only in terms of the countless English words used in Hindi but also in terms of the transformation of Hindi syntax, modes of speech, idiom, and indeed sensibility may not be fully apparent to those of us who operate mostly in English but is a matter of the utmost anxiety to all those others of us who regularly speak, read and even write in Hindi. We will in this conference hear more about it from a couple of speakers, including that long-time Hindi-*premi* Rupert Snell and I shall myself return to this later in this paper.

A History of Hinglish

When did Hinglish begin to emerge and for what reasons? Evidence suggests that this may have begun as soon as Hindi and English began to inhabit the same geographical space— with the coming of the British to India. For languages do not exist in watertight compartments; they are organic things and when placed alongside each other they always interact. In fact, languages feed on each other almost cannibalistically; if they did not, they would die. Allow me to read out a few lines from a *ghazal* illustrating such interaction:

> *Rent Law ka gham karen ya Bill of Income Tax ka?*
> *Kya karen apna nahiin hai sense right now-a-days.*
> *... Darkness chhaaya hua hai Hind men chaaro taraf*
> *Naam ki bhi hai nahiin baaqi na light now-a-days.*

In this *ghazal* what is remarkable is that not only the *qafiya* but also the *radeef* (i.e., not only the penultimate rhyme words, 'right' and 'light' but also the ultimate one, 'now-a-days') are in English—reinforcing the comic and satiric effects. This ghazal was written in 1887 by Ayodhya Prasad Khatri (1857–1905), one of the most vigorous champions that (Khari Boli) Hindi ever had. In those linguistically fluid and fiercely contested times, he distinguished between five kinds of Hindi: Theth Hindi (common mainstream Hindi), Pandit's Hindi (Sanskritized Hindi), Munshi's Hindi (a watered-down form of Urdu that the European administrator-scholars called 'Hindustani'), Maulvi's Hindi (replete with Arabic and Persian words), and Eurasian Hindi, in which 'difficult English words are imported' (Khatri; fuller discussion in Trivedi 2003: 982–83).

So what's new about Hinglish when it was already being written 120 years ago? What is perhaps new in our situation is that the Maulvi's Hindi has withered away, the Munshi's Hindi has shrunk and shrivelled as well, and Theth Hindi has occupied the space vacated by these two obsolete varieties while also taking on elements of Pandit's Hindi. As for Eurasian Hindi— and we mustn't miss the racial slur here—it is now more than a constructed one-off joke as in Khatri, for it has become a cultish dialect with enough practitioners for us to notice it and debate it. Incidentally, Khatri wrote another poem, which contains the line:

Ja ke London mein badal daalenge nation apna

That is a would-be diasporic cry that many of the younger members of the audience may be inclined to echo only too earnestly—though Khatri himself was, of course, mocking such slavish aspirations.

To view Hinglish from the other end, from not a Hindi but an English point of view, Nissim Ezekiel (1924–2004)—long-time poet laureate of Indian English or at least of a coterie of Anglophone poets in Bombay—wrote a string of poems which he called 'Very Indian Poems in Indian English'. That these have proved to be among the most widely cited and most memorable poems of Ezekiel is ironical, for the high serious poet Ezekiel seems to have written them as a lark and in a light, comic, and mocking tone. Let me cite two familiar passages (both from Ezekiel 1988):

> *Why all people of world*
> *Are not following Mahatma Gandhi,*
> *I am simply not understanding.*
> *Ancient Indian Wisdom is 100% correct,*
> *I should say even 200% correct.*
> *But modern generation is neglecting—*
> *Too much going for fashion and foreign thing.*

Or a passage even more pertinent to our purpose:

> *That shopman he's giving me soap*
> *But I'm finding it defective version.*
> *So I'm saying very politely—*
> *though in Hindi I'm saying it,*
> *and my Hindi is not so good as my English,*
> *Please to excuse me . . .*

Of course, Ezekiel makes one laugh—that's the first reaction—because he unerringly catches some common characteristics of low-competence Indian English such as the use of present continuous instead of the simple present and a shadow of the Hindi word-order even in English. (It is notable at the same time that he seldom uses a Hindi word so that, strictly speaking, this may not be Hinglish.) He also hits squarely—if he does not clobber with a sledgehammer—some other nails on the head, such as sanctimonious piety, simple patriotism, pretentious diction, and even attitude. But the trouble is that all this comes tied up as part of the same package, and the medium is for most readers the more comic because it delivers that kind of message. The implication is: this is how people think who think in incorrect and un-pucca Indian English.

It has been argued by some critics, including G.J.V. Prasad (who is present here), that these are 'tragic poems' as their protagonists are obliged 'to use the very language that is both the cause and the symptom of their dispossession' (Prasad 2008: 505). But then, in the second poem cited above, the protagonist is self-avowedly speaking not in English but in Hindi—because in the kind of commonplace everyday situation described in the poem, even his kind of English would be utterly incomprehensible to his interlocutor, the shopkeeper. In other similar poems too, it appears that if such low-class characters presume to speak in English at all, they are committing a major social transgression.

Put simply, this is arrogance and snobbery of the worst order and a condescending joke that Ezekiel asks his readers to share who, like him, are assumed to be smug in their belief that unlike these poor hoi polloi, they use an English that is not 'Indian English'; nor are they themselves 'very Indian'. Incidentally, if these poems are—in Ezekiel's own description—written in 'Indian English', what did he think all his other poems were in—British English? Did his own English become un-Indian forever after just because he had lived in Britain for a few years, from 1948 to 1952, but then was obliged to return to India with his diasporic tail between his Indian legs, having to travel as 'a deck-scrubber and coal-carrier aboard a cargo ship'? (Anklesaria 2008: xvii)

Khatri and Ezekiel represent the two poles of Indian attitudes to English and its Indianization. Khatri has the sturdiness of a propagator of Hindi, and though he lives in an India under British rule at the high noon of Empire, he displays a robust native confidence with which he satirizes the anglicized upper-class Indian, his little upper-class worries (rent law, income tax), and his ultimate cloud-cuckoo escape clause—the ship to London: *Ja ke London mein badal daalenge nation apna.* Ezekiel, on the other hand, *is* that anglicized Indian, leaving a free India to go and try out London and only too willing to laugh at Indians whose English is not as good as his own.

The Uses of Hinglish

The earliest example of a sustained, non-parodic use of Hinglish I encountered was in the 1960s in Shobhaa Dé's gossip column 'Nita's Natter' in the film magazine *Stardust*; it became her first claim to a sort of cliquish fame. In talking about Hindi films and film stars, she peppered her text with common Hindi words just to spice it up. As I recall it, the cattiest words were in Hindi, not because Hindi has a better vocabulary in that regard (or perhaps it does!) but because in gossiping about that most popular of all our forms of entertainment—the Hindi film—only Hindi words could convey the real zing and sting. The films were all in Hindi but the magazine was all in English, and it was in an attempt to resolve this linguistic misalliance that natty Nita felt obliged to go slumming in the language of the masses. It was high culture stooping of necessity to low culture.

This was, of course, well before the rise of cultural studies—the highly jargonized and theoretically abstruse academic discourse in English, which must pay (often patronizing) attention to forms of popular culture in a popular language. This was also before the rise of horribly expensive and exclusive multiplexes, which have increasingly snatched movie-going away from its earlier popular constituency, the proverbial rickshaw-wallas in their six-anna seats, clapping and whistling through the show and watching the same film ten or twenty times so that some films celebrated silver, golden, or diamond jubilees; *Sholay* ran in the same theatre here in Bombay for seven continuous years. For those who now pay more like 150 rupees for a seat, and a lot more for popcorn and soda, movie-going is not a popular carnival but what in English is called an evening out—a phrase for which, incidentally, there is no Hindi equivalent. The elephant of popular movie-going in India has been turned into a poodle, and only reruns and song-and-dance clips on TV now reach the poor masses.

If the duchy of Hinglish ever needed to have a capital, it would have to be Bombay—founded by the British and always more culturally vulnerable than Chennai or even the old British capital Calcutta, where the local languages were far more deeply entrenched. Mumbai (and thank God—and especially Mumba Devi!—that the local name in the local language that has always been in use by an overwhelming majority, together with its Hindi variation Bambai, has now dethroned the nonsensical British name) is now the most commercial, the most anglicized, and also the most linguistically mixed of all our major cities, and thus the ideal breeding ground for Hinglish. It thus seems no coincidence that while Shobhaa Dé, the Queen Mother of Hinglish, has flourished here, the reigning King-Emperor of Hinglish, Salman Rushdie, was born and brought up here in 'Bombay' as well (for he is the kind of person one cannot imagine being born in 'Mumbai')—until he left at the tender age of thirteen for a place even more *angrez*—England, actually!

It is Rushdie who claimed that it was his linguistic agenda and practice to 'chutnefy English'—a *chatpati* self-enacting phrase for linguistic hybridization which has attained international academic currency and is, perhaps predictably, emblazoned on the banner of our conference here. Let us stop and analyse this phrase for a moment. What proportion of a meal can the chutney be—2 per cent, 5 per cent, more? Has chutney by itself ever filled a stomach? Does chutney offer substantial nutrition and sustenance or does it merely stir up the taste buds? And isn't chutney an optional extra, a relish on the side, and indeed a luxury for those still starving millions among our fellow citizens who can't even raise two bare meals of *roti–daal* every day?

Let us also see how, though it is a familiar part of our own cuisine, *chutney* proved to be heady stuff for the Englishmen who ruled us and helped redeem their own bland food from its notorious inedibility. *Hobson-Jobson,* a 1,000-page dictionary published in 1886 of words from the Indian languages that were already in use by then by the British in India, describes 'chutny' as 'a kind of strong relish ... the merits of which are now well known in England' (Yule & Burnell 1986). But what are the merits of the *chutney* of Indian words that Rushdie sought to supplement his English with (which is presumably even more British and bland than Ezekiel's) and what was the effect he intended to produce on his implied reader through this stylistic innovation?

It appears that the effect of Rushdie's Hinglish has been quite different from that achieved by Shobhaa Dé, because Rushdie's reader is very different. Dé wrote right here for us in India; Rushdie has been writing over there for them lot. Dé used Hindi words to reconnect with her subject matter and her reader; Rushdie uses Hinglish to exoticize his subject matter as well as the Indian languages. More important, he uses the small change of a few Hindi words to authenticate himself in the eyes of his Western readers, for he knows these words and they do not—and never mind that they do not know just how little he knows of Hindi or indeed of India. I had occasion once to demonstrate how in *Midnight's Children* he repeatedly gets wrong the meaning of a simple word such as *funtoosh,* a popular word made current by the film of the same title starring Dev Anand, in whose own description the film was 'a farcical comedy to the hilt' and 'fun, fun, fun all the way', with the title (which itself incorporated 'fun') being a characterization of the hero as basically a 'buffoon' (Anand 2007: 154–55). This film was released and became a hit in 1956 when Rushdie was nine and still living in Bombay, though he apparently continues to believe that its title word means 'finished', which is the sense in which he repeatedly uses it in his novel (Trivedi 1999: 69–94). This is an abyss of ignorance that Hinglish speakers are often likely to fall into, of not knowing not only the connotations but even the primary denotation of the Hindi words that they garnish their English with. What is intended to authenticate one's knowledge may end up demonstrating one's very lack of authenticity.

Hinglish in Cinema and Advertising

In current non-literary contexts, Hinglish has come to be used increasingly in dialogues in Hindi cinema and in advertising. To take an early example of this trend, in the film *Biwi No. 1* (1999), Salman Khan says, '*Tu kya mujhe* henpecked *samajhta hai?*' Here, the one unpleasant word is in English while all the rest is in Hindi. Sushmita Sen, in the same film, says, '*Yeh kutta jagah jagah* shit *karta rahta hai,*' and here too we observe the same pattern of what the linguists call code-mixing. Apparently, to utter the Hindi word for 'henpecked' or 'shit' would have been far too embarrassing for the kind of upper-middle-class characters Salman Khan and Sushmita Sen play in this film, the kind who go for a holiday to Switzerland where much of the film is set (further examples in Trivedi 2008: 200–10). In most such cases, it is not randomly but out of some particular kind of cultural and class compulsions that English words are used in Hindi, and a detailed and systematic study of just what these situations may be would certainly prove illuminating.

But the one area of our life where Hinglish seems now to be not the exception but the rule is advertising. So what are the hidden persuaders trying to persuade us of now and why do they need a new kind of language for that? English, as used in India until a couple of decades ago, was the queen among our languages, at least among the affluent classes, and neither consumers nor advertisers would touch the Indian languages with a bargepole. Why does that all-consuming English now feel obliged to descend from its throne to mix with and be contaminated by the languages of the untouchable poor?

Obviously, for the bottom-line reason that the poor are no longer so poor and have acquired the only badge of privilege that the sellers in the market recognize and chase—purchasing power. India's middle class has risen and risen in numbers, for it is now estimated to be over 200 million strong—a number far in excess of those who know English and spend their money in that language. One of the telling signs of the modern times was an advertisement that *The Times of India* ran some years ago to advertise, of all things, its sister newspaper in Hindi, *Navbharat Times*, not to its own readers who could hardly desert English but rather to its advertisers. Under the heading *Hindi Paathakon ki Barhti Zarooraten* ('Growing needs of Hindi readers'), it showed airline tickets and a car and other similar appurtenances once associated exclusively with English speakers, to prove that the Hindi reader was now quite as much worth targeting commercially as the English reader always had been. Another similar development is the fact that the most widely watched news channel in India for the past many years has been a channel in Hindi and, precisely for that reason, it attracts commensurate advertising revenue.

Who among us of a certain age—and I am one of the so-called midnight's children though I feel rather more like a child of the dawn that followed—would have thought that this would ever happen? It would be an exaggeration to call it a social revolution but it does mark a significantly wider spread of affluence and consumption. It is customary in high-minded discourse to always speak of the market forces as evil, but because the market more than any other force cannot afford to stick to outdated attitudes and stand on snobbish dignity, it is obliged to reflect quickly and then to exploit any shifts in socio-economic patterns. That is why we see now the market advertising its wares more and more not only in Hinglish but actually in Hindi and in all the other major Indian languages. English has gone down in India in terms of its economic and social clout, Hindi and the other Indian languages have come up, and thus are the twain able to meet and mate and generate Hinglish.

An advertising slogan that came early on in this development was '*Yeh dil maange more*'; it remains resonant beyond its immediate context and can be regarded as symbolic, for it captures memorably the induced urge to want and to consume more and more—of whatever! (Actually, as with many striking advertising lines, I cannot recall just what it advertised.) I must admit that when I first came across it, I was a little horrified. What kind of *dil* is it, I asked myself, which is obviously discontented with what it has got, and so shamelessly and brazenly wants more! I had thought the only kind of person who was morally justified in asking for more was someone like Oliver Twist, who is being exploitatively starved, who is a little child, who is totally dependent on oppressive strangers, and who yet not quite demands more but merely begs and pleads for more: 'Please, Sir, may I have some more.' In our case, however, it is the *dil*s of persons who already have a full stomach, or, as that rightly reproachful Hindi phrase has it, who are *khayaay-piyaay-aghaayay* ('well fed, well drunk, and quite surfeited'), who are asking for more, without a care in the world for those who actually need more. And the new language of such heartless covetousness is only too aptly Hinglish.

The Right Uses of Hinglish

It is not as if there are no justifiable situations in which words from English can be domiciled and domesticated in Hindi. All languages are born hybrid and they retain and renew their expressive power and vitality so long as they are in an interactive discourse of give and take with other languages. To ask for high 'correctness' or purity in this regard is to ensure that one's language becomes quickly antiquated, indeed fossilized. It is often claimed on behalf of English that one of the reasons for its ever-increasing capability and spread is that it freely borrows from all languages and has incorporated many words even from Hindi. While that is true, it is not half as often pointed out that Hindi has begged, borrowed or stolen a far larger proportion of words from English that are in daily use (unlike most Hindi words in English which remain redolent of exotica), to an extent that most speakers do not notice or even know that these were once English words.

All over the Hindi-speaking parts of the country, for instance, if you try to haggle with a sabziwalla, he will say, '*Nahiin saahab, yehi* rate *hai*.' There is no common Hindi word for 'rate' in this sense that I know and it would be foolish to try and invent one. Incidentally, the proof that Hindi owns this word in this sense lies in the fact that in contemporary English, the word primarily means 'quantity' or 'frequency', as in 'crime rate', then 'the speed at which something moves or happens', and only then 'a fixed price' (Concise Oxford Dictionary, 11th edn, 2004).

In the matter of linguistic borrowing, a rule of thumb would be to use foreign terms mainly for foreign objects, especially when both the term and the object have arrived at one's doorstep together. Thus, one buys a ticket or 'tickut' in Hindi when one travels by 'bus' or 'train' or 'rail' (some Hindi speakers think that 'rail' is a native Hindi word, perhaps because it sounds like *rela a*—a 'throng'—as in *aisa rela aaya ki paon ukhar gaye*). The inspirational socialist leader Ram Manohar Lohia, the ideological light of my student days, suggested that we should similarly adopt other words like 'platform' except that we should retain the right to localize it by pronouncing it as 'laatphaaram.' (A historical precedent here, with its own special local resonance, is 'Laat sahib' for 'Lord sahib'.) Another area of our national life, which transports many of us to remarkable levels of either delight or despondence, in which large-scale import of English words has been welcomed and is fully justified, is cricket— except that at the ground level, there are some local modifications here too. The highly gentlemanly and quaintly polite English enquiry, 'How's that?', for instance, is often turned by little boys playing in subaltern Hindi streets into the broadly similar sounding but jubilantly question-begging assertion: 'Out hai!'

To laboriously and artificially translate in such cases would be plainly absurd; that's why the British haven't translated chutney or biryani or indeed what they claim to be their national dish now, chicken tikka masala. A common joke at the expense of Hindi is that a train is called 'lauh-path-gamini' and a cigarette 'dhoomra-shalaaka'. Well, I must say that in all my life, I have heard these phrases only from the lips of mocking antagonists of Hindi, and never from a Hindi-speaker! It is true that the Government of India set up in the early days of independence a commission to establish Hindi equivalents for many official/ technical terms, and that some of the words suggested by scholars such as Dr Raghuvir were indeed heavy Sanskritic neologisms. But, at the ground level, the model that has prevailed is the one provided not by Nehru's government but by that radical opposition leader of Nehru's time—Lohia. And many Sanskritic neologisms have also, through constant use, become quite naturalized (as much, say, as many English words in Hindi?), and come trippingly off the tongues of the educated middle-class in the cities of north India. *Sva-vitta-poshit yojna ke antargat bhuu-khandon ka aavantan kab hoga?* is no tougher for those brought up on Hindi and educated through school in Hindi than 'When will the allotment of plots of land under the self-financing scheme take place?' for convent-educated English users.

The Perils of Hinglish and the Example of Urdu

The use of Hinglish seems likely to grow in India especially among the young and upwardly mobile—in advertising, where it would obviously be wonderfully economical if just one slogan in Hinglish could be used as a stone to kill the two birds of Hindi and English, and in an area I do not have the time go into, the news media, where again, each channel and newspaper, whether in Hindi or English, keeps beckoning in a more and more mixed language to entice members of the other linguistic constituency. (In fact, during a coffee break in this conference, I was told by a sales executive of a major group of newspapers that it is their policy to actively encourage editors of their English and Hindi publications to cram in as much Hinglish as the reader would take without choking.) It does not seem to concern anyone that such a mixing of languages at a minimal popular level would seriously dumb down the content by imposing obvious limitations of what can be said in it.

But the major peril of thus promoting a demotic dialect like Hinglish is that we may soon be left with neither Hindi nor English but just Hinglish. It is the kind of thing that has already happened through an interaction between native languages and colonially imposed English in several parts of Africa and the West Indies. A consequence of pidgin or a creole becoming the lingua franca in these countries is that this fractured, fragmented language is the only one most of their population has any access to. They can speak it and get by in it in their daily lives but it is doubtful if it can facilitate serious engagement of any kind or expression of any intellectual inquiry or creative conceptualization. When characters speaking in it are put into books, as for example in V.S. Naipaul's early novels including that masterpiece, *A House for Mr Biswas*, many characters sound irredeemably comic and half-witted just because they say things such as 'What you doin', man?' When the Barbadian postcolonial author Edward Kamau Brathwaite decides to write poetry in a creole in what he calls his 'nation language', he runs the risk of not being understood by anyone outside this small island though, on the face of it, he is still writing in some kind of English.

We have known a similar linguistic phenomenon in the history of our own country. Persian was the ruling language of the country for some centuries (until 1837 when an order was passed that English would replace it) and, like English, it had always been spoken and written by a minuscule, privileged minority. Through a commingling of elite and cosmopolitan Persian with local Indian languages such as Hindi, which were based on Sanskrit, a rough-and-ready pidgin was born—mainly in the peripatetic soldiers' camps—and became popular at that level of necessary communication. This was Urdu, which later acquired a high status (higher than Hindi, for example) because it was closer to Persian, just as Hinglish is socially superior to Hindi now because it is closer to English.

When Urdu came into existence, it was not as if many Persian words had not already been accepted into Hindi, even at the highest level of usage. In the *Ramcharitmanas*—and there is no work higher than that in Hindi—Tulsidas in the sixteenth century was already using phrases such as this to describe landscape: *bana-baag-koop-tadaag-sarita* . . . where each word comes straight from Sanskrit, except one from Persian—*baag[h]*, a formal garden, for the good reason that perhaps that kind of geometrically laid-out garden too came to us from Persia. And a robustly humorous Hindi poet, Bodha, later went so far as to play around with the Persian word *maghroor* to form a new word that sounded distinctly Hindi and produced a new and striking effect: *maghroori.* (In both meaning and formation, though perhaps not in effect, it's comparable to forming 'prouding' from 'proud'.) Such playful interlingual wit is of course one of the more delightful justifications for code-mixing, especially in literature. James Joyce's supreme reputation rests partly on his ability in this regard, and an Indian winner of the Booker Prize with a reputation for playful use of language was brought down a peg or two when she was described by a Hindi journalist as a *bookeraai hui lekhika*, which would seem to mean 'a Booker-ed writer', except that Hindi speakers would promptly connect *bookeraai* to the Hindi homophonic *thukraai*—meaning 'dishonoured' rather than honoured by the award of that alien distinction.

The eventual outcome of Urdu having developed as a language that was neither Hindi nor quite Persian was that though it remained quite close to Persian, the two languages proved to be mutually unintelligible. Urdu remains a language spoken and written only in the Indian subcontinent and, though some of the greatest Urdu poets such as Mirza Ghalib and Mohammad Iqbal wrote a major proportion of their poetic corpus in Persian, Persian speakers in Persia have paid them hardly any attention at all. Meanwhile, Urdu has lost out steadily to Hindi even on home ground, mainly because it retained the courtly sophistication of Persian and thus remained largely incomprehensible to the masses who spoke Hindi.

Hinglish and Bilingualism

A parallel to this would be if a future Salman Rushdie were to write a novel entirely in Hinglish, rather than just throwing in scraps of Hinglish, and then could not be shortlisted for the Booker Prize because no one in Britain could follow him, and had an ever-dwindling readership here because such a language had branched too far away from the local soil and was still too upper class for most people. It is doubtful if Hinglish (as used currently) is going to be any more accessible to most of India's population, about one-third of which is still illiterate, than English itself; when and whenever they learn to read, it will inevitably be in their mother tongues. Despite its air of relative laxity, Hinglish is quite as anti-democratic as English itself so far as the great demographic majority of India is concerned.

The fact is that there are, as linguists recognize, two kinds of bilingualism—additive and subtractive. Those who can speak two languages independently, without mixing them, are truly competent in both. But those who start a sentence in one language and cannot finish it in that language without habitually and helplessly taking recourse to another are perhaps not competent in either. They do not know two languages—they only know bits and pieces of each while they use the fact that they know bits of each to tell themselves that they know both.

Over the years, I have devised two simple tests to establish whether someone is really bilingual. One is to ask: Do you read a newspaper or watch the TV news in both the languages you claim to know? If you read say ten books in a year in your language A, do you also read three books in your language B? When did you last write two full pages in your language B? And if it was back in school or perhaps never, is your claim to knowing language B justified just because you can fling around, often in a syntax- and grammar-free fashion, a couple of hundred words of language B, which is the limit of your vocabulary?

I have a simpler test too—easier to administer but perhaps not to pass. Can you spend the next twenty-four hours of your life using just one of the two languages you think you know, either language A or language B, without using a single word of the other language? I have found that anyone who survives this test for twenty-four hours comes out having lost about 10 kilos of linguistic flab within that short period and a corresponding quantity of mental slackness accumulated over the years through the use of saturated Hinglish. Mentally, this person emerges with a leaner, fitter mind and finer-tuned thinking machinery, and discovers that s/he has linguistic muscles s/he never knew existed.

Well, your twenty-four hours start ... now! Or, if you still prefer that needless and almost mindless jumble—*Aapke twenty-four hours ka start hota hai ... now!*

INTRODUCTION

Rupert Snell and Rita Kothari

Most discussions on Hinglish are too deeply enchanted by the spell of this vivacious form of speech to engage critically with the questions that surround it. What are its antecedents in the history of the Indian nation state? What reception has Hinglish enjoyed in different parts of the country: is it truly pan-Indian, or even potentially so? Is it a unique phenomenon, or are similar patterns emerging from other combinations of languages in India? What is the difference between a sprinkling of English in an otherwise Hindi sentence, and a sprinkling of Hindi in an otherwise English sentence? To what extent is it possible to assess the emergence of Hinglish in terms of sum 'loss' or 'gain'? It was questions such as these that made the two editors of this book decide to convene a discussion that might throw some light on the whole phenomenon. The idea quickly grew into a proposal for a smallish workshop, and then a largish conference, and we soon found ourselves in an excited discussion of possible speakers and topics. Armed with the emerging list, Rita Kothari took the idea to her home institution, MICA (the Mudra Institute of Communications, Ahmedabad), and quickly gained enthusiastic support from her colleagues there. The resulting conference, held in Mumbai in January 2009, offered a podium to academics, journalists, people from the film world, students of many subjects including language and communications, and members of the general public.

Introductions to books of collected papers usually attempt the difficult task of evoking the principle of 'unity in diversity'. Our subject here, however, is one that is better addressed by multiple voices rather than by unitary harmony, reflecting a wide variety of disciplines, approaches, research areas and linguistic attitudes. Hinglish cuts across many contexts and we felt it necessary to allow its various aspects to be visited freely, the better for us to appreciate the many complementary aspects of the matter. In a preface based on the keynote address with which he opened our conference, Harish Trivedi initiates our bookish debates with a shrewd discursus of the matter of Hinglish. Trivedi's habitation at the *sangam* of English and Hindi studies (with postcolonialism the abstract third element) made this well-known son of Prayag an obvious choice for providing such an overview. In inviting him to revise his address for publication, the editors of this book did not suspect that he would raid their pre-conference correspondence so egregiously, bringing privately held views on language into the public domain; but the robust Trivedian view that emerges from his paper proves to be the ideal catalyst for a wide-ranging discussion of themes. Trivedi poses a number of questions about the origin, constituents, nature and future of Hinglish; but he also charts more dangerous waters by asking the most controversial question of all: 'Is Hinglish a good thing?' Such qualitative enquiry threatens the careful objectivity of the discipline of linguistics, and takes the issue to its natural habitat, that of lay opinion; but the resolution of the question itself is left primarily to readers of these essays, who must decide for themselves whether to rejoice in the demotic vitality of Hinglish, or to lament the further layers of hybrid complexity that it brings to the language map of the subcontinent.

Examining the components of hybridity in Hinglish, Trivedi regards the language as a Hindi stock with an English graft, rather than vice versa. He locates antecedents of today's phenomenon in comedic nineteenth-century examples; but he then turns the spotlight on more recent times through an unexpected critique of Nissim Ezekiel's 'Very Indian Poems in

Indian English'. Prosecuting the condescension with which Ezekiel derides the imagined perpetrator of these English lines (through whose translucent English skin the bones of Indian-language diction are all too visible), Trivedi asks rhetorically what mode of English the Indian poet Ezekiel had resort to *other than* 'Indian English'.

Such a question gets to the heart of the matter of acceptability in language use, showing that in matters of linguistic style we necessarily deal with a sliding scale rather than a fixed benchmark. Few users of language would be happy with the sobriquet of 'purist', but questions of appropriateness and normative style arise every time we open our mouths or touch a keyboard. Such issues have arisen frequently in the editing of this volume: To what extent is it necessary or desirable to homogenize different varieties of written English to an international norm? Should all the flowers bloom, or is a particular style uniquely suitable for academic prose?

Trivedi's survey of linguistic hybridity invokes such names as Shobhaa Dé and especially Salman Rushdie (who 'repeatedly gets wrong' the meanings of Indian words in his English writing), and also spotlights the role played by Hindi cinema and advertising—sites visited by several other scholars in this book—in the dissemination of the code-switching habit. Far from censuring or censoring such usage, Trivedi finds that the admixture of English in the Hindi lexicon is a component of the hybrid richness of the language; and yet his enthusiasm is muted by a fear of a process of creolization in which 'we may soon be left with neither Hindi nor English but just Hinglish'.

Devyani Sharma's essay 'Return of the Native: Hindi in British English' transports us, if not quite to Egdon Heath, at least to those more urban areas of the United Kingdom where Hindi and other South Asian languages are currently making their presence felt. Referencing Prince Charles's acknowledgement of the word 'chuddies' (an item of underwear also appearing in Pramod Nayar's paper) as part of the new English lexicon, Sharma skilfully lays out for us the long history of the infiltration of Indian words into British English preceding this royal imprimatur. She examines historical and contemporary British forms of Hinglish found in dictionaries, fiction, popular media (such as the comedy series *Goodness Gracious Me*—the source of Prince Charles's example), rap lyrics by Apache Indian, social networking sites, press reporting, and original conversational data in the form of socio-linguistic and interactional recordings with over 70 'British Asians'.

Going beyond such broad concepts and terms as 'mixed code' and 'hybrid identity', Sharma explores 'the particular interactional stances that speakers achieve by mixing languages in a given situation'. This is done with reference to two distinctive but complementary senses of the word 'native', the first alluding to the native Englishman returning home to England with Indian words in his baggage, and the second to the 'Hindi-bearing Asian migrant' who makes his home in the British Isles. Sharma's survey extends as far back as the seventeenth century, and finds that at every stage during this long history, the idea of authority over languages has been contested by various different types of speakers, leading to a situation that can be exploited strategically by speakers of a mixed style. She shows that the complex linguistic choices made by individuals depend on much more than just ethnicity: status (including class) is an important element here, with terms such as 'competition wallah' and the contrastive 'sahib' crossing, with ease, the dividing line of race. But if there are continuities here, there is also difference in the overall register: 'colonial loans' typically indexed social boundaries, whereas the speech of young British Asians not only tends towards the 'simple and juvenile' but also marks differences of generational attitude between such speakers and the generation of their more conservative parents.

Introducing the concept of 'the multilingual mind', Tej Bhatia examines its ability to maintain both language *separation* on the one hand and language *integration* on the other. He argues that these two types of bilingual capacity result in language mixing of the kind that linguists term code-mixing and code-switching. He distinguishes code *mixing* (the mixing of linguistic elements from diverse languages within a sentence) from code *switching* (the switching of language between sentences); both of these are further distinguished from the simpler process of linguistic borrowing. Bhatia reveals various facets of bilingual creativity through language mixing as it manifests itself in the day-to-day verbal behaviour of speakers who are bilingual in English and Hindi. The paper is grounded in the Optimization Hypothesis which the author has proposed in his recent published work; it argues that in language-mixing in general, and in Hinglish in particular, we see what is essentially an 'optimizing' strategy that renders a wide variety of new meaning(s) beyond the capacity of the separate linguistic systems working by themselves. The topic is presented from the perspectives of recent developments in linguistics and socio-psycholinguistics.

'Prescriptivists and the "guardians" of the language decry mixing,' declares Bhatia; and in his paper 'Hindi: Its Threatened Ecology and Natural Genius', Rupert Snell does indeed take just such a protectionist stance towards what he sees as threats to the cogent articulacy of Hindi. While recognizing the inexorability of language change, he argues that if the economy of Hindi is liberalized to the extent of allowing the free importation of limitless influence from elsewhere, its innate powers of articulacy and nuance may be eroded; and that in fact this process is already well under way. His argument is that loans, especially when used in large numbers, cannot be seen as innocent additions to the language, because far from sitting modestly alongside their synonyms they actually *displace* established words and expressions, eventually making a natural and vibrant Hindi lexicon seem unfit for everyday use. Who says *gusalkhaana* any more, he asks, now that 'bathroom' has been so resolutely plumbed into the speech habits of northern India? Hindi is seeming to lose both its palette (as when Hindi-speaking shopkeepers offer their wares in '*yah* red colour, madam ... *yah* blue colour') and its direction (as when metropolitan taxi drivers are directed to 'right *maaro* ... left *maaro*'). While many speakers may delight in Hinglish as a modern lingo whose global frame of reference seems a comfortable fit for a real or wished-for lifestyle, the cost that is being paid for this novelty is the erosion of an established lexicon equipped with rich allusions developed over centuries of usage. This is not to champion a purist stance such as that taken up by the advocates of a so-called '*shuddh*' Hindi, because the achievement of that imagined 'purity' itself involves flooding the vernacular with Sanskritic loans and neologisms that make it sound artificial and strained. Rather, the 'natural genius' of Hindi rests on its true nature as a vernacular language that has its own depth and dignity, and which is imbued with subtle characteristics that can be obscured when its lexicon is swamped with loans from any external source.

'Purity of language is a chimera; our languages are born and thrive in hybridity,' notes G.J.V. Prasad in his paper 'Hindi, Tamil and English: The New Ménage à Trois'. Adopting an autobiographical mode for the opening of his paper, Prasad describes the cultural and behavioural reasons for the spontaneous choice of one or the other of this linguistic trio in the various contexts of a Delhi childhood; the borders between the languages were porous, and the momentary attractions of one language over another were defined by the pragmatics of communication rather than by any self-conscious awareness of (or deference to) cultural hierarchy. Prasad paints a picture of India's language map as being like a rainbow, with adjacent languages blending into one another and accommodating a full spectrum through a continuous series of gradual changes that are hardly to be contained by the boundaries of any kind of map.

Contemplating the influx of Indian words into English, Prasad notes that while Hindi words such as 'lathi' and 'kurta' have established themselves as pan-Indian, words from other Indian languages are regarded as having a *regional* flavour when used in an English context. (Interestingly, then, Hindi surreptitiously achieves through this route a pan-Indian role that it has been denied on the broader stage of Indian polity.) He investigates the ways in which regional flavours tinge the writing of such writers as R.K. Narayan, whose English is 'a language born in and constantly recreating itself in the interface of different cultures'; Narayan strives for pan-Indian intelligibility 'by using Hindi words that have currency even in Tamil country' and only occasionally moves into the specificity of actual Tamil words themselves. And because of a desire to sidestep the local politics of caste, Prasad observes, Tamils speaking to each other outside Tamil Nadu may choose a 'neutral' language such as Hindi in which to converse; meanwhile, Tamil itself has taken on many loans from Hindi, enabling a *vastatu* to do his *kasrattu* (an *ustad* to do his *kasrat*) and then display his *dillu* (*dil*, i.e., his guts). An engaging encounter with the mixed language of Tamil magazines charts the ways in which language use indexes social class: thus a catering contractor advertises in English because, Prasad explains, 'if you need caterers, you know English'. Here too, as in the reflections of his childhood experiences, Prasad shows how language choice follows communicative need.

We return to the discipline of linguistics in the work of Shannon Anderson-Finch, who argues that Hindi–English code-mixing is a linguistic resource used by bilingual speakers to express themselves strategically and creatively in everyday interaction. Following Peter Auer's work, she agrees that bilingualism 'has its foremost reality in the interactive exchanges between the members of a bilingual speech community'. Anderson-Finch offers a micro-analysis of naturally occurring Hindi–English conversations to reveal interactive strategies that she terms 'bilingual repetition', in which the semantic content of a phrase in one language is repeated nearby in the other language, as in '*Main aaj soch rahi thi, aadha semester khatam ho gaya*, half the semester is gone'. Anderson-Finch finds this phenomenon to be ubiquitous in South Asian multilingual contexts ranging from casual conversations to Bollywood dialogues to printed advertisements and beyond. She shows how investigation of bilingual repetition contributes to the understanding of code-mixing in general by focusing on a particular interactive strategy and conversational structure.

Taking us 'Towards a Political Economy of Hinglish TV', Daya Thussu shows the development of Hinglish as part of the strategy of global media interests as they move into the highly profitable market of South Asia. India's enormous market offers fascinating possibilities for researching how the global interacts with the national, and the national with the myriad variations of the local, given its multilingual and multi-layered media scene. Thussu examines the exponential growth of the Indian television market in the past decade—from Doordarshan, a notoriously monotonous and unimaginative state monopoly, to more than 300 digital channels, covering most genres of television from sports to comedy, from children's programming to news and documentary, and catering to a huge Indian market as well as a large Indian (and indeed South Asian) diaspora, estimated to be 24 million strong.

Thussu argues that the rapid liberalization of media and cultural industries in India and the increasing availability of new and sophisticated communication technologies has created a market of an increasingly Westernized and culturally hybridized audience, with growing purchasing power and aspirations to a consumerist lifestyle; and that this process has attracted transnational media corporations into India. While initially successful, their largely Hollywood-based programming did not prove profitable as it was being watched only by a tiny English-speaking minority. Recognizing the limitations of this strategy, transnational networks first Indianized then localized their programming to suit the range and variety of cultural and linguistic tastes encompassing the Indian market.

Focusing on the example of global media magnate Rupert Murdoch's television channels in India, Thussu's paper shows that its dominant position has largely been achieved through specific localization strategies, including a move beyond Hindi into other regional languages such as Bengali and Tamil; the local has been skilfully prioritized over the global through the localization of content and the adoption and adaptation of Indian languages, such as mixing Hindi with English to provide the hybridized media language of Hinglish. The media's tendency to 'go native', while celebrating this process with active support from increasingly vocal local media corporations, has helped them present themselves as an acceptable, even nationalist, face of globalization. However, in the name of defending the national interest, are these channels propagating dominant neoliberal ideology, and helping legitimize a media marketplace in which global corporate clients can consolidate and expand, while the rural poor move further to the margins of a rapidly globalizing India?

Rita Kothari historicizes Hinglish in the arena of Hindi cinema. She argues that English in Hindi cinema from the 1950s to 1980s flows into Hinglish today, but generates new social meanings. Titled 'English *Aajkal*', her essay is a document of English/Hinglish in Hindi cinema, whilst constantly drawing upon the social attitudes surrounding them in both real and reel life. Kothari detects various distinctive (but not necessarily chronologically successive) patterns. On the basis of films like *Julie* (1975), in which English became a marker of cultural difference, 'it seemed the Anglo-Indians always spoke English, and that you could "romance" only in English'; Parsis and Christians received similar linguistic treatment as anglicized communities, and the use of English was just one symptom of a Westernized lifestyle that remained beyond the pale for the majority communities. Thus language played a part in distancing the Westernized few from the core of Indian society: English was an exotic other. A different kind of othering is at work in films such as *Shree 420* (1955), where English becomes the language of the casino, indexing notions of wealth, decadence, and an abandonment of normative social behaviour. A kind of variant of this image is found in villainous characters who stood apart from the moral universe of the audience; and in the comic vein, the attempts of Hindi-speakers to master the ABC (or rather, C-A-T) of English became a source of ready humour.

Against this backdrop of distinctive values for the image of English-speakers in Hindi cinema, Kothari examines the ways in which Hinglish developed as a 'language of commodities' in the 1990s. This is the mode of speech that is branded, presented and celebrated in the cinema of today. Whereas English had earlier been seen as a language of difference, marking and perhaps judging this or that element of Indian society through cinematic characterization, an increasingly widespread view of consumerism as legitimate has established the new style of mixed language as something unmarked and morally neutral. Hinglish, as Kothari puts it, 'constitutes the possibility of having fun and fulfilment on Indian terms'.

Difficult as it may be to segue from 'fun and 'fulfilment' to the hard grind of earning one's daily bread, we turn next to Mathangi Krishnamurthy's essay 'Furtive Tongues: Language Politics in the Indian Call Centre', which examines a complex of linguistic issues around the controversial phenomenon of outsourcing. Krishnamurthy points out that both the media and scholarly attention have focused on the English-language usage and training central to the commercial mission of the call centre, largely ignoring the more interesting role played by the vernacular, except perhaps in the bids to erase its influence. She contends that understanding the persistence of the local vernacular(s) in everyday communication around the call centre is an important opportunity for workers to resist language homogeneity and hegemony. Further, such examination of the vernacular on a purported transnational site may chart a path to the new English of urban India—to Hinglish, local English and Indianized English.

Making a much-needed disruption in a popular view of Hinglish as a 'pan-Indian' language, Rohini Mokashi-Punekar tells a story from an India that has no Hinglish. Her paper 'Views from a Different India: Not Hinglish but Nagamese' takes us to a contrasting area of India's language map, and casts light on the phenomenon of Hinglish from the (north-eastern) side. Mokashi-Punekar examines the history, scope and usage of the pidgin languages, Nagamese and Nefamese, against the background of a brief history of the linguistic situation prevailing in North-East India and infer the common grounds of their comparison or contrast with Hinglish.

If Hinglish is the register of the upwardly mobile and aspiring urban middle class of contemporary India that has grown in economic and political strength since liberalization, asks Mokashi-Punekar, what about the politics of speech in underdeveloped, remote and politically fraught regions of the nation such as the North-East? Years before television shows, advertisements and Bollywood made Hinglish the swinging lingo of the Indian market, there were All India Radio news broadcasts from Dibrugarh in Nagamese and Nefamese, pidgin languages of Nagaland and Arunachal Pradesh respectively, born of contact between the Assamese and various tribal languages, with Hindi and English loanwords. Diverse even by Indian standards, the North-East is home to some 220 languages belonging to three different language families. Linguistic debates have been intrinsic to the region since colonial times: the Assamese struggle against the imposition of Bengali by the British administration and the controversies over the adoption of the Roman script for Khasi are cases in point. The gradual reorganization of the region into seven states after Independence, the growing disenchantment of different groups within these states with the policies of the Indian nation and their assertion through linguistic and cultural identity—all these factors have resulted in a mêlée of increasing antagonism amongst linguistic/tribal communities. This is over and above the insurgency against the Indian state which showed itself in the recent attacks on Hindi cinema and Hindi-speaking people in parts of Assam.

If Rohini Mokashi-Punekar disrupts synonymy of one kind, two young students help question simplistic equations between 'all' youth and 'Hinglish', that inform media representation of the subject. Soumik Pal and Siddharth Mishra show through self-reflection how urban Indian youth respond to a brand called 'Hinglish', and also complicate the idea of its 'naturalness'. Meanwhile, Pramod Nayar brings the discussion of Hinglish into the digital domain, a necessary intervention that helps question Hinglish as an interaction only between Hindi and English. His essay 'The Vernacularization of Online Protests: A Case Study from India' explores the employment of local language and linguistic registers alongside English in online protests in India. Using the example of the 'Pink Chaddis' campaign it demonstrates how the protests make use of the multimodal digitextuality of New Media. Humour and bilingual satire characterize the vernacularization of online politics, and Hinglish, his essay suggests, is a form of cultural transcoding which, by conflating the local with the global, presents the possibilities of a vernacular cosmopolitanism.

The essays discussed so far have emerged from scholars and, in one case, students working on Hinglish from within institutional contexts of academia. Although the conference did not make such partitions between academic and practitioners' views, the discussion panels and interviews form a distinct cluster to which we turn below.

Nayar's discussion of Hinglish in the context of digital media extends into practitioners' experiences of using Hinglish as a language of the radio, television, Hinglish songs and advertisements. Prashant Panday relates the experiments with Hinglish that were launched by Radio Mirchi and asserts the immediacy of success. Cyrus Broacha 'performs' the hybridity of language through a comical defiance of rigid positions on language, and underscores television's need to 'communicate'. Rahul Dev, also associated with the media, expresses strong misgivings on the depletion of Hindi vocabulary. The subject of Hinglish is invested with almost irreconcilable ideologies, a fact surfacing rather sharply in the first panel discussion. Interestingly, the discussion between Santosh Desai, Kandaswamy Bharathan, Raj Rao, Urvashi Butalia and others takes this for granted, and makes overt the different meanings Hinglish holds for different people. The gay writer Raj Rao finds Hinglish most appropriate as a language that helps blur hegemonic class divisions, while Kandaswamy hints at its potential in Tamil cinema. Nuanced analysis by Butalia and Sharma complicates the idea of Hinglish as a single language, and stresses its multiple meanings that depend upon the interlocutors in the dialogue. Meanwhile, Shuchi Kothari & Nandita Das, Mahesh Bhatt and Gulzar form a triad and offer an insiders' perspective on the constraints and joys of working with language from within Bollywood. Nandita Das and Shuchi Kothari mention how inadequate is the label of 'Hindi' film when you wish to present multiple languages for multiple identities, sometimes even within the same person. The constraints of definition they faced are not dissimilar from Mahesh Bhatt's admission that his Urdu-speaking scriptwriter felt the need to expand her English usage in her recent scripts. Gulzar's own oeuvre of lyrics in Hindi film songs shows a rich repertoire of Urdu–Hindi–Hindustani that is difficult to consider as disparate, and he strongly rejects those definitions. His comments on a more generous use of English words are refreshingly different from what is commonly understood as 'Hinglish'.

All in all, the book has attempted to provide as many perspectives as possible on a subject that is just beginning to be taken seriously. We offer here a view of a state of flux, perhaps fuelling rather than extinguishing the flames of controversy that rage in this excitingly vexed context of language use.

A NOTE ON TRANSLITERATION

How should Hinglish be written and spelt? In recent years, the use of Romanization—once merely a route around the impasse between Urdu's Persianate and Hindi's Devanagari characters—has come into its own through the electronic media: early versions of email etc. knew no Indian scripts, and we all became accustomed to writing roman Hindi emails in whatever approximate phonetics appealed to our ears and eyes. In this book, we have tried to reduce the resulting anarchy by establishing some ground rules. Thus a long vowel is shown as doubled (so that *kam kaam* unambiguously means 'less work'), though long vowels at the end of the word do not seem to need doubling: *maine kam kaam kiya*. Similarly we distinguish *din* 'day' from *diin* 'faith'—preferring *ii* over *ee* in this context (with apologies to the alumni and staff of the Deep Children's Academy). With 'u' we parted from our rule: it was felt that *khoon* did less 'murder' to the eye than the unfamiliar *khuun*, and thus we have admitted such spellings as *zaroorat* and *phool*, of 'necessity' allowing all the 'flowers' to bloom. We have not adopted the common convention of capitalizing retroflex consonants (as in *kaaraN*) for the simple 'reason' of preferring graphic simplicity. English words retain their English spellings rather than being transliterated from Indian scripts: thus we go to *school* rather than *skuul* or *skool*. English versions of Hindi film titles, sometimes influenced by numerology, follow a logic all of their own, as in the doubled final consonant of *Darr*, the serendipitous final 'e' in *Kabhi Kabhie*, or the formulation *Sholay* which begs to be mispronounced as 'Show Lay'; these established spellings are of course inviolate. The result is a system of transliteration that has enough inconsistencies to bother the purists, but not enough to prevent the kind reader from understanding our romanized citations.

RETURN OF THE NATIVE: HINDI IN BRITISH ENGLISH

Devyani Sharma

KISS MY CHUDDIES! (WELCOME TO THE QUEEN'S HINGLISH)
The Observer, April 2004
Asian 'yoof-speak' is spicing up English, with Hindi words such as 'gora' and slang such as 'innit' soon to enter the dictionary and experts predicting an explosive impact of the language used by second-generation immigrants . . .

HINGLISH MAKES ITS DEBUT IN ENGLISH DICTIONARY
The Independent, June 2005
For centuries French and Latin have been dominant influences on the English language. Now, though, the popularity of mainstream BBC TV programmes such as *The Kumars at Number 42* and *Life Isn't All Ha Ha Hee Hee* has brought with it a new phenomenon—the introduction of Hinglish . . .

IT'S HINGLISH, INNIT?
BBC News Magazine, November 2006
Hinglish—a hybrid of English and South Asian languages, used both in Asia and the UK—now has its own dictionary. Is it really a pucca way to speak? . . .

The substantial South Asian presence in Britain since the mid-twentieth century has led to a remarkable rise in the visibility of Hindi mixing in British English. In November 2007, Prince Charles noted in a speech that among the 'splendidly unstoppable' South Asian contributions in Britain, *'chuddies*

1

seem to have crept into the English language, if that is the correct way to put it'.[1] While delicately distancing the Queen's English from such usage through strategic ineptitude, his remark acknowledges a rich and tangled history of Hindi–English mixing in British English.

But contemporary British Asian Hinglish is only the latest phase of Hindi infiltration into British English. Since at least the seventeenth century, Indian words have populated British English, either travelling back to England in the mouths of returning Englishmen or staying within India, in the form of an inexpert—often derisive—variety employed by British colonists in superficial exchanges with local Indians. The small selection of British English uses of Hindi explored here—from early colonial encounters to sophisticated contemporary hybridizations—illustrates why speakers mix codes at all, and how linguistic form and social status are fundamentally co-constitutive.

Uniting these diverse language practices under such intractably broad terms as 'mixed code' or 'hybrid identity' runs the risk of obscuring important differences in the forms and functions of language mixing. Instead, I explore the particular (often very distinct) interactional stances that speakers achieve by mixing languages in a given situation. These fleeting acts can, in turn, serve to index broader social affiliations or contestations. Such acts afford their users strategic advantages only because the use of a word or a language *in a specific discourse context* can accrue specific and recognizable rights, ownership, or authenticity to the speaker, whether ratified in the interaction or not. Particularly in colonial and postcolonial language-mixing, this can equip a speaker with powerful tools to impose or subvert structures of nativeness and authority.

The term 'native' itself offers a useful starting point to understand the conflicting power dynamics of British Hinglish, depending on the user. The deictic ambiguity, particularly in colonial usage, of the word 'native'—signalling either entitlement or bondage—is evident in this selection of Oxford English Dictionary (OED) definitions (many now obsolete):

NATIVE, *n.*

    i.   A person born in bondage; a person born to servants, tenants, etc., and inheriting their status . . .

    ii.   Austr., N.Z.: A white person born in Australia or New Zealand, as distinguished from first-generation immigrants and aborigines . . .

   iii. A member of the indigenous ethnic group of a country or region, as distinguished from foreigners, esp. European colonists. Freq. with a suggestion of inferior status, culture, etc., and hence (esp. in modern usage) considered offensive . . .

   iv. In Britain and the US during the period of colonialism and slavery: a black person of African origin or descent . . .

    v.   *(adj.)* Of a person: entitled or qualified by right of birth to some status, title, etc.

Of interest to the interpretation of Hinglish here, in terms of transport and exchange of linguistic material, is the duality of nativeness: Hindi in British use can involve either a return to Britain of the 'native' Englishman with new linguistic baggage (having 'gone native'), or a postcolonial return to British soil of the colonial 'native', the Hindi-bearing Asian migrant.

In the discussion that follows, I explore two historical types of Hindi use in British English. First, the use of Hindi by white British English speakers in the seventeenth–twentieth centuries (importing linguistic material of the 'other' into their 'own' English) and, second, the use of Hindi in the English of British-born Asians in contemporary Britain (involving the importing by Asian subjects of their 'own' material into the 'other's' English). The language mixing I examine ranges from isolated loanwords (borrowing of occasional words from another language) to profound code-mixing (admixture of segments of varying lengths from two or more languages). In all time periods, a tension arises between competing claims of authority over the languages (and, by extension, the identities) in question, a tension I argue is exploited strategically by speakers who mix.

Cannadine (2001) has argued that the aristocratic British in

India identified more with Indian royalty than with their own 'blackened' nineteenth-century industrial classes, whom they disdained alongside lower-class Indians, and that class and social status were, in fact, as important as racial concerns in the colonial relationship.[2] In the cases that follow, historical as well as contemporary, I suggest that the choice of a given phonetic, morpho-syntactic, or lexico-semantic alternative in a particular moment constitutes symbolic capital that speakers use to signal specific class or status (as well as ethnic) affiliations (Bourdieu 1977), and to manipulate the relative status of their interlocutor.

Colonial British Hinglish

Loanwords

Loanwords in colonial British Indian[3] usage offer plenty of evidence of British elaboration of class hierarchy in colonial India. In Cannadine's (2001: 41) terms, 'the British colonies of settlement were about the export of hierarchy; India, by contrast, was much more about the analogues of hierarchy'. Indigenous and hybrid terms, such as those in (1a), helped to reinforce and refine extant boundaries of social status in both cultures.[4] For instance, the hybrid term *competition wallah* did not draw a line in the sand between ethnic groups; it applied equally to Indian and British members of the Indian Civil Service who entered via an open competition rather than elite channels such as Haileybury and Imperial Service College. Similarly, definitions of *sahib, memsahib*, and *nabob* eventually cross ethnic boundaries in order to preserve class denotation; in the case of *memsahib* we see a literal reinforcement of two class systems: the English/French *ma'am* and the Urdu/Arabic *sahib*.

(1a)   **competition wallah**: 'An English–Hindustani hybrid, applied in modern Anglo-Indian colloquial to members of the Civil Service who have entered it by the competitive system first introduced in 1856. The phrase was probably the invention of one of the older or Haileybury members of the same service.' (Yule & Burnell 1886)

sahib: 'The title by which, all over India, European gentlemen, and it may be said Europeans generally, are addressed ... In other Hind. use the word is equivalent to 'Master'; and it is occasionally used as a specific title both among Hindus and Musulmans.' (Yule & Burnell 1886)

memsahib: 'A married European or upper-class woman.' (OED)

nabob: 'The word is used in two ways: (a) simply as a corruption and representative of *nawab* (a delegate of the supreme chief) ... (b) It began to be applied in the 18th century, when the transactions of Clive made the epithet familiar in England, to Anglo-Indians who returned with fortunes from the East.' (Yule & Burnell 1886)

The trajectories of other Hindi loans from this period similarly trace a history of deep class divisions. British intellectuals' esoteric loans as in (1b) remain in higher registers of British English today; By contrast, barrack loans can still be found in working-class British English. Today, it is specifically Cockney dictionaries that list the words in (1c).[5]

(1b) *avatar, sandhi, Buddha, pundit, guru, karma*

(1c) *blighty:* England   (Ar. > U. > H. *bilayati, wilayati* 'foreign')

     mufti: Civilian clothes   (U. *mufti* 'Muslim cleric' or 'freedom')

     dekko: To have a look around   (H. *dekho* 'see', imperative verb)

     cushy: Comfortable   (H. *khushi* 'comfort, pleasantness')

     doolally: Crazy   (Deolali, site of a British sanatorium or transit camp)

Even within the British intellectual and upper classes, differences in loans reflect differences within British culture and in the nature of colonial relationships. For instance, scholarly loans as in (1b) stand in contrast to exotic loans that fed British Romanticism, as in the following extract by Sir Walter Scott, writing in Scotland in 1827:

(1d) Happy Dog! To India! Oh, Delhi! Oh, Golconda . . . where men are making **lacs** of **rupees** . . . in the land of **cowries** . . . I shall be relieving some **nabob** or **rajahpoot** of his plethora of wealth! . . . The luxuries of a **nautch** . . . and of changing sheep-head broth and haggis for **mulagatawny** and **curry**! (Lewis 1991: 24)

Scott, a nineteenth-century Scottish writer associated with Victorian Romanticism, never visited India; his reliance on superficial lexical loans betrays a lack of participation in any real Indian speech community. Far from constructing a fused identity, as in the contemporary examples discussed later, Scott's hyperbolic use of exotic cultural loans magnifies the distance between the two cultures, reinforced by the explicit contrast between *sheep-head broth and haggis* and *mulagatawny and curry*.[6]

The selective adoption of lexical loans—among scholars, military men, Romantics—gives us a first impression of the underlying power dynamics among different classes of British colonists. Instances of more elaborate British Hinglish style from this period allow a more detailed understanding of the construction of status in interaction.

Code-mixing

Hindi mixing in the English of middle- and working-class British residents in nineteenth-century India became a recognized discourse style, much to the amusement of the domestic British public. Lewis (1991: 13) describes this variety as a 'frontier language', constructed on the fly in superficial interactions and never even approaching expert ability in the foreign code. Its users were the *qui-his*, 'the popular distinctive nickname of the Bengal Anglo-Indian, from the usual manner of calling servants in that Presidency, viz. "*Koi hai?*" "Is anyone there?"' (Yule & Burnell 1886).

A turn-of-the-century novel (Steele 1900, discussed in Lewis 1991) parodies this colonist style, mixing working-class British dialect markers with inexpert, fragmented use of Hindi. Although a fictional monologue, the early date suggests that the extract in (2a) draws on personal familiarity with this style.

(2a) ***Decko***, you want this ***admi abhi***, but you ain't goin' to get 'im. ***Tumhara nahin***. He's mine, ***mehra admi, sumja***? If you want to ***lurro***, come on. You'll have a bellyful, and there'll be plenty of you to ***phansi***. But wot I say is don't be a ***pargul soors***. I don't do your temples 'arm. It's ***durm shester ram-ram*** an' ***hurry ganga***, so far's I care. But this man's my guv'nor. You don't touch 'im ***kubbi nahin***. I'm a ***nek admi, burra ussel***, when I'm took the right way, contrariwise I'm ***zulm*** an' ***ficker*** an ***burra burra affut***? (Steele 1900, cited in Lewis 1991: 12)

(Word translations: look, man now, yours not, my man, understood, fight, hang, crazy pig, faith scripture Ram-Ram, praise Ganga, ever not, virtuous man, very gentle, tyrant, trouble, big big misfortune)

The second example is also one step removed from a natural instance of spoken language. Charles Allen interviewed 'survivors' of the British Raj for a popular BBC radio series and book in the 1970s, in which he includes the 'well-known admonition' in (2b). Again, this example represents an artificial but informed parody of the style.

(2b) You ***dekko***ed me ***giro*** in the ***peenika pani*** and you ***cooch-biwani***ed. You ***soono***ed me ***bolo***. ***Iswasti*** I'll ***gurrum*** your ***peechi***. (Allen 1975: 273)

(Word translations: see, fall, drinking water, no-concern, hear, speak, hence, warm, backside)

Finally, Sadaf (2007: 81) cites Kipling's example in (2c), also within the realm of fiction but with the weight of personal experience behind it.

(2c) The ***choop***er you ***choop***s and the ***jild***ier you ***chel***s, the

better **kooshy** will that **sahib** be. (Kipling, 'The Three
Musketeers' in *Plain Tales From the Hills*, 1888)
(Word translations: quiet, fast, walk, happiness)

Scholars distinguish between lexical borrowing, a process
available to monolinguals, and code-switching, practised
primarily by bilinguals (Myers-Scotton 1993). Borrowing usually
involves the adaptation of a loanword to the phonetic and
morpho-syntactic constraints of the recipient language, while
code-switching (or code-mixing, when intra-sentential) is more
spontaneous, frequently retaining the original phonetic and
grammatical characteristics of the material in question.

Allen's original sound recordings confirm what the
transliterations in (2a) imply: English working-class dialect is
prevalent in this mixed usage (*wot, 'arm, guv'nor, ain't, goin',
'im, took*) but there is no evidence of Hindi phonology anywhere
in the loanwords or the accent.[7] Hindi words are completely
incorporated into English phonology (*decko, kubbi, burra, durm,
pargul, shester, hurry, ficker*).

The first salient feature of the colonial Hinglish examples,
then, is their strict integration into English phonology, a hallmark
of loanwords and greater monolingualism, or at least asymmetric
code-switching.

The grammar of the variety reinforces this impression of
limited familiarity (or effort) with Hindi. Bilingual code-switching
usually involves a matrix or dominant language that provides
the morpho-syntactic frame for the sentence, for example, word
order and all grammatical structure and inflections (Myers-
Scotton 1993, see Bhatia in this volume). Words from the
embedded or subordinate language are generally content words
only, sometimes accommodated through the use of standardized
templates, for example, (VERB-*ify*) in Indian English or (VERB
karna) in Hindi. In (2b) and (2c), English is clearly the exclusive
matrix language; all function words and inflections are in English
(*soono-ed, dekko-ed, this admi, a pargul, choop-er, chel-s*). In
(2a), we see a few longer Hindi sequences, but only short, fixed
phrases (*tumhara nahin, mehra admi*). Further, Hindi switches

in these extracts, though creative, do not always resemble structured bilingual code-switching: violations of Hindi word classes abound and very few structured templates are evident (*cooch-biwani, choop,* and *gurrum* used as verbs, *kooshy* as an adjective). All of these traits suggest limited familiarity with Hindi.

The one highly regular template is the familiar (as opposed to polite) imperative form of the verb as the base form (*lurro, decko, soono, bolo, giro*), bearing the imprint of the primary 'servant-ordering' function of this register for its users. Remarkably, this template was so widespread that it is now the standard loan template for contemporary Hindi–English code-switching (e.g., 'College principal gheraoed', headline from *The Hindu,* 12 January 2008).[8]

Social psychological studies have shown that adopting the linguistic traits of one's interlocutor increases solidarity and positive evaluation between speakers (Sachdev & Giles 2004). The above discussion shows that, in terms of phonetic and syntactic structure, this variety is marked by a spectacular lack of accommodation to the other code. This is accompanied by an equally spectacular lack of mitigating devices and negative facework that usually accompany limited competence (e.g., laughter, apology, self-deprecation, respect terms; Goffman 1967, Brown & Levinson 1987).

So why use Hindi at all? In other situations of severe status asymmetry, slavery conditions for instance, we do not witness the use of the subordinated code by the superordinate group. In other situations of low proficiency, tourists for instance, we either see earnest attempts to approximate the non-native system or copious negative facework to signal the foreigner's lowered status due to lack of proficiency.

Here, however, we see widespread and authoritative use of highly inexpert Hindi. Contemporary parallels of this type usually involve the explicit intent of mockery or injury. Racist parodies of African-American vernacular English by non-speakers ('mock Ebonics') fail to attend to phonetic and grammatical rules of the dialect (Ronkin & Karn 1999), and 'mock' or 'junk' Spanish in monolingual American parodic usage is characterized by pejorative language, hyperanglicization, and bold mispronunciation (Hill 1993). Some British speakers had more command over the 'other' code than some of these cases, but they share many of the same properties, such as bold hyperanglicization and explicit insults. Code-switched insults do not always reduce solidarity, as we will see in the next section, but in (2) they have this effect partly because of the accompanying mispronunciation and other markers of social distance.

As we will see through a comparison to high solidarity uses of similar forms in the next section, it is not simply linguistic form alone but the combination of *form* and *context of use* that conveys high speaker status and low inter-speaker solidarity here. The ostentatious anglicization of Hindi forms first divests the speaker of any authentic alignment with Hindi, forcing an interpretation of the code as other-directed. Interlocutor distance initially remains ambiguous, however: anglicized Hindi could potentially construct solidarity, for instance in humorous banter or tourists' attempts to use a foreign language. It is the use of anglicized Hindi specifically in confrontational or authoritative *discourse contexts,* with no mitigation, that violates the expectation of lower status for a non-native speaker, construing the imprecise use of Hindi as a careless, derogated 'other' code and conveying a face-threatening stance. Bourdieu (1977: 655) proposes that an agent's 'chances for profit' using a given linguistic strategy derive from 'his specific competence and his authority'; even 'imperfect mastery' (p. 659) can accrue symbolic profits as long as it is marked by sufficiently empowered or authoritative conditions of formation. To some extent, junk Spanish, mock Ebonics, and what we might term 'junk Hindi' all constitute such cases.

Two period extracts cited by Sadaf (2007) support the view that Hindi was employed by these speakers as a status-marking 'other' code. The first, (2d), uses *Hindustani* metonymically as a verb to mean 'berate indigenous servants' and the second, (2e), describes a pejorative attitude to Hindi, reserved for orders and scoldings.

(2d) The spring of the carriage was broken ... (so) he
      Hindustani'd the syces ...
(Letter, 17 April 1837. *Miss Eden's Letters*. London: Macmillan,
1919, cited in Sadaf 2007: 74)

(2e) He said he'd see the natives hung
      Before he'd learn their lingo;—
      If he'd his way, the British tongue
      He'd teach them all, by Jingo!
      His Hindostanee words were few—
      They couldn't well be fewer—
      As '**Jeldy jao!**' and '**Deckho, do!**'
      And '**Kupperdar**, you **soor!**'
(Word translations: go quickly, look, give, don't you dare, pig)

(Walter Yeldham, 'The Wonderful Shikaree', in *Lays of Ind*,
Bombay: Thacker, Vining & Co. 1907, cited in Sadaf 2007: 75)

Contemporary British Asian Hinglish

Colonial Hinglish clearly involved vari-directional voicing
(Bakhtin 1981; Rampton 1995), in which Hindi was used to
denigrate a devalued voice of the other, not align with the self.
By contrast, contemporary British Hinglish favours uni-
directional voicing, such that the speaker's use of Hindi asserts
a valued alignment of the self with the borrowed voice.[9] Although
contemporary uses thus stand in stark contrast to colonial uses,
both sets of speech acts surprisingly achieve their divergent
goals through the same linguistic mechanisms of form, context,
and inference.

All the examples in this section come from individuals born
and raised in Britain. Although the historical and contemporary
cases are not directly comparable (a closer parallel to the
colonial variety would be asymmetric, Hindi-dominant users of
English), the comparison here illustrates how dramatically
different the meaning of mixing of the same two languages can
be, given different contextual conditions.

Loanwords

As earlier, I begin with loanwords, perhaps the more visible and widespread form of mixing in Britain. The British newspaper extracts at the start of this article focus primarily on loanwords and a dictionary of British Asian slang now exists (Mahal 2006). The first examples, listed in (3), are from popular British Asian fiction and comedy.

(3a)   From *Londonstani* (Malkani 2006):

(The narrator Jas is a twenty-year-old boy in an Asian gang from West London)

  (i)   . . . As soon as they've taken all their photos, sung *Heppi birday* and then passed round ***thookafied*** (spit-afied) slices a birthday cake. (p. 62)

 (ii)   You seen dat bitch in action when she is surround'd by *munde* (boys)? (p. 61)

(iii)   'Or wudyu prefer it if I threw up in da street? ***Oolti*** (vomit) out on da pavement here where u cud slip in it?' How ***gandah*** (dirty) is that? (p. 37)

 (iv)   Amit takes one look at it an gives it—***Ehh ki hai?*** (What's this?) Wat's wid all dis ***gandh*** (filth), man? You best gets your mum to do your laundry quick time or you'll have to wear da same smelly ***kachha*** (underwear) every day. (p. 52)

  (v)   U sound like a poncey ***gora*** (white person). Wat's wrong wid'chyu, ***sala kutta*** (bastard dog)? U 2 embarrass'd to b a ***desi*** (Indian)? (p. 21)

 (vi)   Right up until Hardjit raised his hand as if was gonna give me a ***thapparh*** (slap) across the face. (p. 61)

(3b)   From *The Bhangramuffins*, a rap parodying young British Asian youth style, in comedy sketch show *Goodness Gracious Me* (1998):

  (i)   Fierce place to pick up the ***rasmalai*** (sweet dish, attractive girl) . . .

He's total ***besti*** (shame, embarrassment) man, whereas
we are cool

(ii)   And we don't drink, and we don't smoke,
If we do we get a ***thapparh*** (slap) from the old folks

An immediate difference between these loans and the colonial
British loans noted earlier is in lexical domains and registers.
Where colonial loans frequently filled cultural gaps or marked
new social status boundaries, many of the loans in (3a-b) denote
familiar, common, indeed base, concepts (*oolti, kachha, thapparh,
gandah*). The voice of such loans is simple and juvenile, evoking
the predominant functional register through which these young
speakers acquire Hindi/Punjabi—childhood home life, an
intimate register, unlike the highly asymmetric 'servant-ordering'
register of colonial Hinglish. Not all aspects of this 'childish'
register reduce status difference, however; the use of *thapparh*
when a perfectly common English word is available—as in
(3a.vi) and (3b.ii)—voices the status and conservatism of the
parent generation.[10]

Structural properties also contrast strikingly with colonial
Hinglish. In (3a-b) there is a complete *lack* of anglicization of
Hindi in transliteration and a strict conformity to Hindi/Punjabi
morpho-syntactic constraints. In my sound recordings with
over seventy members of this community, the overwhelming
majority of Hindi/Punjabi material retains its original phonology,
often emphatically, when embedded in English.

Greater bilingual skill among these speakers is marked by the
retention of not only phonetic but also grammatical detail from
the embedded language. Word class violations in the colonial
examples suggested a lack of familiarity with Hindi; word class
in the present examples respects the constraints of Punjabi and
loans are adapted using structured templates, as in *thookafied*
(the standard Indian template additionally indexing
transnational networks).

Another grammatical retention from the embedded language
can be seen in *munde*, where the speaker uses the Hindi/
Punjabi plural inflection. This is a sign of genuine code-switching,

as opposed to borrowing, which would use only the matrix language inflection, *munda*-s. We can even see evidence of a greater processing cost in mixing inflectional material from both languages in (3c). In line 3, the speaker corrects *gora* to *gori* to conform to Hindi gender agreement, but only with some disruption in speech production. The speaker is willing to take on this processing cost possibly in order to signal mastery of both codes through the use of Hindi grammatical agreement. Notice how dramatically this contrasts with the ostentatious signalling of disaffiliation through lack of skill in colonial Hinglish.

(3c)   (Eleven-year-old British Asian boy)

she does the tuition for my other cousin,	1
he's a ***gora***, half ***gora*** half Punjabi	2
cos his mum's a ***gora*** er- ***gori***	3
and the other one er- dad's a Punjabi.	4

In (3d), we see another example of this practice of actively employing Hindi grammatical agreement (in this case plural agreement in line 7) where the simpler route cognitively might be to use the English plural -*s* inflection.

(3d)   (Twenty-year-old British Asian girl and interviewer discussing language use)

Lavanya:	what about at work?	1
Rita:	er- totally depe- if I'm working where Basma's	2
	working which is for BA (British Airways)	3
Lavanya:	yah?	4
Rita:	then I'd be um English.	5
Lavanya:	mmkay	6
Rita:	cos they're all flippin ***gore*** there, innit?	7

Notice how, in line 2 of the extract in (3e), a white boy uses *gora* as well but uses English, not Hindi, agreement. His adoption of Hindi—and its corresponding cultural capital—is thus subtly shallower.

(3e)   (White British teenager and interviewer, Rampton 1995: 498)

Peter: ***gora*** ... I always call the people who didn't go to   1
         Southleigh (school) ***gora***s, yet I'm white myself   2
Ben: the kids who didn't go to Southleigh you say   3
Peter: yeh, cos we reckon they're, you know,   4
         a bit upper class

The examples above also offer a striking parallel to the colonial instances of race terms shifting to signal class. On the surface, *gora* is a race term. However, in Rampton's example in (3e) the form has explicitly shifted in local usage to denote class. Even in (3d) and (3a.v), the choice of modifiers (*poncey, flippin*) articulates deeper class ideologies. *Poncey gora* and *flippin gore* can both be construed as signalling class as much as whiteness. A significant proportion of airport workers for British Airways are Asian and Rita in (3d) may well be using *flippin gore* to describe the Standard English speech environment there, including both white and Asian employees. Precisely as with *competition wallah* or *memsahib*, the mixed-code forms *poncey gora* and *flippin gore* have acquired the potential to group individuals by class status, not simply ethnicity.

Code-mixing

As in the colonial case, more profound mixing of the two languages affords further devices for the negotiation of status. The examples in (4a-b) are both instances of English mixing with Punjabi and both examples come from conversational speech recordings conducted as part of a larger project on dialect variation and change in the British Asian community.[11]

(4a)   (Twenty-year-old British Asian girl [Rita], her friend [Basma], and interviewer [Lavanya] discussing her use of English and Punjabi when younger)

Lavanya: what about in nursery?   1
Rita: in nursery. did I used to talk in nursery?   2

	I used to chew on my brush in nursery	3
Basma:	boys used to talk to you	4
Rita:	oy shut your face =	5
Basma:	= (*inaudible*)	6
Rita:	= *TU* SHUT UP *HO JA*, RIGH'?	
	TU SHUT UP *HO JA!*	7
	(you shut up become) (*smiling voice*)	
	hhhehhehh	8
Basma:	(*inaudible*)	9
Rita:	is that why you're my best friend, inni'?	10
Basma:	yeah	11
Rita:	*sali* (bitch)	12
Lavanya:	(*laughing*) so she was there in nursery	
	with you?	13
Rita:	no. thank the lord. i'd have been pretty	
	psychologically	14
	disturbed	15

As with the loanword examples, the two switches to Punjabi in lines 7 and 12 in (4a) show no incorporation into English phonology. This maintenance of distinct phonologies is typical of bilingual code-switching as opposed to borrowing.

Line 7 involves a particularly fine example of balanced bilingual skill, as Rita maintains the two distinct phonologies and grammars across no less than six language boundaries in a single utterance: *tu* and *ho ja* in Punjabi phonology and grammar, *shut up* in Indian English phonology and grammar, and *righ'* in urban London style (using a vernacular diphthong and glottal stop). Her production of *shut up* in Punjabi-accented English adds a layer of irony, whereby the mixed utterance *shut up ho ja* invokes a comedic contemporary Indian English voice. To some degree, the switch in line 7 is vari-directional, mockingly addressing her friend in a kind of authoritative Indian parent voice (see Rampton 1995 on the functions of stylized Asian English). However, her choice of a vernacular British form *righ'* at the peak of pragmatic force couches the violent Punjabi imperative within a solidarity-building local British 'friend' code.

Similarly, in line 12 Rita uses an insult, *sali*, but its embedding within mitigating laughter, solidarity, and complimenting (lines 8, 10) conveys solidarity and uni-directional voicing of Punjabi as a powerful self-aligned voice. At other points, Rita even Indianizes her English; at moments of high emotion or performance (lines 14–15), her British accent gains retroflexion, monophthongization, and lack of aspiration, all features of Indian English. This contrast with a very standard British accent in formal speech (line 2).

Thus, where in colonial usage English completely overshadowed Hindi in terms of phonology and syntax, here Punjabi infiltrates English at all levels, at times blurring the boundary completely and even becoming the matrix language in places.

And where colonial mixing unambiguously constructed social distance and status asymmetry, here exactly the *same* Hindi forms—the familiar (versus polite) imperative form and an insult—have precisely the reverse effect. The imperative and insult in Rita's usage serve to *build* solidarity and *reduce* social distance. Bourdieu (1977: 655) observes that 'the same linguistic productions may obtain radically different profits depending on the transmitter'; in this case, the contextual differences that permit the radically different effects in Rita's usage are (1) the extensive phonetic and grammatical evidence of her own skill in the language, indexing her as an authentic Punjabi user; (2) the English-dominant environment, where Punjabi serves as an in-group code; and (3) conversational cues of playfulness (volume, laughter, the London vernacular tag *inni'*, positive facework). As in all successful play confrontation, the playful use of face-threatening acts here proves that the relationship is beyond the threat of such acts; in (2e), by contrast, no such disambiguation is offered by the speaker, leading to a genuine face threat.

The example in (4b) shows an even richer cycle of stance alignments and indicates a wide range of functions of code-switches in the British Asian community.

(4b) (Middle-aged Muslim British Asian businessman talking on the phone with a Sikh school friend; only the businessman's speech is included)

o kiddaan bhai? thik hai? how's i' going man?	1
nah phone aa gaya si ga- o bande da phone aaya si haan.	2
hor kiddaan? everythin alrigh'?	3
yeah listen listen righ'? you started up in business	4
and eh i though' i'd give you a li'le head start as well	5
yeah i give you the yeah you take the balloon	6
orders from me all the balloon orders the arches and that	7
tu kuchh changi job kariye da jab- er- fuck about *na kari*	8
changa sahi sahi kam kari	9
to m- dassi phir	10
how much is i' a balloon?	11
come on *yaar!*	12
sasta kar!	13
achha thik hai thik hai thik hai	14
alrigh' then okay tha's fine	15
nice one	16
yeah yeah yeah yeah	17
tha's good yeah yeah yeah yeah	18
yeah we need these balloons you know	19
jiddaan tin balloon *honde a ik* tree *de ich*	20
yeah *haan haan kar le idda phir*	21
thik hai accha	22
yeah do it like that then	23
i don't mind	24
they gotta look nice you know with nice pretty	25
colours you know sometimes you get pinks and blues	26
and reds and yellows	
byah de rang jede honde a	27
tennu pata hai yaar	28
hor kiddaan what's going down man everything cool?	29
how's things at the yard	30
the old lady alrigh'?	31
you're not giving her any trouble are you?	32

yeh be'er behave yourself man   33
kick your arse in otherwise   34
yeah don't want any more complaints from you yeah?   35
yeah don't go out my home pissed   36
telling you   37
yeah you gon regre' it man i'm telling you bloody   38
behave yourself right
nahin te tennu jutiyaan maar ke bahar kar dena tennu   39
banda ban ja   40
nah nah nah seriously man look listen hear   41
me ou' man look

(Line translations:

what's up brother? you okay?   1
i got a phone call. that guy's phone call came.   2
what else is up?   3
do a good job. don't fuck about.   8
do a good, proper proper job.   9
so tell me   10
friend   12
make it cheaper   13
good okay okay okay   14
the one where three balloons are in one tree   20
yes yes do it like this then   21
okay good   22
the ones that are wedding colours   27
you know, friend   28
what else   29
or she'll throw shoes at you and kick you out of the house   39
be a man   40)

In brief, the broad stances, acts, and personae that this speaker evokes include: in-group solidarity-building (lines 1–3, 29), a haggling Asian businessman (8–10, 12–14), shared cultural knowledge (20–22, 27–28), a middle-aged traditional Asian woman (39), and honourable Asian masculinity (40). In each case, affiliation rather than denigration is asserted; these voicings build solidarity, reduce social distance, and uni-directionally affiliate the speaker positively with recognizable aspects of Asian culture. This speaker, like Rita, has crafted a flamboyantly alternating linguistic repertoire—combining elements of Punjabi, Standard English, London vernacular, and Creole—to index a composite meaning of bicultural authority, claiming each culture as his own.

As with Rita, part of the solidarity-marking force comes simply from the displaced context of using Punjabi in England. Even in confrontational encounters, an element of solidarity persists: In (4c), despite the speaker's intent to demote the addressee's status, his code-switch necessarily marks a shared in-group membership within the UK context and contests the positioning of the foreigner as powerless just as the reclaiming of the insult term *paki* contests its asserted injurious value.

(4c) *Londonstani* (Malkani 2006: 21):

(British Punjabi boy heckling a Westernized Asian boy from his car)

Tu ki samajda hai? (What do you think?) U a Paki jus like me. Even tho u b listenin to U2 or someshit. Are u 2 scared 2 look at us?

A final, crucial element in the construal of Hinglish utterances is the *type* of English used. Young British Asian Hinglish almost obligatorily co-occurs with London vernacular and London Jamaican forms.

(4d) *Londonstani* (Malkani 2006: 16):

Kiddaan, man, 'sup, homeboy?

For instance, typical greetings among British-born members of the London Asian community—as in lines 1, 3, and 29 in (4b) and the extract in (4d)—combine Punjabi (*kiddaan*), urban vernacular (*man, 'sup, homeboy*) and creole forms (*whagwan,* 'what's going on') in a single utterance. Similarly, in (3a) the English included creole and African-American vernacular forms (absence of *be* in *she surround'd*, *dat/da/wid* for *that/the/with*, non-standard verb agreement in *gets*) as well as London vernacular forms (absence of auxiliary in *you seen*). In (3d), Rita uses *flippin* and *inni'*. In (4b) we see vernacular and creole forms such as glottal stops (*be'er, righ', li'le*), *man, fuck about, nice one, tha's, cool, going down, the yard, the old lady, pissed, arse, gon*. In the extract in (4e)—from the lyrics of a song by Birmingham-born British Asian bhangra reggae ('bhangramuffin') musician Apache Indian—the entire English component is Jamaican creole (complementizer *say*, subject pronoun *me*, *fe*, past participle *dress, wan, gal*).

(4e) *Arranged marriage* (Apache Indian)

> Me wan gal fe me Don **Rani**
> Me wan gal dress up in a **sari**
> Me wan gal say **soni lagthi**
> Me wan gal sweet like **jalebi**

(Word translations: queen, sari, looks pretty, Indian sweet)

The composite meaning becomes paramount here—a unified, multi-ethnic, street-smart identity rather than a foreigner inadvertently mixing two languages. Without the high prestige urban elements in young British Hinglish, the risk of construal of Hindi/Punjabi switches as signalling direct alignment with older, first-generation Punjabi-speakers would be very high. Once more, the linguistic and cultural *context* of code-switches or loans constrains, but also potentially enriches, interpretation.

Colonial and contemporary forms of British Hinglish reveal that the structural choices made by speakers encode assertions and contestations of highly specific, historically situated identities, in particular relating to societal and interactional status. At the societal level, both colonial loans (*nabob*) and contemporary loans (*gora*) were seen to shift from a narrow ethnic denotation to optionally indexing primarily social class. At the level of interaction, Hindi–English code-mixing by both groups strategically exploited comparable linguistic devices, but differences in form, context, and cues, to produce diametrically opposed functions for Hinglish in British speech.

HINDI: ITS THREATENED ECOLOGY AND NATURAL GENIUS

Rupert Snell

The Old Language

England, what have you done to make the speech
My fathers used a stranger to my lips,
An offence to the ear, a shackle on the tongue
That would fit new thoughts to an abiding tune?
Answer me now. The workshop where they wrought
Stands idle, and thick dust covers their tools.
The blue metal of streams, the copper and gold
Seams in the wood are all unquarried; the leaves'
Intricate filigree falls, and who shall renew
Its brisk pattern? When spring wakens the hearts
Of the young children to sing, what song shall be theirs?

—R.S. Thomas

I have to watch my language in my adoptive home of Austin, Texas. How much of my native British English—with its 'fortnights' and 'pavements' and 'chalk-and-cheese' distinctions—will cut the mustard in America? Perhaps only people from England or India will understand me there. Eventually one becomes used to reining in one's idiom, and to playing it safe by using universally applicable expressions; such is the price of stepping outside the magic circle of one's mother tongue in its original locale. But in another part of my modest linguistic experience I see a far more insidious process at work: thanks to the influence of English on Hindi, that would-be national language is year by year sacrificing its own heritage of articulacy, and is becoming a stranger in its own land. Looking at the broad sweep of history, this is surely one of the strangest and saddest fates to befall any member of the great Indo-Aryan family of languages.

As an outsider to Hindi, I am constantly struck by two things: the enormous depth of field and expressive power of the language, and its strange readiness to compromise its own articulacy by blithely capitulating to the easy seductions of English. In terms of cultural politics this whole area is a minefield where only fools rush in; but the angels' preferred strategy of sheltering within a discipline such as linguistics does not always give the breadth of vision needed for a view of the broad picture, so I shall risk some folly here. My argument is that one effect of the influence of English on Hindi is to erode Hindi's natural articulacy and elegance by making its own innate lexicon seem exotic, esoteric and eccentric even within its own geographic territory. The juxtaposition of these two differentiated abstract concepts—'articulacy' being pragmatic, and 'elegance' aesthetic—is deliberate, since the expressive power of a language can only be judged with reference to both its high-flying usage in, say, literature, *and* its effectiveness in the array of everyday contexts and registers demanded by contemporary circumstances both specialized and domestic. Though many metaphors and parallels come to mind, it is the trope of ecology that provides the most satisfying model for understanding the situation surrounding Hindi: a certain amount of outside influence can be enriching, but the nice ecological balance begins to be threatened at the point where the imported material starts to displace—and render obsolete—the native strand.

With such an opening, my argument may seem about to deal

in the coin of linguistic 'purity', a currency associated with a reactionary cultural conservatism and a nostalgia for an imagined golden period remote from the benighted present. In order to show that my anxiety about the lading of Hindi with excessive English freight is not an exercise in Indic xenophobia, let me begin by unravelling the three major *gunas* or strands that comprise the body of modern Hindi.

It is well known that modern languages from the northern part of South Asia—languages such as Hindi, Bengali, Punjabi and Urdu—are all essentially and historically derived from Sanskrit; and that (with the exception of Urdu) the development of their modern forms has depended quite heavily on the addition of Sanskritic loanwords and neologisms. In terms of lexicon, this major strand itself provides Hindi speakers with two types of words: *tatsama* or 'unchanged' Sanskrit words such as *kshetra* 'field' and *karma* 'action', and their *tadbhava* derivatives, *khet* and *kaam* respectively. Most usefully, such doublets often serve two different contexts or registers: we can plough a *khet*, but not a *kshetra*, which is reserved for abstract 'fields' such as education or psychology. Ever since its first recorded usage, Hindi has been enriched by these paired variations of lexical function and register. Contrarily, as modern Hindi has become more and more remote from the period in which Sanskrit was any kind of spoken language, the lure of the old Sanskritic forms has garnished today's vernacular language with a 'classical' *tatsama* flavour: thus in modern standard Hindi, *mitra* ('friend') is now preferred over its *tadbhava* form *miit,* which spoke so sweetly of friendship in Hindi's earlier vernacular lexicon. In the field of pre-modern poetry, doublets such as the *tatsama* word *hridaya* and the *tadbhava* word *hiya* would offer poets a choice of register and variances in rhythm and euphony, even if the two words share, at heart, the same meaning.

Thus throughout its history, Hindi has enjoyed the benefits of varied registers; and it was in this context that new sources of words began to enrich the language even further when the Perso-Arabic lexicon became available in the subcontinent. Thus the second of Hindi's three *gunas* is the great gift of the Persian lexicon (itself including words of Arabic and Turkish origin), which gradually and slowly became grafted on to the Sanskritic stock through the very centuries in which north India's regional vernacular languages developed and their discrete but related literary traditions came into being. Sanskritic and non-Sanskritic words began to rub shoulders very comfortably from an early stage, certainly well before the phenomenal growth of the literary corpus in Braj Bhasha and Awadhi in the sixteenth century: thus it was a small thing for Tulsidas to use such words as the Arabic loan *gariib* (and *gariibi*) many times in his works. In many a situation, modern Hindi can choose from a rich menu of synonyms; for example, there are no less than five choices for the conjunction 'but'—Sanskritic *par*, *kintu* and *parantu*; Persian *magar* and Arabic-derived *lekin*.[1] But if fastidious speakers of Sanskritized Hindi can readily avoid non-Sanskritic words by sticking to their *kintus* and their *parantus*, they have no such opportunity in the equally essential function of a conjunction meaning 'that', for which Hindi now[2] offers no choice but the Persian-derived *ki*. So even if commonplace words as *bachcha* 'child' and *baad* 'after' are found objectionable on the basis of their respectively Persian and Arabic origins, the little word *ki* has embedded itself so deeply into the body of Hindi as to refuse extraction even by the surgical skills of the *shuddh* Hindi purists; and similarly, but for the Persianate name 'Hindi', the language itself would have no name at all.[3] Thus the desire for a process of linguistic cleansing that would rid Hindi of its non-Sanskritic lexicon has no chance of success; it is as though English, through overzealous devotion to its Germanic roots, were to eschew all Romance words—a ridiculous situation in which the word 'word' would be acceptable but the word 'sentence' would be sentenced to exile.

(The so-called 'purity' enshrined and fossilized by the term *shuddh* Hindi calls for some analysis. *Shuddh* Hindi is not 'pure' in terms of an honest and natural characterization of Hindi as a vernacular tongue—a concept that we might think of as the horizontal axis of Hindi, and which would proudly include the mixed palette of features that make Hindi such a subtly articulate and flexible language; rather it relates to an understanding of purity as relating to ancestry, a *vertical* axis in which anything that is seen to dilute the pristine sacred character of the language is regarded as a threat from an alien 'other'. It is, in other words, a kind of *ritual* purity rather than a pragmatic one, making *shuddh* Hindi better suited to the pomp and circumstance of ceremony than to everyday life.)

Following the importation of Persian vocabulary, ships and sailors from Europe began to unload Hindi's third strand at various trading ports, especially on the western seaboard of India: they added Portuguese and English words to India's already complex language map. First of all, coastal languages such as Konkani, and then interior languages such as Hindi (and thence, eventually, even such thoroughly landlocked languages as Nepali)[4] began to feel the influence of Portuguese, as domestic Hindi's *chaabi, kamra* and *almaari* remind us each time we use a 'key' to lock a 'room' or a 'cupboard'. It is hard to know exactly how such words displaced any Sanskritic equivalents in everyday use, but we must note that these European guests were never admitted to the hallowed halls of the higher registers: *kamra*, for example, must give way to a Sanskritic word such as *kaksh* in a formal context, and an abstract 'key' to an exercise or theorem is a *kunji* rather than a *chaabi*.[5] Such elevated registers have consistently been a Sanskritic preserve, even more than the higher registers of English are dominated by Latin and Greek.

If the grafting of non-Indic words on to the Hindi stock has been restricted to certain specific registers, it has also been subject to some *structural* limitations: few of the new arrivals were allowed to become verb roots, or to be admitted into the inner sanctum of word-making through such processes as affixation. The Persian *gair-* 'without' almost always partners Perso-Arabic components, yielding results such as *gair-qaanooni*), rather than with Sanskritic ones; and similarly the Sanskritic negative prefix *a-* will usually choose a Sanskritic marriage partner, as in *avaidh*. Mixed forms such as **gairvaidh* or *aqaanooni would be linguistically illegal—as filmic fathers must invariably say, *yah shaadi nahiin ho sakti!* Similarly, only a very few non-Sanskritic or non-Indic words have followed the pattern of *intazaarna* or *talaashna* in forming an infinitive verb; *filmaana* is a rare (and rarely used) Anglo-Hindi example. The late Rajiv Gandhi lost popular credibility one day in the run-up to elections, when he spontaneously coined the verb *loozna* 'to lose'—*'chaahe ham jiiten ya loozen . . .'* The rarity of such organic formations is readily explained by the fact that the Hindi habit of forming phrase verbs with either *karna* or *hona* renders them unnecessary: why create such a form as *talaasho* when the ingredients for *talaash karo* are already to hand? The formula of 'loanword + *karna* or *hona*' has proved spectacularly successful, leading to the freest possible mixture of languages: not only such sets as *koshish karna, prayatn karna,* and 'try' *karna,* but also the more freewheeling 'fry' *karna,* 'adjust' *karna, bachchon ki* 'look-after' *karna,* anything-you-like *karna.*

Adjacent to this tendency is the production of calques, or 'loan-translations' as they are often called. As V.R. Jagannathan has pointed out with characteristic insight,[6] the translated Hindi term for this, *udhaar-anuvaad,* is an example of its own class, with the two component words, 'loan' and 'translation', being separately translated into the target language to form a new expression (whose meaning can perhaps be understood only by reference to the underlying English original, since the concept of the 'loanword' is not common currency in the Hindi medium). The process has led to countless English expressions being admitted into Hindi with scant regard for the appropriateness of the resulting Hindi expression: the English term 'bus service' is rendered *bas seva* (with implications of service *of* buses rather than *by* them); a *stambh-lekhak* is a newspaper 'columnist' (rather than, for example, a graffitist prone to defacing the columns of buildings).

In some contexts, an English pattern supports or endorses a Sanskritic neologism, as in such participial adjectives as *likhit* 'written' and *prakaashit* 'published', in which the word-ending -*it* provides a closer match to the '-en' or '-ed' endings of English

than do such Hindi equivalents as *likha* (or *likha hua*); examples
are legion—*paricit* 'acquainted', *aashcharya-cakit* 'astonished',
sthagit 'postponed', and so on.[7] Such Sanskrit or Sanskrit-derived
words have become standard in Hindi during the last 150 years
or so: tracing the imprint conventions in books published in the
nineteenth century, one sees such words as *prakaashit* gradually
taking over from older expressions such as *chhapa hua*
'printed'—expressions in which the term is less specialized in
sense, and more modestly vernacular in form. The true
significance of this process is not to be seen at the level of the
individual word, but rather in terms of the associated syntax:
these Sanskritic participles often allow for constructions which
parallel English ones, such as *main aashcharya-chakit tha* 'I was
surprised', in which the grammatical subject in both languages
is the 'self', whereas a less self-consciously formal Hindi would
typically frame the *experience* rather than the experiencer as
the grammatical subject, saying something like *mujhe aashcharya*
[or *taajjub*] *hua*. With the inception of such processes, involving
grammar as well as lexicon, Hindi is on the slippery slope
towards forfeiting part of its natural character; for while it is a
characteristic of English to invest a strong sense of agency in
the individual, the traditional preference of Hindi has been to
subjugate the individual to the experiential world—hence its
rich range of constructions on the pattern of *mujhe X hua*, in
which 'X' is the experience, and *mujhe* the obliquely referenced
actor.

Other loanwords have been admitted into Hindi because they
fulfil a palpable need. The neat and clipped English word 'sorry!'
is unmatched as a social disclaimer—a perfect blend of concision
and insincerity—and has found a ready place in Hindi speech. A
more celebrated shibboleth lies in the etiquette of 'please' and
'thank you': Hindi relies on the sophistications of its inherent
honorific system and largely dispenses with the tacked-on
phrases favoured in English. (Learners of Hindi err on the safe
side, with too many a *kripa karke* and *dhanyavaad*.) Here is the
Hindi poet Raghuvir Sahay, simultaneously celebrating and
subverting the usages of Hindi etiquette:

भारतीय

हम भारतीय हैं
धन्यवाद, धन्यवाद, क्षमा कीजिएगा, नहीं कहते हैं
हम सिर्फ़ देखते हैं अपनी आँखों से
और ले लेते हैं पानी भरा ग्लास
फिर से उधर एक बार देखकर[8]

Indian

We are Indian;
We don't say *thank you, thank you, excuse me*:
We just look shrewdly,
And take the glass of water,
And glance that way again.

Latterly the process of globalization, along with a slew of Western images through American and British media and other sources, has hastened the import of loanwords into Hindi. Their selection seems to have followed many different kinds of logic, going well beyond the requirement of finding words for new concepts and artefacts: the Hindi lexicon hardly needed another word for 'death', already having such multiple synonyms as *mrityu, maut, dehaant, nidhan* and countless others (including a host of highly expressive euphemisms), and yet the loanword *deth* stalks the Hindi-speaking world just as determinedly as any of these native avatars of Yama. For many speakers, Hindi words for such items as relationship terms, colours, left/right directions, kitchen, bathroom, garments, table, time, and an almost infinite number of other such items have been all but displaced by their English equivalents in everyday usage. *Daddy ki blue shirt bathroom ki table par padi hai.* An unfortunate side effect of this process is that the Hindi words themselves begin to sound quaint and exotic (who says *gusalkhaana* any more?). What is truly egregious here is that the new imports do not merely *supplement* existing words, but also *replace* them, just as the wheezy, arthritic harmonium (wholly unsuited to the fine glissando technique of Indian music) replaces the sublime sarangi.

Faced with this onslaught of English since the early twentieth century, the self-appointed champions of Hindi have fought back by developing the Hindi lexicon through the formation of neologisms, typically based on Sanskrit roots. This has led to a situation in which the so-called 'purity' of the language is measured on a scale that privileges Sanskrit as the primary altar, font, source and model for the modern language: *Shuddh* Hindi pretends that Hindi is in some way a classical language, a kind of contemporary Sanskrit, rather than a vibrant vernacular in which various strands have blended together organically over time. As noted earlier, what is meant by *shuddh hindi* is far from being a pristine vernacular unchanged by influence from elsewhere: rather it is a supercharged Sanskritized Hindi, a culturally conservative register artificially enhanced with Sanskritic loanwords and neologisms. The attitudes around this enhancement collapse the timescale of linguistic history and regard the Sanskrit lexicon as a fully legitimate source of vernacular words: that is, it sees no boundary between the Hindi lexicon and Sanskrit, and does not regard Sanskrit loanwords as 'loans' at all but gives them a welcome that is fastidiously denied to imports from any other source. To regard *pratiiksha* as in some way truer to the character of Hindi than *intazaar* is to rewrite history, for in many such cases the Sanskrit loanword is a much later import into Hindi than its Perso-Arabic equivalent.

The admission of loanwords into the *active* lexicon of Hindi-speakers has been patchy, with some of the more absurd formulations (such as *lauh-path gaamini* or 'iron-path traveller' for 'train', and *kanth-langot* or 'larynx loincloth' for 'necktie') the butt of well-earned mockery. Some coinings seem to reflect a desire to build on phonetic as well as semantic connections between an English term and its Sanskritized Hindi equivalent: thus 'pollution' yields *pradooshan*, 'survey' yields *sarvekshan*, and 'navigation' yields *nauvigyaan* (in which the *nau*/nav parallel artfully exploits an old Indo-European cognate). In terms of language development, the difficulty here has not been to create requisite neologisms, but to make them a real part of actual usage in spoken Hindi: speakers who know English are entirely at home with 'pollution', and would not necessarily feel themselves to be more articulate or comprehensible by jettisoning it in favour of its encoded Hindi version, *pradooshan*. And because of the social cachet of English, some speakers would even regard such Hindi terms with disdain: Anglophone Hindi-speakers who claim to be unable to follow the Sanskritized Hindi of the news media often do so with pride rather than regret.

One context in which the *shuddh* register has developed freely and productively is the field of literature—*arthaat, saahitya ke pavitra kshetra men iska vishesh evam asiimit vikaas sampann hua hai*. This is a space which need not be concerned about a general or widespread comprehensibility, or about the broad currency of vocabulary: indeed it can *revel* in its highly Sanskritic register, and tends to be the preserve of an educated class whose credentials are in any case likely to include a knowledge of English alongside Hindi, meaning that readers may decode difficult loanwords, understanding them on the basis of the English words that underlie them. To take a single example, the literary prose developed so successfully by writers like Mahadevi Verma exploits an ironic disjunction between the elevated, Sanskritized tone of the prose on the one hand, and the humbly domestic nature of the characters (especially children and servants) being described on the other: the author colludes with the reader in the use of a linguistic register that would be wholly impenetrable to the subjects themselves. Though Mahadevi's example may smack of a loftily patrician superiority, there is no doubting the importance of the Sanskritic element in Hindi *belles-lettres*. The literary corpus of Hindi has been enriched beyond words by this high-culture element, which brings to the vernacular language precisely that element of 'refinement' which is enshrined in the very name of 'Sanskrit'. In literature of this kind, Hindi exploits its birthright to the full, making profitable claim to the unparalleled riches of the Sanskritic heritage.

But alas, literature is not the world, and although often

evoked as a 'mirror' of society, it is one that can both colour and distort the natural picture. What we might define as 'the literary' has acquired a perhaps disproportionate dominance in the broader institution of Hindi because of the very close symbiosis that has developed between the fields of language and literature in academia. Literature—'acquaintance with books; polite or humane learning; literary culture' as one definition has it[9]—has become the primary and often sole focus for scholars interested in language, the language–literature connection being far more exclusive in Hindi than it is in, say, an equivalent European situation. Consequently, academics and writers monopolize linguistic authority in the Hindi sphere. The problem here is that in speaking to and for the artistic priorities of the literati, literature may disregard the pragmatic needs of everyday language use (the higher registers are privileged at the cost of the demotic, with 'confidential beverages' being regarded as superior to 'free drinks'). To concentrate exclusively on literature while ignoring the needs of the quotidian is to develop aesthetically pleasing handicrafts while ignoring the many other industries on which society depends.

In summary, then, my argument here is that the development of Hindi in the twentieth century has been very largely the preserve of high-register, Sanskritic contexts and usages, and that this process has been aided and abetted by the high status accorded to literature as the highest accomplishment of language use. Faced with a multiplicity of new social contexts, and given the absence of any sustained institutional attempt to develop a middle-of-the-road Hindustani, the Hindi-speaking public has had just two main options: to learn and accept the Sanskritic neologisms, or to pick up the English loanwords. The more extreme and 'difficult' the neologism, the greater the appeal of the pre-existing English: thus terms such as *vaataanukoolit*[10] and *pratham shreni*, intended to enrich the language, in fact drive the Hindi-speaking public into the arms of 'air conditioning' (or more likely 'AC', given India's penchant for abbreviations and acronyms) and 'first class' respectively. Far from developing Hindi from within as intended, such processes of Sanskritization have actually aided the importation of English words. The overwriting of a historical 'Hindustaan' with a national 'Bhaarat' has played its part in the widespread acceptance of the English word 'India'[11] as a name for this country; and Bhaaratiy, whether adjective or noun, seems to be a much more heavily loaded and portentous word than national nomenclatures in common use elsewhere in the world.

The *Dhvani* of Hindi

One of the cornerstones of the articulate use of language as recognized by the Indian tradition has been the concept of *dhvani*—a term referring to the allusive meaning implied by a statement, or the full burden of information carried by the totality of words (including their sounds) used in particular combinations. The context in which this concept is usually invoked is that of literary theory, and it may seem out of place in a discussion of contemporary colloquial language. But in assessing the rhetorical effectiveness of language, and in exploring the idea of the ecology of a language, such a concept has a useful relevance. Linguists explain that even a simple sentence or 'speech act' is a highly complex piece of communication; and part of what makes speech articulate is the deeply rooted grounding of its words in a culture that houses and sustains it. Take, for example, the prose of a writer such as Premchand, whose language is composite and varied in terms of its word origins, but which achieves an impressively orchestrated coherence, a masterfully organic rhetorical effect which constitutes a discrete world of meaning.[12] Premchand's Hindi manifests an entire world of experience, in which words and concepts bolster and support each other. It might be said that to invoke an author who died over seventy years ago is to indulge in archaism, so let us take a more recent work, a contemporary poem by Vinod Kumar Shukla, and consider what makes some sixty words into such a satisfyingly coherent human statement:

हताशा से एक व्यक्ति बैठ गया था

हताशा से एक व्यक्ति बैठ गया था
व्यक्ति को मैं नहीं जानता था
हताशा को जानता था
इसलिए मैं उस व्यक्ति के पास गया
मैंने हाथ बढ़ाया
मेरा हाथ पकड़कर वह खड़ा हुआ
मुझे वह नहीं जानता था
मेरे हाथ बढ़ाने को जानता था
हम दोनों साथ चले
दोनों एक दूसरे को नहीं जानते थे
साथ चलने को जानते थे।[13]

A man

me, but
amiliar
went up to that man
I reached out to him
He took my hand and stood up
I was a stranger to him, but
Reaching out felt familiar
We set off together
We were strangers but
Setting off together felt familiar.

We find here a wonderfully articulate quality in the use of language: self-aware to a fault, and largely domestic in register with just two *tatsama* words—*hataasha* and *vyakti*, neither of them particularly obscure or literary. The idea of 'knowing' (*jaanna*) a person in lines 2, 7, and 10 is paralleled or capped by the 'knowing' of an abstraction (despair, the extending of a hand, walking together) in lines 3, 8, and 11. Thus the fulcrum of the poem, the feature that gives it leverage, is the bringing together of two kinds of knowledge: to 'know' (appreciate, be connected with, feel for, value) a person, and to 'know' (recognize, be familiar with, understand, value) a shared experience; like the biblical 'acquainted with grief', the phrasing forces us to see the act of 'knowing' anew, commuting between subjective and objective modes of knowledge, and yielding meanings of a deeply humane connectedness. Much of this is lost in (my) translation, where a single verb to render the Hindi *jaanna* seems ineffective. When Hindi has such rich powers of expression, why should it capitulate so blithely to the compromises of today's Anglophile usage?

What has this to do with language development, and with Hinglish? My argument is that the organic cohesion of this poem is achieved through a very careful control of lexicon, in which the sense of everyday sharedness of experience is of a piece with the well-established, vernacular familiarity of the words that constitute it. Each word and each experience in a poem such as this has a thousand echoes in the sentiments of the reader. It is language at its most brilliantly communicative: an act of genius, a contemporary statement with roots running deep into the culture of the land, and deeply imbued with *dhvani*—a quality which depends on the integrity of a linguistic ecosystem in which words relate to each other as long-acquainted members of an established world of meaning.

Language is of course a dynamic entity, and those who resist change are on a hiding to nothing. Etymologies and origins cannot count for everything: after all, the name 'Cambridge' has successfully travelled from its native England to Massachusetts, USA, where there is no Cam river to be bridged, while Oxford has travelled to many American states having neither fords nor oxen to ford them. As I noted in an earlier paper,[14] calque-based phrases and expressions such as *prashna poochna* and *doosre shabdon men*, slated as solecisms half a century ago in R. Varmma's admittedly conservative *Acchi Hindi*, are now fully assimilated into the rhetoric of contemporary Hindi; and even such esteemed Hindi authors as Nirmal Verma use calqued expressions such as *prem men girna* (to 'fall' in love). Such usages reflect the deep penetration of English influence into the Hindi soil, and in many cases the language may develop and flourish as a result. But as the process of change continues, my argument is that the process includes also a definite loss.[15]

We are encouraged, within the pages of this book and elsewhere, to celebrate the new, zippy Hinglish as a fun thing that echoes the buzz of youth culture, and all that. But the point I want to make is a more sombre one: the unattractiveness, for whatever reason, of the over-formal register of Hindi promoted in official circles has turned a long-term trickle of English words into a monsoon flood; the result is a dilution of the genius of Hindi, and irreversible damage to its ecological balance. Hindi aspires to be a national language but is in danger of becoming little more than a *notional* one as people turn to English or Hinglish in droves. As Hindi orientates itself increasingly to the compass of English, it devalues its own genius as a language with innate individuality and articulacy. Beyond the obvious comedy, the character and genius of Hindi is inexorably eroded year by year. The Welsh-English poet R.S. Thomas, lamenting the ascendancy of the latter language over the former, was not laughing when he asked 'When spring wakens the hearts / Of the young children to sing, what song shall be theirs?' Is it not timely to ask the same rhetorical but serious question in the context of India?

THE MULTILINGUAL MIND, OPTIMIZATION THEORY, AND HINGLISH

Tej K. Bhatia

Introduction

Given the long history of language contact in India, the phenomenon of language mixing is not just inevitable—it can be considered natural. The language contact situation of Hindi with Sanskrit, Persian, Arabic, and other Indian and European languages has led to the fusion of these languages with Hindi over its approximately ten-century history. Different names and labels such as Hindvi, Rexta, Rexti, Hindustani, and Urdu are in fact more reflective of the mixed nature of Hindi than of language differentiation. Bhakti poets of Hindi celebrated and characterized such fusion as 'sadhukari boli' or 'khichari boli'. The most recent addition to this long inventory of mixed systems is Hinglish, a blend of Hindi and English.

This paper will examine Hinglish, particularly through the lens of the bi/multilingual mind and linguistic creativity. It will argue that bilingual creativity can best be explained by what I propose as the Optimization Theory. Salient aspects of the theory will be introduced along with underlying mechanisms that render the formal and functional (e.g., socio-psychological) meaning in bilingual language mixing. Both universal and

37

language-specific aspects of Hinglish and bilingual creativity will receive specific emphasis as our discussion will focus on the linguistic, sociolinguistic, and psycholinguistic treatment of Hinglish usage in Indian media and advertising. The paper is divided into two parts—the first briefly lays the conceptual foundation of the Optimization Theory and the bi/multilingual mind while the second is devoted to Hinglish. It is vital to note that the term 'bilingual' or 'bilingualism' is used in a wider sense to cover both bilingualism as well as multilingualism.

I: The Bi/Multilingual Mind: Language Organization, Optimization, Creativity

A bilingual's organization of the verbal repertoire in his/her mind is quite different from that of monolinguals. When a monolingual decides to speak, his/her brain does not have to make complex decisions of language choice that a bilingual faces. According to Chomsky (1988: 188),

> Every human being speaks a variety of languages. We sometimes call them different styles or different languages, but they are really different languages, and somehow we know when to use them, one in one place and another one in another place. Now each of these languages involves a different switch setting. In the case of [different languages] it is a rather dramatically different switch setting, more so than in the case of different styles [of one language].

In other words, the decision-making process for a monolingual is restricted to choosing from a limited number of varieties/styles (say, informal versus formal). Monolinguals do not realize that a multilingual person, take me for instance, has to make a choice from among four languages and their sub-/mixed varieties while communicating even within his family in India. Language choice is not random but unconsciously governed by a set of factors. I am a speaker of Multani (also called Lahanda or Saraiki), Punjabi, Hindi, and English. When growing up, I would use Multani to talk with my brothers and parents, Punjabi with my two sisters-in-law, Hindi with my nephews and nieces, and English with my children. In short, each language in my mind is associated with a well-defined domain. A violation of this domain allocation has serious implications not only for communication alone but also for interpersonal relationships. In addition to the language–person domain allocation, other factors such as topics, setting, social structure, and emotions determine language choice. While discussing an academic topic, I switch from Multani to English with my brothers and, if the context is emotive, from English to Hindi with my children. In short, the determinants of language choice, let alone language use, are very complex among bilinguals, which in turn, presents evidence that the scope and the degree of a bilingual's organization of verbal repertoire are different from that of a monolingual's. Interestingly, language choice (or 'language negotiation') is a salient feature of bilingual linguistic competence and performance. The Markedness model (Myers-Scotton 1993) attempts to capture such social motivations that trigger and determine language choice in bilinguals.

From this discussion, it follows that the differential domain allocation holds a key to the representation and access to languages in the bi/multilingual brain. The complexity of differential domain organization/allocation and its unconscious determinants poses a serious challenge not only for the psycholinguistic theory of bi/multilingual language production and processing but also for exploration of deeper insights into the socio-psychological motivations for bilingual language use.

Another fascinating feature of bilingual speech is that though bilinguals are capable of keeping the two linguistic systems separate, they often mix them either within a sentence or inter-sententially. This behaviour, exhibited by both bilingual children and adults, is termed 'code-mixing' or 'code-switching' in sociolinguistic literature. What explains this behaviour? Earlier research attempted to explain it using the **language deficiency hypothesis**, claiming that bilingual adults in general, and children in particular, have language/vocabulary gaps. In other words, they possess limited language proficiency either in one or both languages. Whenever they experience difficulty retrieving a word from their non-dominant language, they tend to substitute a word from the native or dominant language. There is no doubt that at times both monolinguals and bilinguals might experience temporary difficulty in retrieving a word from memory—reminiscent of what is termed the 'tip of the tongue' phenomenon. However, this hypothesis fails to explain observed natural occurrences of bilingual language mixing. A cursory examination of bilingual verbal behaviour worldwide shows serious limitations of this hypothesis—for instance, bilinguals often substitute words both from their dominant as well as non-dominant languages. Interestingly, they might even mix synonyms from both languages in the same utterance to underscore or paraphrase a point they are making. For example, in the Hinglish phrase *cintaa na kiijiye, koii worry nahiin* (do not worry, no worry), the use of the Hindi word *cintaa* (to worry) is followed by its English counterpart 'worry' to reinforce the point. In other words, the lack of proficiency in either one or both languages (i.e., 'semi-bilingualism') or memory recall is not always the primary motivator for language mixing.

The **language augmentation hypothesis** can offer deeper insights into the bilingual mixing behaviour and, in turn, constitutes a basis of the Optimization Theory proposed here— it states that bilinguals are basically very discriminating, very skilled users of their linguistic resources. The unconscious and conscious consideration of optimization leads them to mix language with the aim of achieving maximum efficacy from the two linguistic systems at their disposal. This can explain, for instance, the immense popularity of the Hindi song, '*Crazy kiyaa re*' 'Hey, (you) drove (me) crazy'. The underlying reason for mixing Hindi with English is not the lack of a translational equivalent of *crazy* in Hindi. In fact, Hindi dictionaries and Bollywood films offer a rich vocabulary to capture a range of denotative and connotative meanings expressed by the English term *crazy*. However, due to the differential domain allocation/ appeal of English and Hindi in the mind of Hindi–English bilingual, the socio-psychological weight assigned to the degree of craziness by the two translational equivalents is not the same. The English word is capable of invoking the premium form of craziness witnessed in Hollywood movies in addition to underscoring a Western association (and thus its overt behaviourist attributes) that Hindi translational equivalence lacks. The discussion in the second part of this paper will further highlight the range and scope of augmentation effects of Hinglish.

There are two main facets of the Bilingual Linguistic Optimization Theory: (1) accommodation or neutralization of paradoxical or opposing features of two participating languages and (2) enhancement by drawing mutually exclusive or overlapping features from the two or more languages. If two languages stand in an opposing or paradoxical domain relation, their mixing results in the reconciliation of the two domains. Bhatia & Ritchie (1996: 346–47) illustrate this point by identifying the hedging (e.g., taboo suppression, de-intensification, or vague 'sort of' expression; also see example 11) function of language mixing. Another manifestation of accommodation is by compromising on one feature but making up for that deficiency by incorporating a new positive feature. For instance, English is a prestige language in India but Hindi is not. That is why a prestigious English periodical or an advertisement for a luxury product will avoid mixing Hindi. However, the reverse is not true (e.g., Hindi periodicals will not shy away from using English both in Devanagari and Roman scripts). As a result, a Hindi–English mixed ad might fall short on the scale of its exclusive appeal or diminish the prestige effect marked by an English-only ad. However, a mixed Hinglish ad is ultimately capable of reaching out to both English and Hindi speech communities instead of exclusively marking membership in either. When languages stand in mutually feeding relation with respect to a particular feature or domain, they can enhance each other's effect either by intensifying a feature (gradational enhancement) or providing a mosaic of features drawn from the input languages. The mixing of the English word *crazy* or the use of the English word *new* in global advertising exemplifies the gradational enhancement rendered by English. It is not that either Hindi or other languages of the world lack the concept of *new*. However, the degree and nature of newness afforded by the English word is distinct from its corresponding word in another language. Such optimization is somewhat similar to what happens in metallurgy or material sciences—a new product is developed by mixing, by thus reducing the weakness of one by mixing it with another to strengthen it.

The cumulative effect of accommodation/augmentation in the context of optimization of linguistic meaning can best be explained by an analogy drawn from the beverage industry. The separation of juices (e.g., apple versus orange juice) renders two distinct tastes. However, if one mixes the two juices, the result is a new taste, distinct from the two pure juices. To get an optimal yield from mixing, it is imperative for the mixture to have the correct ratio, not just a random mix. The mixture has to follow a set of rules, forcing it to be systematic. A competent bilingual has a set of integrative rules which, in turn, assure a systematic mixed output. In short, whether languages are in conflict or harmony, language mixing results in a win–win unless it fails to obey the formal grammar of the resultant mixed system. The formal grammar provides the much-needed glue to linguistic units assembled from two or more languages.

Optimization Theory can not only add explanatory power to both the Linguistic Accommodation Hypothesis (e.g., Giles 1984 and his colleagues over the past twenty-five years) and the Markedness/Differential Domain Hypothesis (Myers-Scotton 1993), but it also relates them as different manifestations of the same basic principle. The theory predicts the limitations of single-language discourse in attaining multiple appeals and high semantic potential; a mixed language system can ensure a win–win situation by combining resources of two languages. Further, the theory is grounded in the generative conception of human languages.

The linguistic and sociolinguistic motivations for language

mixing include deeper creative needs, including considerations like semantic domains and complexity (an item less complex or salient in one language), stylistic effects, clarification, elaboration, relief strategy (i.e., a linguistic item is temporarily unavailable in one language), interlocutor's identification, discourse strategies of participants/topics, the addressee's perceived linguistic capability, and the speaker's own linguistic ability. It can also be used to convey other complex socio-psychological meanings such as attitudes, societal values, and personalities. This list of motivations is by no means complete (see Bhatia & Ritchie [1996] for details).

The hybrid system resulting from mixing English and Hindi is popularly named Hinglish, which begs further discussion of the fundamental bilingual brain capacity and language naming. Any theory of the bilingual brain has to account not only for the capability of integration/separation of linguistic systems but also for its capacity to distinguish between the 'matrix' and the 'embedded' languages. Consider the following sentences:

1. *Daddy* kii *blue shirt bathroom* kii [*corner*] *table* par pari hai (Snell, this volume) 'Daddy's blue shirt is sitting on the table.'
2. *Filmi raajaas kii duniyaa* is not worth *ek paisa.* 'The world of filmi royalty is not worth a single paisa.'

Interestingly, despite the fact that sentence 1 contains less Hindi lexical items than English ones (and vice versa in 2), Hindi–English bilinguals will judge sentences (1) and (2) as examples of the Hindi and English language, respectively. This is because, in most cases of language mixing, it is possible to identify one of the two languages involved as playing a more dominant role. In linguistic research, it is customary to refer to the dominant language in mixed utterances as the *matrix* (host, base) language and the non-dominant language as the *embedded* (guest) language (Myers-Scotton 1993). The matrix language is the one that gives the sentence its basic character, and the embedded language is the one that contributes the 'imported' material. For this reason, Hindi–English bilinguals will claim on intuitive grounds that in (1), the matrix language is Hindi and the embedded language English—and vice versa in (2). What unconscious criteria do bilinguals employ to distinguish the matrix from the embedded language? This is the subject of debate in linguistic research (see Bhatia & Ritchie 2009: 594–95). Before we proceed, I should add that the term Hinglish is an ambiguous label used as a cover term for both Hindi–mixed English (matrix English, embedded Hindi) and English–mixed Hindi (matrix Hindi, embedded English)—yet another aspect of bilingual optimization.

II: Bilingual Language Mixing System: Key Theoretical Questions

Any unified treatment of the bilingual mind has to account for the language separation and integration aspects of bilingual verbal competence, capacity, use, and creativity. It needs to address the following key questions, central to understanding the universal and scientific basis for the linguistic creativity of bilinguals. I will attempt to answer them with special reference to Hinglish (Hindi as matrix) as used in Indian advertising.

   i.   Is language mixing a random phenomenon?
   ii.   What kind of linguistic elements can be mixed? Where and how?
   iii.   Does mixing exhibit varying degrees of complexity? If yes, what is the difference between high-level (complex) mixing and low-level (simple) mixing?
   iv.   What is the social evaluation of this mixing and alternation?
   v.   What motivates bilinguals to mix and alternate two languages?

The answer to (i) is self-evident from the grammaticality of (3) and the ungrammaticality of (3a)—language mixing is not a random phenomenon.

(3)   Aap yahii brand *choose* karengii.
      (You will certainly choose this brand.)
*(3a) Aap yahii brand *choose*-engii.

Interestingly, if the English verb *choose* in (3) is replaced by the corresponding Hindi verb, *cun*, it results in an ungrammatical (4) while the corresponding Hindi version of the ungrammatical (3a) will yield a grammatical output as in (4a). This presents further evidence that language mixing is systematic and is subject to highly complex rules of the interaction between grammars.

*(4)   Aap yahii brand cun karengii.
       (You will certainly choose this brand.)
(4a)   Aap yahii brand cun-engii.

The rule is that the English verb *choose* cannot take the Hindi tense-aspect marking (-engii and its other number, gender and person manifestations—uungaa, egaa, egii, etc.) without the insertion of Hindi *karnaa* 'to do', which functions as a semantically light verb carrying little or no meaning. The corresponding Hindi verb *cun*, however, does not require the insertion of a dummy verb; it can take Hindi tense-aspect marking directly. In fact, if the light verb *kar-* appears with a Hindi verb, as in (4), the result is an ungrammatical output. (For a formal discussion of this rule within the framework of Chomskyan generative grammar, see Bhatia & Ritchie 2001; for universal constraints on the grammar of language mixing, see Bhatia & Ritchie 2009: 597–608.)

To answer (ii), let us consider data from Media Hinglish, which permits the mixing of such units as grammatical morphemes, words, phrases, clauses, sentences, idioms, and cultural expressions drawn from Hindi.

(5)   matlabi*ness* 'selfishness', masko*fying* 'to flatter', bahan*s* 'sisters', *wife*-jii 'wife' (honorific), *ex*-biivii 'ex-wife'

In words such as matlabi*ness*, masko*fying*, and bahan*s*, the English derivational and inflectional morphemes are added to

Hindi base morphemes. However, the expression *wife*-jii allows the Hindi honorific particle jii with the English base morpheme *wife*. The prefixing of the English *ex* with a Hindi base morpheme yields the expression *ex*-biivii. The mixing of Hindi nouns, pronouns, adjectives, adverbs, and verbs with English sentences is the norm in Hinglish. Even chunks of Hindi sentences and clauses are not immune to mixing with English sentences. Moreover, the use of Hindi idiom and proverbs is frequent in Indian English media sources, as exemplified in (6).

(6) I thought it was a charming thing to be—all those aankhon aankhon mein baaten (eyes eyes in talks).
      'I thought it was a charming thing to be—all those talks with eyes.'

Further analysis of formal units of Hindi reveals that Hindi mixing constitutes a complex system of Hinglish. The most preferred sources of mixing are: (1) familiar terms; (2) markers of respect; (3) cultural terms; (4) idioms and common expressions of Hindi; (5) use of Hindi *vaalaa*; and (6) emotive and gossip vocabulary. This does not exhaust the inventory of lexical types employed in Hinglish (Bhatia 1989). The incidence of Hinglish is so pervasive that no genre is immune (Bhatia 2000, 2007 for Hinglish in advertising; Kachru 2006 for pop music; Bhatia 2006 for comic books). Any conscious attempt to filter out English in Hindi fails miserably and results in linguistic absurdity. A case in point is loan translations into Hindi from English in domains such as recorded messages.

(7) Aap ke dvaaraa *dial* kiyaa gayaa *number* abhi vyasta hai. Kripayaa dobaaraa *phone* kiijiye.
      'The number that you have dialled is currently busy. Please call again.'

The oddity of this sentence is the result of avoiding the English word *busy* in the target Hindi utterance. Notice also the violation of the selectional restriction on vyasta 'busy', which is usually reserved for humans.

Linguistic integration which manifests itself word-internally is particularly intriguing for linguists because it requires a complex integration of the two linguistic systems within a word. Consider the expression '*Chutnefying* English'. It is possible to derive a past tense form (chutnefied) from the Hindi noun. Hindi nominal stems that don't end in -ii require the English derivational suffix -*fy* to intervene between the obligatory vowel -**o**- and the past-tense marker (mask-**o**-*fi-ed*). In addition to the formal complexity, Bhatia (1989) shows that the hybrid verb formation allows Hinglish to introduce a systematic dichotomy between formal and informal stems, thus adding another dimension to Hinglish creativity.

Concerning (iii), linguists distinguish between borrowing (low-level phenomenon) on the one hand and code-mixing and code-switching (high level) on the other. The term code-mixing refers to the mixing of various linguistic units (morphemes, words, modifiers, phrases, clauses, sentences) primarily from two or more participating grammatical systems *within a sentence*. In other words, code-mixing is intrasentential, constrained by grammatical principles, and motivated by socio-psychological factors. Code-switching, on the other hand, is intersentential. (For details concerning the motivations for positing the difference between code-mixing and code-switching in formal linguistics, see Ritchie & Bhatia 2004: 337.) I should add here that this paper employs 'language mixing' as a cover term for both code-mixing and code-switching, but does not refer to other mixed systems such as pidgin and creole languages. (See Bhatia & Ritchie 2009: 595–97 for the distinction between code-mixing, code-switching and other related mixed systems.)

Not only is language mixing a natural activity of the bilingual mind, it is also reflective of the underlying 'optimization' strategy that I have already sketched. For this reason, one would expect human societies to hold an extremely positive view of this phenomenon. However, just the contrary is the case—the social evaluation of language mixing (iv) is largely negative which is, in turn, a remnant of the linguistic deficiency hypothesis discussed in Part I. Prescriptivists and 'guardians' of the language decry mixing. They get a further boost from contemporary media (in the US, for instance), which follows the ideology of linguistic purism. Language mixers are often ridiculed for their 'bad' and 'irregular' linguistic behaviour. The backlash to mixing is not restricted just to societies, even governments get on to the bandwagon. Some countries such as the newly freed nations of the former Soviet Union and even France regulate (or even ban) mixing either by appointing 'language police' or passing laws to wipe out the perceived negative effects of 'bad language' in the public domain. Asia is no exception. Table 1 illustrates the anomaly between the scientific reality of language mixing and its social perception, which translates into the negative evaluation of mixed speech.

Table 1: Language-mixing Anomaly

Natural Fact	Social Fact/Perception
Systematic behaviour	Unsystematic behaviour
Linguistic augmentation	Linguistic deficiency
Natural behaviour	Bad linguistic behaviour
Motivation in creative needs	Memory/recall problem, clumsiness
Language change	Language death

Needless to say, Indian society shows much more openness to language mixing than other societies. Therefore the stigma of language mixing is minimal, but not totally absent. What motivates bilinguals to mix and alternate two languages? The rule of thumb is that mixing triggers a socio-psychological change or new situation of some type. Socio-psycholinguistic research reveals that language mixing is motivated by the following three types of factors.

1. Speech accommodation, multiple identities, social distancing
2. Situational factors
3. Message-intrinsic factors

The primary social function of language mixing is speech accommodation (Giles 1984; see discussion in Sharma, this volume; Khubchandani 1997). While a pure linguistic system establishes the interlocutor's membership in one group or the other, language mixing marks his dual or multiple identities. These identities, in turn, determine participants' roles and their relations. Motivated by the consideration of participants' relations and roles, it is not surprising that a businessman in Ahmedabad will use Gujarati with one customer and turn around and speak Hindi with another and yet another mixed variety with another.

In bi/multilingual societies, languages normally do not duplicate each other's roles; instead, speakers cut the communication pie into mutually exclusive pieces and allocate a piece (role) to each language. Consequently, some languages are viewed as more appropriate for some domains (topics), participants, social groups, and/or relations than for others. In that process, a complex division of linguistic labour begins to shape communication. In terms of marking relationships and identities, usually one language indexes intimacy (the we or private code) while another indexes distancing (the they or public code).

Message-intrinsic factors also play critical roles in language mixing or shifting. Linguistic and pragmatic factors such as quotations, reiteration, message qualifications, hedging, rhyming, and interjections trigger mixing. The following examples illustrate this point.

Quotations

The direct quotation or reported speech function of language mixing is attested to in a wide variety of empirical studies, and in Hinglish too.

Reiteration

Reiteration or paraphrasing is another function of language mixing.

(8) Father commanding his son utters:
Abhii jaao *right away!* 'Go right now, right away!'

Message qualification

The disjunctive clause in the following example serves as a source of qualifying message of the preceding sentence:

(9) *I'm going there,* dost se milne.
'I'm going there, to meet (my) friend.'

Rhyming and other literary effects

(10) Chaahe ham jiiten ya *looz*en (Snell, this volume, p. 27)
'Whether we win or lose.'
(Also observe the violation of the dummy verb requirement.)

Hedging/Taboo suppression

Language mixing serves an important function in hedging. Though the formal and functional range of hedging is quite wide and both languages of a bilingual can contribute, the language allocated as the 'they' code is often used for this purpose, particularly when hedging performs the function of taboo suppression. This aspect of language mixing is often deliberate and, by and large, conscious. The passage in (11) concerns a veterinarian doctor's attempt to explain to villagers in rural India the process of artificial insemination. When the listeners fail to understand the English term, the doctor attempts to explain the concept by paraphrasing it figuratively into Hindi. The dilemma regarding how to suppress the tabooness via Hindi is clear from his hesitation and halting speech.

(11) Doctor to villagers (Hindi–*English*)
'*Artificial insemination*' Dekho ise kyaa kehte hain hindi men . . . Barii aasaan ciiz hai . . . Jab bhains garam ho rahii ho . . . To use *A.I. centre* le jaaiyee aur uskaa A.I. karva daaliye.

'Artificial insemination' Look, what do people call it in
Hindi ... It is very easy (to explain). When a buffalo is in
heat, take her to the A.I. centre and have her artificially
inseminated.' (Literally: Have A.I. done on her.)

Table 2 summarizes the socio-psychological and other
motivations for language mixing.

**Table 2: Language Mixing: Socio-psychological, Interpersonal,
and Linguistic Motivations**

Participants	Situational Factors	Socio-psychological Factors	Linguistic and Pragmatic Factors
Indexical (social class, gender, ethnicity, race, age of speaker/ listener, etc.)	We versus they code Private versus public code Informal versus formal code	Neutrality, speech accommodation, multiple identities	Repetition, clarification, quotation, message qualification, hedging, language trigger

Adapted from Ritchie & Bhatia (2004: 347)

The socio-psychological, situational, and message-intrinsic
optimization of meaning through language mixing underlies the
linguistic creativity of the bilingual mind, which in turn allows
language mixing to bypass its negative social evaluation. (For a
detailed treatment of the determinants of language mixing and
optimization of social meaning, see Ritchie & Bhatia [2004:
339–48] and Romaine [1989]; also see Finch, this volume.)

Conclusion

Language mixing, indispensable for creativity, is a defining
feature of the bilingual mind as shown in our account of the
Optimization Theory. It is the bi/multilingual brain's attempt to

attain the optimal result from its input of two linguistic systems by accommodating and augmenting linguistic and socio-psychological meanings of the message. It is not surprising then that Hinglish fulfils the creative needs of Hindi–English bilinguals. While there is no question that such creative needs cannot be filled either by English or Hindi alone, it is also important to realize that Hinglish is undergoing rapid and significant changes in both qualitative and quantitative terms. So pervasive is the influence of Hinglish in the verbal repertoire of Hindi–English bilinguals that the balance is shifting more and more in favour of English, thus reducing Hindi to some functional words, dummy verbs, and tense-aspect marking. Are these changes induced unconsciously or by design? Do they reflect a linguistic reality in the age of hyper-globalization or a transient fad? Will these changes take a toll on the bilinguals' ability to keep the two systems separate? These questions remain to be answered.

MORE THAN THE SUM OF ITS PARTS: HINGLISH AS AN ADDITIONAL COMMUNICATIVE RESOURCE

Shannon Anderson-Finch

A major theme emerging from this collection of papers and the related conference is that Hinglish represents a broad spectrum of linguistic practices in South Asia and among the diaspora. These heterogeneous practices are unified as Hinglish in that all phenomena involve the integration of Hindi and English at various levels of linguistic organization, including sounds, structures, and words. Hinglish can mean Indian English, a fully nativized variety of English involving phonological transfer, structural borrowing, and calquing from Hindi and other Indian languages. Hinglish can also refer to lexical borrowing and single-word switches, as in an English grammatical frame with a Hindi word, for instance, 'To get an idea of what the *tamaasha* (uproar) is all about, listen to a typical Hinglish advertisement.'[1] Hinglish often also refers to code-switching, a more dynamic mixing that occurs turn by turn in conversations, phrase by phrase in sentences, even morpheme by morpheme in individual words, for example, *filmein* (films). Further, the diversity of linguistic practices comprising Hinglish is accompanied by a wide range of sociolinguistic ideologies and attitudes. In circulating discourses, Hinglish is variously viewed as a jumble, an arbitrary mixing of languages, twisting words, survival communication, an unholy union between English and Hindi, a

53

new, hybrid language, natural language change, youthful exuberance, hip, playful, market-friendly, injurious to Hindi, an insult to English, and more.

I argue that Hinglish, as Hindi–English code-switching, is a structured, systematic, and strategic linguistic and social resource uniquely available to bilinguals. Based on bilingual conversations, I demonstrate that Hinglish expands options speakers have for expressing linguistic and social meanings. My claims contrast sharply with prescriptive approaches to language that primarily view code-switching as indiscriminate and inappropriate boundary crossing, as evidence of lack of linguistic proficiency, as necessarily detrimental to the languages involved, as a reflection of cultural or cognitive confusion, or as dissolving the distinctiveness of Hindi and English. In my research, Hinglish ultimately emerges as a *skilled strategy* of linguistic, cognitive, and social simultaneity.

Bilingual Repetition

The systematicity and dynamism of Hindi–English code-switching are particularly apparent in what I have termed bilingual repetition (Finch 2005). In bilingual repetition phenomena, the semantic content of a message in one language is repeated nearby in another language, as in the following exchange.[2]

Example 1 (AYR/SDM—'semester')

1 S d- **do mahiine khatam ho gaye** *(.)*
      'Two months are over already.'
2   ⌈already *(.)*
3 A ⌊*maiN gayi aur abhi phirse* (.)
      'I went and again,'
4 S *maiN aaj soch rahi thi* ((clears throat))
      'Today I was thinking,'
5   **aaddha semester khatam ho gaya**,
      'Half the semester is over,'
6   **half the semester is gone**.

In this example, the speakers have been discussing how quickly the semester is passing. Note that the noun phrases '*do mahiine*' and '*aaddha* semester' are synonymous, and that '*aaddha* semester' and 'half the semester' are equivalent. The verb phrases '*khatam ho gaya*', '*khatam ho gaye*', and 'is gone' are also equivalent. Bilingual repetition raises interesting questions regarding synonyms within languages and equivalents across languages, but the debate about the existence of true synonyms or equivalents is beyond the scope of this paper.

I first encountered bilingual repetition as a learner of Hindi. Instructors often gave the same message in both Hindi and English, for example, '*kitaab kholiye,* open your book'. Ensuring comprehension seemed to be the goal. But then I began to notice that lines of dialogue in Bollywood films were quite often delivered in both Hindi and English. In *Chupke Chupke*, for instance, a character says, 'What nonsense! *Kya baqwaas hai!*' Such examples abound in Bollywood dialogues and, at first glance, appear to be a kind of translation for the benefit of non-English-speaking audiences. As I began considering the use of English in and alongside Hindi in everyday speech, I encountered many instances of bilingual repetition in Hindi–English code-switched conversations. In these cases, with similarly proficient speakers, it seemed unlikely that bilingual repetition was being used to ensure comprehension. It also seemed unlikely that instances of bilingual repetition were simple redundancies or disfluencies. Close analysis of naturally occurring conversations has indeed revealed that bilingual repetition achieves various rhetorical and interactional effects, such as cohesion, contrast, and focus. Bilingual repetition is not so much about re-transmitting a message as it is about expressing communicative intentions above and beyond the semantic content of that message.

Not only is the phenomenon of bilingual repetition ubiquitous in South Asian multilingual contexts, it has also been encountered in a wide range of other language contact situations. However, mentions in literature are relatively limited.[3] Due to the unique side-by-side presentation of alternative ways of making meaning both within and across languages, a closer look at bilingual repetition holds promise for contributing to the understanding of code-switching and discourse structuring.

Background on Code-switching

Code-switching is defined as an individual speaker's use of two or more language varieties within a single communicative exchange, including spoken and written as well as spontaneous and pre-planned communication. Some researchers (Kachru 1978) additionally use the term code-mixing to refer to intra-sentential switching, that is, language mixing *within* sentences, and to distinguish it from inter-sentential switching, that is, language mixing *between* sentences. Here, I adopt code-switching as a cover term for language alternation occurring both between and within sentences, and I use the term Hinglish as shorthand for Hindi–English code-switching.

Research on code-switching has expanded greatly since the early 1970s, when Jan Blom and John Gumperz published an influential study of code-switching between standard and regional Norwegian dialects (Blom & Gumperz 1972). Prior to Blom and Gumperz's study, code-switching, particularly within sentences, was typically treated as linguistic interference and social aberrance. Code-switching was thought to reflect the inability or unwillingness of a bilingual to sustain a conversation in a single language. The following, now infamous, quote by Uriel Weinreich (1953: 73) neatly expresses the thinking of the times:

> The *ideal bilingual* switches from one language to another according to appropriate changes in the speech situations (interlocutors, topics, etc.) but not in an unchanged speech situation, and *certainly not within a single sentence* (italics mine).

Blom and Gumperz's study crucially demonstrated code-switching to be a type of 'skilled performance', thus helping establish it as a legitimate research topic (Myers-Scotton 1993).

Research since the 1970s has continued to demonstrate the linguistic skill involved in code-switching and has expanded to investigate code-switching as a strategy for accomplishing communicative and social goals (e.g., Myers-Scotton 1993; Auer 1995, 1998). Interest in the structural and grammatical details of code-switching (e.g., Muysken 2000) and the cognitive and neurological aspects of code-switching and bilingualism (e.g., Bhatia & Ritchie 2008; Abutalebi, et al. 2007; Rodriguez-Fornells, et al. 2002) has also expanded.[4] Despite advances made in code-switching research and the accumulating evidence that code-switching is skilled performance and strategic behaviour, some bilinguals and many monolinguals continue to consider the mixing of languages to be an unstructured linguistic free for all, as shown in the attitudes towards Hinglish mentioned earlier.

Data and Participants

The evidence for my argument comes primarily from my research on Hindi–English code-switching in natural, everyday conversations. This study is based on a corpus of audio-recorded Hindi–English bilingual conversations but also includes examples from popular media. The conversations involve dyads of familiars who all reported using Hinglish as the regular mode of communication. I suggested upcoming or recent trips to India as a topic, and participants were left alone with the recorder. Initial talk referenced the situation, but participants soon began discussing a wide range of general and personal topics. Afterwards, participants often apologized for drifting from the suggested topic, evidence of relatively natural interactions. The recordings were transcribed and translated by me in consultation with native speakers of Hindi and Indian English.

I also conducted sociolinguistic background interviews with participants. All participants attended English-medium schools, and all spoke Hindi and English plus at least one other family and/or regional language. As shown in the following list of participants for examples appearing in this paper, no dyad shares the same family or regional language:

- AYR: mid-twenties, Bengali; SDM: early thirties, Kashmiri (Example 1)
- SDM: early thirties, Kashmiri; MLS: late thirties, Tulu/ Kannada (Example 5, Example 6)
- APP: late twenties, Telugu; MTV: late twenties, Tamil (Example 3)
- DPM: early thirties, Tamil; RKS: mid-thirties, Kashmiri (Example 4, Example 7)

This fact underscores the point that Hinglish is emerging as a shared mode of communication within India, particularly among educated, affluent, and geographically mobile speakers.

Among such speakers, Hindi–English code-switching is itself chosen frequently as the unmarked mode of communication for a wide range of settings and topics. In unmarked code-switching, speakers continuously use two (or more) languages, often intrasententially, and the overall pattern of switching is socially significant (Myers-Scotton 1993). For these speakers, 'pure' Hindi and 'pure' English have become highly marked linguistic options. Studies of code-switching suggest that it is not so much that speakers *cannot* finish a sentence in one language, as many prescriptivists claim, but rather that speakers may *resist* doing so because choosing one language to the exclusion of the other has become so marked (Myers-Scotton 1993).

Hinglish as an Additional Communicative Strategy

My overarching argument is that Hindi–English code-switching functions as an additional resource uniquely available to bilinguals. Hinglish expands, rather than contracts, options for making linguistic and social meaning and expressing communicative intentions. Hinglish is generally structured and systematic, but not necessarily along the lines of *Hindi = India + tradition* and *English = West + modernity* as many readily assume. The primary communicative significance of Hindi–English code-switching is found in micro-level interactions between speakers, rather than in macro-level associations between languages and socio-historical circumstances. Moreover, Hinglish cannot be taken as evidence of lack of proficiency in either Hindi or English or both, because code-switching only tells us that two grammars and two lexicons are working simultaneously. It does not tell us much about proficiency in individual languages, for code-switching requires above all experience using two or more languages together. Finally, Hinglish is not a 'language' but an important mode of communication in South Asia and among the diaspora. Hindi and English clearly retain their distinctiveness as separate language varieties, and this distinctiveness is exploited in a dynamic interplay of linguistic similarity and difference in interactions between speakers.

One way to think of language is as a set of alternatives for communication. Halliday (1994: 15) describes language as 'a network of systems, or interrelated sets of options for making meaning'. Languages allow for different ways of expressing the same meaning, and for the same linguistic unit to have different meanings. Alternatives are available at all levels of linguistic organization. For example, we can express the same proposition with either 'The bear chased the man' or 'The man was chased by the bear' or even 'The bear ran after the man'. Similarly, the words 'sofa', 'couch', and 'davenport' can all be used to denote the same piece of furniture. Of course, each option involves social and pragmatic associations and consequences as well as fine distinctions in connotations among alternatives. But the crucial point is that languages provide many alternatives for making meaning, so that speakers almost always have more than one way of expressing the same meaning at their disposal.

Bilinguals have access to two (or more) languages. Here, 'access' to languages does not correlate with 'proficiency' but refers to a speaker's experience with using the languages in particular contexts, including familiarity with mixing or switching according to community norms. Given that language provides speakers with alternatives for making meaning, and that bilinguals have access to more than one language, it follows that bilinguals have access to more options for making meaning than monolinguals do. Overall, bilingual speakers have access to a larger lexicon, a wider inventory of grammatical structures, a broader range of phonological patterns, and a more extensive repertoire of discourse styles. If community norms allow code-switching, bilingual speakers will have access to these expanded and interrelated sets of options for making meaning *within* individual conversations.

Below are examples that demonstrate how Hinglish expands linguistic options in specific ways. The first excerpt comes from Radio Mirchi. The RJ is discussing an interruption in the production of a film starring Amitabh Bachchan; a cheque given to Bachchan is rumoured to have bounced.[5]

Example 2 (RJ Saloni, Radio Mirchi—'trust')

1	S	Of course AB has agreed to go ahead with the project,
2		which is being directed by Vikram Bhatt.
3		Now that's certainly a show of how much
4		Bachchan **trusts** in the film's viability.
5		That's what we call true *aitbaar.*
		'trust'

In line 4, the RJ says that Bachchan's decision shows how much 'trust' he places in the film and, in line 5, the RJ concludes the report by referring to Bachchan's action as 'true *aitbaar* (trust)'. This example involves complex verbal play, as the title of Bhatt's film is *Aetbaar*. Access to the Hindi option for 'trust' in this context allows her to repeat and emphasize the concept of trust while also invoking the name of the film, and the switch from English to Hindi also helps foreground the word through contrast with the previous English-only lines. Hinglish, with both Hindi and English options, gives speakers the opportunity to make fine lexical distinctions among alternatives for aesthetic effect.

Hinglish also gives speakers the opportunity to make lexical contrasts. In the next example, the research participants have just been left alone with the recorder and are discussing the awkwardness of the situation:[6]

Example 3 (APP/MTV—'suddenly')

1   M   **suddenly**,

2   *abhi kuch aur* topic *baat kar* ⌐*rahe the*,
        'Just now, we were talking about some other topic,'

3   A   ⌐I know, I know,

4   M   *aur abhi* **achaanak** ⌐India *ke baare mein*
        'And now suddenly about India

5   A   ⌐That's right.

6   M   *baat karne ka matlab jara* difficult *hai.*
        'to talk, I mean, it's a little difficult.'

In line 1, M begins with the English word 'suddenly', continuing in Hindi. In line 4, M uses '*achaanak*' ('suddenly'). Though 'suddenly' and '*achaanak*' are conceptually equivalent, the first instance is associated with one state of affairs, namely, talking about another topic, and the second instance is associated with a different state of affairs, namely, talking about the new, imposed topic of India. The juxtaposition of 'suddenly' and '*achaanak*' involves both conceptual continuance and linguistic contrast. The repeat of the concept 'suddenly/*achaanak*' creates cohesion between the two statements, while the language change creates contrast and represents the distinction between the previous, presumably more natural discussion of another topic and the current, awkward discussion of the suggested topic of India.

Hinglish as Structured and Systematic

I have argued that bilingualism and Hindi–English code-switching give speakers more options for making meaning. Options imply choice, so that bilinguals have more alternatives from which to choose in making meaning and communicating intentions. Here I argue that the choice among options is systematic and that it results in structured discourse. This is a key point, as Hinglish is often portrayed as a disorderly, chaotic phenomenon where anything goes.

In bilingual repetition, speakers use both languages to express the same linguistic meaning more than once. Two traditions within linguistics have demonstrated that the choice among options for 'saying the same thing', that is, expressing the same meaning with different linguistic forms from the same language, is orderly and systematic. Within sociolinguistics, variation analysis has demonstrated that, though different forms sharing the same meaning appear to stand in free variation, the choice of one form over another is generally influenced by and aligns with various contextual factors and social characteristics (Labov 1974). Within pragmatics, information–structure analysis has demonstrated that semantically equivalent sentence pairs with different forms, that is, active and passive, are also generally pragmatically divergent (Lambrecht 1994).

If the choice among linguistic alternatives *within* a language is principled and patterned, then it is reasonable to expect that the choice *between* languages in a bilingual, code-switching context is also orderly and systematic. The examples of bilingual repetition in this paper collectively suggest that far from being a linguistic free-for-all, Hindi–English code-switching is systematic and structured, both in terms of linguistic details and overall discourse organization.

In the next two examples, bilingual repetition plays a clear role in structuring discourse. The repeated content appears with specific detail or additional material. First consider example (4); D is making a case for special preparations for guests who arrive the next day:

Example 4 (DPS/RKM—'prepare')

1   D   doesn't *ki– chalo dekha jaayega tab hoga nahiin*
        'That– let's see later, if not,'
2   *to **kuch to** prepare **karna hota hai**,*
        'Then, something should be prepared,'
3   *matlab* **one has to prepare dinner breakfast** (.)
        'I mean, one has to prepare dinner and breakfast.'
4   *parson ka kuch to dekhna par-*
        'We need to think about the day after tomorrow a bit.'
5   *chhe log hain yaar aise* ⌈*nahiin kahenge*
        'Six people are coming, dear, they won't eat like that.'
6   R   ⌊yeah so (.) the- there is stuff
7   in the house to eat

The utterances in lines 2 and 3 both express the obligation to prepare food. The general word '*kuch* ('something')' in line 1 is replaced with the more specific phrase 'dinner breakfast' in line 2, but both utterances are generic statements of obligation. The word 'prepare' appears in both the Hindi utterance in line 2 and the English utterance in line 3, thus creating additional cohesion between the two utterances. Note, however, that line 3 is the only English utterance in D's entire turn, making the form of line 3 contrast with the surrounding material. This has the effect of foregrounding and emphasizing the obligation to prepare food for the guests.

The next example also involves bilingual repetition with specification of detail. M has just asked S whether she has already bought her ticket for an upcoming trip to India:

Example 5 (MLS/SDM—'ticket')

1   S   yeah **I** uh ((*laughing*)) **ticket** *liya tha*.
                  'Yeah, I uh got a ticket.'
2   I- I- **I bought the ticket** um o- **one month ago**.
3   M   okay. *Kitna diya*?
                  'How much did you pay?'
4   because I think S was looking for a-
5   she's got the (.) summer FLAS[7] (.)
6   S   *main ne* uh **one-way ticket** *liya hai*. ((*laughing*))
                  'I got uh a one-way ticket.'

In line 1, S confirms that she 'ticket *liya tha* (took, i.e., bought, the ticket)' in response to M's question. In line 2, she switches to English, repeating that she 'bought the ticket' and adding the detail 'one month ago'. In line 5, she switches to Hindi, again repeating that she 'ticket *liya tha* (took, i.e., bought, the ticket)' and specifying that it is a 'one-way ticket'. The repetition of the message 'I took/bought the ticket' cohesively binds this discourse segment together, while the change in language highlights each new bit of information. Note also that 'ticket' is an integrated cultural borrowing, and that its reappearance in lines 1, 2, and 5 provides further cohesion among the utterances.

Hinglish Not a Fused 'Language'

Hinglish is often referred to as a fused or hybrid 'language'. It is even accused of eroding the distinctiveness of Hindi and English as separate languages. As noted, Hinglish, as Hindi–English code-switching, is more accurately described as a mode of communication rather than a language. Much of the communicative significance of Hinglish lies in the distinctiveness of Hindi and English as separate language varieties. This is seen at the micro level of interaction, where the change of language itself creates various discourse effects as the communicative exchange unfolds.

The communicative impact of alternating languages within discourse is especially well illustrated in bilingual repetition. Gumperz (1982: 78–79, 84) briefly mentions bilingual repetition, calling it 'reiteration'. He argues—and I agree—that 'the juxtaposition of two alternative linguistic realizations of the same message signals . . . information' beyond the semantic content. In this way, code-switching functions as a contextualization cue (Gumperz 1982; Auer 1995). Contextualization cues are surface features of message form, such as intonation, rhythm, gesture, pitch, and volume, which contribute to the situated production and interpretation of language. They allow speakers to express and lead listeners to seek meanings beyond the literal semantic content of the message. Contextualization cues work by marking certain words and phrases through contrast with surrounding discourse, thus making these words and phrases more salient.

In cases of speaker overlap, we see how the change of codes further employs contrast to create focus. In this example, the speakers are discussing S's sister who lives in New Jersey:

Example 6 (MLS & SDM—'where in NJ')

1 S *vahaaN pe* ⌈*pure Bombay ka baazaar.*
    'There, it's a whole Bombay bazaar.'
2 M   ⌊**where does she live in New Jersey?**
3 S ⌈*jaisa lagta hai dilli ka* ⌈*voh*
    'It seems like it's Delhi.'

4	M	⌊*haN*	⌊*haN*
		'Yes.'	'Yes.'
5		**kidhar rehti hai**	⌈**New Jersey meN?**
		'Where does she live in New Jersey?'	
6	S		⌊*dukaane-* sorry.
			'The stores- Sorry.'
7		*voh rehti hai* (.) Plainsboro *naam hai uska* ⌈(??)	
		'She lives (.) Its name is Plainsboro.'	
8	M		⌊*haN*
			'Yes.'

M's question in line 2 overlaps with the end of S's statement in line 1. S does not respond to the question and continues her discussion from line 2 about how New Jersey is like India. In line 5, M reiterates her question, this time in Hindi: '*Kidhar rehti hai* New Jersey *meN?*' S, still discussing New Jersey, interrupts her own speech with a glottal stop. She apologizes in line 6 and answers M's question in line 7. The self-interruption, apology, and eventual response all suggest S's orientation to M's question, demonstrating how the contrast inherent in code-switching contributes to gaining and maintaining the hearer's attention. The use of bilingual repetition in this exchange foregrounds the overlapped, unanswered question, helping the speaker accomplish her interactional goals.

A dynamic and delicate equilibrium exists between repetition (doing the same thing) and variation (doing something different) that is fundamental to meaning-making in human culture and communication. The tension between these forces is particularly exploited in code-switching and bilingual repetition. Repetition draws on similarities in form or meaning, while code-switching engages differences in languages varieties. In bilingual conversation, the dynamic interplay of continuance and contrast frequently assumes an almost poetic quality, as in example (7) below. Speakers R and D are discussing whether bread will sell out at the local HEB grocery store due to predicted inclement weather:

Example 7 (DPS & RKM—'deliveries')

1 R   that's not an issue. bread and all is not an issue.
2 D   *chal* HEB *log-* usually **daily deliveries** *hote haiN.*
       'Come, HEB peop- usually there are daily deliveries,'
3   *abhi* HEB *meN,*
       'Even now, in HEB,'
4   they were saying on the news
5   **every hour delivery** *ho raha hai,*
       'Every hour a delivery is happening.'
6   and they are not able to meet the **demand** (.)
7   they've upped from **every day** to-
8   now they've made it **hourly deliveries** in certain HEBs.
9   *to abhi bhi matlab* **demand** *utna hai.*
       'So, even now, I mean, the demand is that high.'
10   w- water they don't even expect for the next two days.
11   *to maiN bol* ⌈*rahi huN,*
       'So I am saying,'
12 R   ⌊water they expect tomorrow night (.)
13   that's what they said.

In line 1, R claims that bread will not be an issue. In line 2, D expresses a different view. She explains in Hindi in lines 2–5 that there are usually daily deliveries, but now they are hourly. In line 6, she switches to English, concluding that the grocery store still cannot meet the demand. I suggest that the switch sharpens the contrast between the supply and demand of bread. The meaning content of lines 2–6 is repeated in lines 7–9, with the language switched. D explains again in lines 7–8, this time in English, that daily deliveries have been increased to hourly deliveries. In line 9, she summarizes the situation, this time in Hindi: '*To abhi bhi* ... demand *utni hai.*'

Schiffrin (1987: 131) notes that 'once a textual regularity has been developed—even if it is only for a short sequence—a new idea can be introduced by a change from the textual norm'. In example (7) above, language develops a textual regularity for messages A (daily deliveries: Hindi, English) and B (hourly deliveries: Hindi, English). That norm is changed for message C (high demand: English, Hindi), creating a contrast with the previous material and foregrounding the message. The overall pattern of code-switching and bilingual repetition in this example contributes to the representation of multiple contrasting situations: (1) D believes that bread will be an issue, while R does not, and (2) in spite of increased supply, the store is still facing a high level of demand. Far from blurring the distinction between languages, Hinglish actively exploits the differences between Hindi and English in making meaning, as seen in the examples here.

Hinglish as Social Strategy

The systematicity and dynamism seen in bilingual repetition in particular is key to understanding the significance and meaning of Hindi–English code-switching in general. The *juxtaposition* of languages in bilingual repetition and code-switching necessarily involves an *integration* of languages within individual speakers and within words, sentences, and conversations. This micro-level linguistic integration both facilitates and is facilitated by macro-level social integration. Such linguistic and social integration are often discussed in terms of 'hybridization'. The dynamic nature of Hindi–English code-switching underscores the point that hybridization is an active process, rather than a static product. Hybridization happens through face-to-face interactions among community members engaged in creating and negotiating identities and relationships. Following Auer (1995: 115), I agree that bilingualism 'has its foremost reality in the interactive exchanges between the members of a bilingual speech community'. Accordingly, investigation into Hinglish as a linguistic and social phenomenon of hybridization of languages and identities properly begins with a careful look at micro-level, on-the-ground interactions between Hindi–English bilingual speakers.

Anthropological and sociolinguistic studies of code-switching typically favour macro-level issues to the exclusion of micro-level interactions. When the systematicity of code-switching is acknowledged, attempts to account for it frequently appeal to the wider historical, social, and political contexts of the languages involved. For example, it is frequently claimed that code choice and meaning in bilingual discourse are dependent on the languages' associations with dichotomous contexts and that certain languages are used for particular topics and settings (Woolard 2004). In the case of Hindi and English, the claims are usually as follows: Hindi is predominantly used in interactions with family, indexing that which is familiar, traditional, Indian, and indigenous, while English is preferred for peers and official and public encounters, representing that which is Other, modern, Western, and global. English is often claimed to invoke 'authority' and 'social distance', while Hindi invokes 'solidarity' and 'familiarity'. English is additionally said to be the best vehicle for expressing 'rational thought' and that which is in the head; Hindi best expresses 'emotion', 'feelings', and that which is in the heart.

If nothing else, post-Structuralism has taught us to beware of such overly simplistic dichotomies, as they tend to obscure rather than illuminate. And so it is with Hindi–English code-switching. Clearly, Hindi and English are *broadly associated* with differing contexts and 'affective stances', as captured in the language ideologies described above. While these differing social, political, and historical associations are undoubtedly important in understanding the broader significances of the language varieties used in code-switching, it is extremely difficult to argue that each and every switch necessarily indexes juxtaposed social worlds for speakers (Woolard 2004). This is particularly true in cases where code-switching itself has become the unmarked mode of communication, as with the speakers in this study.

Macro-level accounts that appeal to dichotomous worlds primarily offer descriptions of the historical, social, political, and economic conditions that make code-switching possible or likely in a community; they do not adequately account for on-the-ground language choices. Macro-level contexts neither completely determine nor fully account for the regularities and patterns of code-switching in actual interactions (Auer 1998). Claims that Hindi is used for 'personal' topics in 'familial' contexts and that English is used for 'modern' topics in 'official' contexts are simply not borne out empirically at the micro level of interaction between bilingual speakers.

Conclusion

I have presented evidence that Hinglish, in the guise of Hindi–English code-switching, is a resource that systematically expands options bilingual speakers have for making linguistic and social meaning and for structuring discourse. Through micro examination of instances of bilingual repetition, we see that code-switching emerges as a strategy of both linguistic and social integration and hybridization. In short, code-switching has been shown to be interactionally meaningful without understanding individual switches as invoking dichotomous socio-political associations or historical contexts.

A sub-goal of this paper has been to dispel popular myths concerning Hinglish and code-switching. First of all, rather than limiting options speakers have for making linguistic meaning, Hinglish has been shown to expand speaker options in particular ways. Second, rather than being a jumbled, linguistic free for all, Hinglish has been shown to be systematic and structured. Third, macro-level approaches to code-switching that align Hindi with India, familiarity, and tradition and English with the West, formality, and modernity have been shown to be overly simplistic and not borne out in actual practice. Finally, hybridization of Hindi and English is argued to be an ongoing process that takes place in on-the-ground interactions between bilingual speakers through a lively interplay of similarity and difference that relies on the robust distinctiveness of Hindi and English as separate languages.

In sum, Hinglish is a creative solution to the 'problem' of living with two (or more) equally (albeit differently) valued languages. Potentially opposed language varieties and linguistic identities and associations are integrated and displayed through the dynamic interplay of similarity and difference encountered in Hindi–English bilingual conversation. Hindi–English code-switching is ultimately a strategy of linguistic and social simultaneity, offering speakers a way of being *both* Hindi-speaking *and* English-speaking while still making linguistic and social meaning (Woolard 1998: 10). Speakers are not forced to choose *either* Hindi *or* English, which is of particular importance when their home languages are *neither* Hindi *nor* English. Social simultaneity, in the equal valuing of different macro-level socio-historical associations of individual languages, both enables and is enabled by the linguistic simultaneity encountered in Hindi–English code-switching in micro-level interactions and conversation. What has been described here for Hinglish likely also applies to other postcolonial and diasporic settings, particularly where code-switching has become the unmarked norm. The findings of this research align with more recent research on code-switching that increasingly portrays bilingual language phenomena as dynamic, shifting, ambiguous, multivocal, contingent, and emergent (Woolard 2004).

THE VERNACULARIZATION OF ONLINE PROTESTS: A CASE STUDY FROM INDIA

Pramod K. Nayar

The Internet facilitates mainstream as well as subcultural politics. Online campaigns increasingly replicate, extend, expand, and augment offline political action. From Denial of Service (DoS) attacks to hacktivism, online political work has proliferated rapidly since the late 1990s (Jordan 2002; Thomas 2002; Lovink 2002).

In this note, I use one case study to probe the language games that such an Internet politics generates and appropriates. Hinglish, or more accurately a vernacularization of the dominant English-language political campaign, is visible here. If Hinglish, as Crystal (2004) has argued, is likely to soon be a global language, it follows that one of its many uses would be in the domain of political discourse. If Cybermohalla (http://www.sarai.net/practices/cybermohalla) appropriated global technologies to capture local conditions, chronicle local lives, and run local campaigns (Nayar 2008), the political campaign I discuss appropriates local/global cultural codes and language registers for its political agenda.

Online protests also fit into the context of a newer politics. Manuel Castells (2001: 140–41) suggests that the gradual erosion of traditional political formations such as the political party and the trade union has enabled loose coalitions, ad hoc

71

assemblages and spontaneous mobilizations to 'substitute' for permanent and more organized structures. The online campaign reflects this assemblage. Online campaigns relocate political action into a new domain, where the very nature of protests is informed by the nature of the medium (in this case, electronic information and communications technologies). The medium is characterized by links, home pages, blogging, non-official archivization (exemplified by www.witness.org), and user-generated content (aligned with non-official archivization). Social movements and protest campaigns online can be well served by the appropriation of multiple, even conflicting, registers and dialects, facilitated by the nature of New Media. New Media language embodies a 'digitextuality' (a portmanteau of 'digital' and 'textuality')—the collage of forms, registers and signifying systems. This involves the 'absorption and transformation of other texts, but also by embedding the entirety of other texts (analogue and digital) seamlessly within the new' (Everett 2003: 7). In other words, all texts can be potentially multimodal in their language. Online campaigns, such as the one I am about to discuss, make good use of the multimodal language of New Media.

However, there have been conflicting opinions on the political efficacy of online campaigns. For example, it has been argued (Byrne 2007) that, in the case of black social networking sites (SNSes), discussions of community issues have stayed at the level of *discourse* with little active social mobilization. But this reading, I believe, treats online action as a limited space when, in fact, we need to see how SNSes create a culture of dialogue and public debate—deliberations—that is central to *deliberative* democracy. Thus online activism and debates do move beyond the level of a discursive engagement into the public sphere of protests and political action by supplying information for public debate, drawing the attention of a wide spectrum of people, and transmitting complaints and opinions—all of which are key elements in any political culture.

The most recent online campaign (which supplemented offline protests) in India is the 'Pink Chaddi' campaign initiated by the

Consortium of Pub-Going, Loose and Forward Women and S.I.T.A. Sena—both groups formed in cyberspace. The Consortium was created by Nisha Susan on the now-ubiquitous SNS, Facebook (http://www.facebook.com/group.php?gid=49641698651) on 9 March 2009. The campaign blog is available at http://thepinkchaddicampaign.blogspot.com/.[1] Protesting against the 'moral policing' by Rama Sene in Mangalore and other parts of Karnataka in January 2009, the two organizations spearheaded a large-scale campaign, both offline and online. The Consortium has been a massive success, with over 5,000 posts and a news presence worldwide. The campaign is still on, so what I have to say is, at one level, restricted to what has already been done but is likely to evolve and alter. It has since been taken up by other gender-sensitive projects such as Blank Noise (http://blog.blanknoise.org/2009/02/for-pink-chaddi-campaign.html) thereby cobbling together (as Castells theorized) a loose coalition of people around a political issue—all facilitated by New Media. I would like to emphasize that this 'linking' is essentially enabled by the electronic links on blogs and websites that lead visitors on to the Pink Chaddi campaign page, thus expanding the reach of all of them. The cross-referential nature of the political is what is made possible by the very nature of the medium. If the Indian state, or the conservatives, fret over the appropriation of new technologies for porn (compellingly argued in Shah 2007), then they will need to worry about a similar kind of appropriation being made for political protests. In April 2009, the campaign's Facebook profile was hacked into, and instead of dealing with the security issues, Facebook simply shut down the account (see blog entry by Nisha Susan, dated 11 April 2009 at http://thepinkchaddicampaign.blogspot.com/). Susan's (2009) *Observer* feature on the campaign received massive responses, with many linking women's rights in India to issues worldwide.

It must be emphasized that I am looking, in the main, at the cyberspace version of the protest, and that too a minuscule section. A greater depth of analysis will require looking at blog posts and SNS posts on the incident. In the first section, I scrutinize caricature as a mode of protest. In the second, I turn to a more theoretical reflection on what I perceive as a 'vernacular cosmopolitanism' in political discourse.

Humour and Bilingual Online Protests

The Consortium itself is interestingly named. 'Forward woman' is standard Indian English usage, generally a pejorative to describe women considered 'Westernized' and independent. The rather prosaic 'pub-going, loose and forward women' consciously underscores the moral judgements passed on women who go to pubs. Note that the name is not '*drinking*, loose and forward women'. Drawing a finer distinction between 'pub-going' and 'drinking', the Consortium questions the implied (by people like Pramod Mutalik, the Rama Sene leader) association between 'pub-going' and 'loose' or 'forward'.

Its 'officers' are named, again bilingually, 'Pink' and 'Gulabi'. A related group launched to protest the same excesses is S.I.T.A. Sena (http://sita-sena.blogspot.com/).

Central to the Consortium's protest is what has famously been termed the 'pink chaddi' campaign. This consisted of sending to Mutalik pink lingerie in large quantities. 'Pink chaddi' itself signifies an appropriation of (1) the cultural code of pink as a feminine colour[2] and (2) the Hindi word for undergarments into an English-dominated protest.

The campaign's very title, 'pink chaddi', suggests a collocation, a co-occurrence not only of two languages (English and Hindi) but also two cultural codes. Much of the wit within the online version of the protest worked with startlingly effective bilingualism. If all politics demands, primarily, a sensitization then what we can see emerging here is a process of sensitization—of the general population—through a *vernacularization of the online language of politics* itself.

By vernacularization I mean the deliberate and creative mix of registers and languages through collocations, slang, new codes of syntax, and extended semantics used in this campaign. I am less interested in whether Hinglish dominates this linguistic dimension of the campaign than in the creative linguistic acts visible here—acts that seem to appropriate multiple, varied, even conflicting registers. If agency is marked by creativity (McNay 2000), then one of the most significant modes of agency-formation and assertion is in the *language* of protest that is creative, reflexive, subversive.

Caricature has always been a key element in political crusades and protests, and this campaign is no exception. The interesting part is the bilingualism and multicultural coding of the language of caricature.

From the Consortium one can link to an online profile created for Mutalik, the 'Chirkut Profile' (http://www.bigfishmag.com/extra/blog/2/) which opens with a well-known nursery rhyme and its vernacularization:

Chirkut! Chirkut! Where have you been?

Have you been to London to see the queen?

It goes on: 'So you see, even chirkuts have the need to network. Like in the elementary rhyme, the chirkut in question would have to travel all the way to London to see the queen. We have tried to simplify this painful procedure by creating profiles for some of our everyday "chirkuts" and offering them the opportunity to meet their "queens".'

The very term 'Chirkut Profile' signals a link with the once very popular 'Orkut Profile', thus making the name itself a vernacularization. 'Pramod Mutalik' is transmuted into 'Commode MootaLeak'. The bilingual punning here (recalling the 'Ajit jokes' of the 1980s–90s) plays on a scatological image (*moota*, Hindi for 'urine') and an English word ('leak', also indirectly referencing body fluids, physiologies, and the scatological). It carefully positions the Rama Sene leader within a series of associations—of toilets, defecatory acts, seepage. This bilingual caricature of the 'leak' also holds, especially to feminist critics, a singular significance. Women's bodies have traditionally been deemed to be 'leaky' and threats to certainty (Shildrick 1997). Here the reversal of the gendered stereotype of the 'leaky' body, whether intentional or not, is interesting in itself.

Now *chirkut* is a word common to Uttar Pradesh, Bihar, and other parts of northern India. It is used to describe a loser or one who indulges in vulgar or 'cheap' behaviour (to explain this common usage, I have consciously used the bilingual online source at http://www.urbandictionary.com/define.php? term=chirkut). Mutalik has been classified as a loser, but the classification works mainly within the linguistic domain via the term chirkut. On the one hand, the dominant language of this campaign has been English yet its best online components have been *vernacularized*. Mutalik has been culturally coded as a loser, whose behaviour is dubious at best. The cultural code of chirkut resonates with the numerous letters that appeared in English-language newspapers (I refer to *The Hindu* and *Deccan Chronicle* in Hyderabad) describing the Rama Sene's actions as 'cheap' and 'disgraceful'.

The profile then shows a caricature of Mutalik painting the pink chaddis he has received with saffron paint. Hovering in the air are cameras capturing his efforts at saffronizing the campaign itself. This is followed by a spoofy profile created for Mutalik. The language of the profile is again a collocational mix of registers, cultural codes, and languages. It opens with: '*I am a simple, cool, god-fearing man who is the president of a Hindu fundamentalist orgy by accident ... I just gone to that Amnesia pub with some friends to dance to Pappu can't dance saala and hopefully get action just like Pappu. I have some lady-killer dance moves.*'

The profile picks up on a popular song from the 2008 Hindi film *Jaane Tu ... Ya Jaane Na* (incidentally starring one Muslim and one Christian actor—Imraan Khan and Genelia D'Souza, respectively). It also works with the vernacularization imperative where the song—itself *bilingual* in lyrics—is adapted with slang and everyday speech styles: 'get action' and 'lady-killer dance moves'.

It continues: 'So I wear my best lungi, and gorge on the linseed oil for that perfect side partition ...' Note the collocational mechanisms here. The dress code is Indian, but the caricature does not use any native name for 'linseed oil'. The 'side partition' is a typical Indian expression for a particular kind of hairstyle. Extending the collocations from the opening paragraphs, we see more creative uses of language and cultural codes here.

Mutalik's level of acquaintance with the English language, especially its colloquialisms, is also caricatured. The woman at the pub door mistakes him for a 'nariyal delivery man' and asks him to go round to the back. When he says he is there to party, she laughs and says, 'Sorry, no stags today!' Mutalik is confused about what that means and thinks: 'Yes, yes I know but I am human being, though area friends do call me "pig" and "donkey", but no "stag" ever!'

When she laughs, Mutalik's caricature *start[s] to live last night's wet dream*. The everyday English term 'stag' sits in juxtaposition with the commonplace 'wet dream'. Mutalik is shown as unable to comprehend the first, but able to think up the second! The careful, if slightly droll, caricature shows how Indians have adopted the English language; the 'dirty', eroticized, non-formal *sexualized* expressions have found their way into the lexicon of the moral police even as more 'technical' or 'pure' terms for sex-related topics have become inexplicably commonplace. This argument is borne out by the very next set of sentences.

The caricature proceeds to describe, in Mutalik's own words, their violence against the women in the pub: 'Very soon, we grapple with women trying spanking and enjoying BDSM (bondage and discipline, dominance and submission, sadism and masochism). But they still not content, scream for more. These liberated women I tell you!!'

The right-wing Hindu moral cop understands the technical term for a form of alternative sexuality (BDSM). Their prejudice against emancipated women uses the language of political discourse (in English and metropolitan India)—*liberated women*.

The power of this caricature lies, I believe, not only in its vernacularization of protest language—or what can be termed its 'footpath bilingualism', collocating local-language variants of sexual terms, the language of protest, and cultural codes. The droll humour—and I can be easily accused of overrating and overinterpretation here—is excessive indeed but serves a useful purpose of drawing attention to the exaggerated (misplaced) nature of the Rama Sene's reactions itself.

Transcoded Politics: A Vernacular Cosmopolitanism?

The Consortium campaign marks in protest politics a 'vernacular cosmopolitanism', which Werbner (2006) defines as the question of whether 'the local, parochial, rooted, culturally specific and demotic may co-exist with the translocal, transnational, transcendent, elitist, enlightened, universalist and modernist'. The vernacular upsets any *elitist* cosmopolitan—it marks the insidious, subversive and often violently rebellious cultural interactions, and an appropriation of the global by the local. It is also an act of transcoding. As Manovich (2001: 64) defines it, transcoding—a central feature of New Media language—is the process of translating something into another format. For instance, cultural categories and concepts are 'substituted ... by new ones which derive from the computer's ontology, epistemology, pragmatics'. What we see in the bilingualism of these protests is more than a shift between languages. We perceive a 'translation' of cultural codes for a political agenda.

In one sense, transcoding and vernacular cosmopolitanism become responses to the very charge that the right wing levels against Valentine's Day or so-called 'loose women'—that of Westernization. I see vernacular cosmopolitanism achieved through transcoding and the melangé of Indian/Western, local/ global discourse as a localization and nativization of universal concerns such as women's rights, democracy, and civil society freedoms.

Cybercultures enable this through their 'network sociality' (Wittel 2001)—the simultaneous sense of 'integration' and 'disintegration' in a network, where one is separated without face-to-face interaction and yet together through constant communicative acts. The Consortium's 'network sociality' is facilitated through the sharing of a social condition—the oppression and circumscription of women. If sociality demands a shared sense of the *social*, then the vernacularization of the global, the nativization of international codes, and the transcoding of native cultural symbols constitute a new sociality.

Rama Sene had threatened to disrupt any Valentine's Day activity in Karnataka. The general argument, seen earlier in the Bharatiya Janata Party and Akhil Bharatiya Vidyarthi Parishad's rhetoric, is that Valentine's Day is against Indian traditions, that boys and girls who 'celebrate' the occasion are 'importing' Western values into India. This is a charge of transcoding—Western symbols and (abstract) values (supposedly) being translated into an Indian format.

Mutalik declared that boys and girls seen together in public would be married off—this triggered the next phase of the Consortium's campaign. Posters for Valentine's Day were circulated online; the posters showed a pink undergarment against a backdrop of radially widening golden yellow stripes/rays, clearly recalling the halos around idols and icons in mythological TV serials and *their* posters. The legend said: 'This Valentine's Day, send the Rama Sene a pink chaddi.' At the foot of the poster ran another legend, the punchline: 'Because chaddis are forever.'

The poster campaign marked a vernacular cosmopolitanism, achieved through transcoding—it translates cultural and symbolic codes into a different format, a different language, a different register. First, it utilizes a very *local* mode of visual rhetoric—the radiating rays. Second, 'Because chaddis are forever' references a recognizable *cosmopolitan* cultural code—'Diamonds are forever'. The latter, of course, reiterates the standard aphorism for diamonds (as also the tagline for De Beers, the diamond mega merchants) but it also reinforces the cultural code of diamonds being a woman's best friend. The clever interweaving of cultural codes enhances the campaign's cosmopolitanism yet rendering it local/vernacular. Here, transcoding works to 'reformat' a well-known native visual rhetoric into a global commercial one.

The campaign gained the attention of activists and supporters of women's rights from across the world. On International Women's Day, 8 March 2009, the online campaign helped engineer a public rally and protest in Bangalore. On the blog was a direct response to Mutalik and company's (questionable) campaign to 'protect Indian culture', inviting one and all to 'Reclaim Indian culture one chaddi at a time'.

In what is surely a concrete example of my argument (Nayar, forthcoming), network, online, and cyberspace activism and cultures have *material* consequences, whether job layoffs for women workers or stalking by paedophiles. The Consortium persuaded people to send not just online petitions but real 'pink chaddis' to Mutalik. Collection boxes were set up in major cities for people to drop off their gifts. So, to say that online activism stays at the level of discourse is to ignore the very real material dimension of these cybercultural acts.

Let's move on to a related campaign on this issue, again created primarily online but now also engaged in offline protests, that of S.I.T.A. Sena.

S.I.T.A. Sena's posters declared: *We'll still use pepper sprays and chilli powder, but first we'll whistle* (http://sita-sena.blogspot.com/). The vernacular cosmopolitanism references the culture of protests from the feminist movement to state measures here. It is a new register of political discourse in India where local cultural practices and symbols are enmeshed with global rhetoric. It is an instance of transcoding. A local cultural/symbolic code is recast within the language of feminism, political protest, and caricature. It appropriates the language, nomenclature, and connotative aspects from a different tradition and places it elsewhere for a political purpose. A good example of the transcoding mode of vernacular cosmopolitanism would be the bilingualism of the protests discussed so far. But far more significant is the relocation of symbols from Indian tradition into a new site, a process I term, after Manovich, 'transcoding'.

S.I.T.A. stands for Sensitivity in True Action. It also references several local and 'Indian' contexts. First, it is a nod to that icon of Indian womanhood, Ramayana's Sita. (Yes, the underlying

Hindu angle to even protest rhetoric cannot be ignored. A respondent, Sidhu Saheb, identifying himself as male—http://www.blogger.com/profile/08428201823375343016—on Shobhaa Dé's blog suggested a change of nomenclature because, as he put, 'The name suggested in the title doesn't go too well with tanking up on booze'. Another suggested using a 'non-religious name'.) Second, it gestures at the *state* measure to protect women, the Suppression of Immoral Traffic Act instituted to prevent trafficking in women. The blog received massive posts on International Women's Day, thus linking up local cultural codes to a global movement, a local protest campaign to international symbols. This is a transcoding, where a symbol of (Hindu) femininity is shifted into different format—(1) specifically the law, with a state-sponsored measure being used as a new acronym, S.I.T.A. and (2) a protest campaign about a different kind of woman (Ramayana's Sita appropriated to defend the rights of pub-going, loose and forward women).

The referencing of native traditions while simultaneously embedding them in global frames such as feminism (Dé's post at http://shobhaade.blogspot.com/2009/02/sita-sena-join-now-speak-up.html) constitutes a bilingualism and multiculturalism, even if it occurs exclusively in cyberspace. The provocative footpath bilingualism of caricature (as discussed earlier) and the more affective bilingualism of the polemical texts in these recent campaigns are undoubtedly metropolitan—since bilingualism could hardly be the register of political discourse in rural or even semi-urban India. Yet this does not detract from the significance in the multilayered appropriation of discourses, of symbols, of rhetoric.

The 'network sociality' of the campaign transcodes local cultural symbols into and against a global one to create a new sociality. A new *social* relation (or *space*) is forged through a common *language* (bilingual, Hinglish), *medium* (cyberspace, instant messaging, blogging), and *genre* (emails, post, poster) where the local and the global intersect. Cyberculture's multimodality—its ability and facility to merge audio, video, and text forms—and its transcoding powers clearly push the possibilities of the language of politics.

FURTIVE TONGUES:
LANGUAGE POLITICS IN THE INDIAN CALL CENTRE

Mathangi Krishnamurthy

> *I know your head aches; I know you are tired; I know your nerves are as raw as meat in a butcher's window. But think what you're trying to accomplish. Think what you're dealing with. The majesty and grandeur of the English language, it's the greatest possession we have.*
>
> —Henry Higgins, *My Fair Lady*

> *The biggest obstacle is that you have to make them speak in English. English is a major problem for these people. They are reluctant towards a new language.*
>
> —Bipin Deo, call centre consultant

On any given day at the call centre, customer service agents open their mouths wider, enunciate their syllables stronger, and seek to create out of a recalcitrant lexicon, the possibility of meaning. Sitting through training sessions on accent, tone, emphasis, and grammar, the worker's attempt at rendering the English language seems relentless. One could mistake this for a language immersion programme, intent on indoctrinating willing subjects into an economy of English. The business of the transnational call centre based out of India does indeed depend largely on workers' English language abilities along with the organization's technological infrastructure and capacity to develop business relations and confidence. Scholarly work, media accounts, and business propositions have all focused on the advantage that a large, urban, middle-class, English-speaking population has conferred on the voice-based Indian outsourcing economy. Two areas, however, remain ambiguous in this supposition. The first is the question of the middle class, in itself both a discourse and an inadequately defined and broad population possessing varied levels of cultural capital (Fernandes 2006); and the second is the tenability of attempts to harness and commodify such cultural capital into a homogeneous linguistic offering.

In examining English language usage in the call centre, this paper will eschew the widely examined and debated question of accent training. Instead, I concentrate on the ways in which workers are identified as possessing different linguistic abilities and how the call centre attempts to flatten regional differences and varied histories of English language education into a 'good, professional and efficient'[1] process of language deployment. Scholarship has expanded on the question of accent in the call centre, especially in its recent tendency to 'neutral' inflection and speech (Cowie 2007). By neutral, I refer to the ostensible homogenization of speech. This essay will concentrate instead on the processes of language training and deployment that define such neutrality even as they seek to create a universally understandable worker. My primary argument is that attempts to homogenize workers into uniform English-speaking agents are doomed to failure and inadequacy in conforming to the avowed goals of a noise-free clarity. While clearly embedded in the belief that the colonized in this instance are not 'passive actors of a Western script' (Sharpe 1995), this paper is, however, not about resistance. Instead of classifying such failure as the worker's act of agency, I examine how the day-to-day work of the call centre is nevertheless rendered possible. I use ethnographic analyses and read the linguistic codes of the call centre in their changes, norms, and accommodations to talk about linguistic capital in the Indian service economy.

The ethnographic research on which this paper is based was carried out over eighteen months in 2006 and 2007.[2] During this period, I conducted in-depth interviews with agents, managers, trainers, and consultants in and around the university town of Pune, India. I also worked in a call centre as a communications, and voice and accent trainer for four months.

Talking the Talk

Call centre workers or customer service agents interacting with American, British, and Australian clients are expected to make themselves clearly understood in English, while intoning a modicum of appropriate accent or markers of accent, and communicate effectively in a phone conversation that, most often, lasts between five and ten minutes only.[3] The content of the conversation is often repetitive and involves providing solutions for a fairly limited set of issues and queries. While it is difficult to define 'effectiveness', one can concur at the very least that this means being able to speak clearly and express oneself in English. Most agents are between eighteen and twenty-five years of age, and enter the call centre armed with varying and varied levels of English language fluency. As a result, all call centres provide training in communication. There has also risen around the call centre a burgeoning business in English language training, often coupled with 'soft skills'[4] variously labelled 'personality development', 'effective communication', and 'professional communication'. Several agents enter the call centre already equipped with some form of training. While workers were earlier trained to reproduce an ambiguously defined American or British accent, the emphasis has now shifted to an equally nebulous 'neutral' accent.

Training in language and accent forms one of the core support functions of the call centre. Depending on the size of the organization and the kind and number of business processes it supports, the training department may consist of five to fifteen employees providing anywhere from a week to three months of training in communication. These are often codified into initialisms to indicate specific expertise that the training department of any one organization has developed. So, for example, ECT trainers provide training using 'Effective Communication Tools' while V&A personnel deliver modules dealing with 'Voice & Accent'. The difference in monikers does not, however, extend into training content; most call centres provide similar lessons in language usage, grammatical structure, sentence construction, and process-specific terminology. While the last is often jargon that refers specifically to the task at hand—billing cycle for credit cards or phone bills, itinerary for air travel, premium payments for insurance queries—clients in the US and UK, who outsource these services, often insist on their own trademarked sentences as opening or closing lines that are mandatory for agents to spout. An agent may have to begin every call with, 'Thank you for calling [name of company], my name is Howard. How may I help you today?' and end with 'Have I managed to address your concern today?' and 'Thank you for calling [name of company], have a wonderful day/ evening.' Training processes can be broken down into (1) basic sentence construction, (2) voice coaching (clear speech, enunciation, word flow), (3) tone management, (4) accent (American, British, neutral), and (5) standard phrases and specific terminology.

During my stint as a communications trainer, I encountered various levels of fatigue among fellow trainers. My colleagues often lamented the fact that it was getting increasingly difficult to train workers—their batches of trainees had to be taught everything from constructing a sentence to the appropriate tone of speech. Given the increasing demand for workers,[5] high levels of attrition, and the consequent search for new caches of labour populations in provincial India, the call centre had been recruiting young workers with a regional language education in the hope that they could be trained to communicate in English. The assumption was that workers could be trained in the minimal language skills required to deal with a defined set of problems in a business situation. Thereafter, experience on the job was expected to provide enough repetitive instances that the workers could then effectively communicate within the said range of business situations.

I walked out of my training session one sunny Tuesday afternoon in March 2007 to see a crowd of young men and women clustered around the reception area. They were all waiting for results from their psychometric tests. Workers who successfully made it through this test would then be asked to undertake a voice profiling test—typically a ten-minute session conducted by voice and accent trainers who then classify workers into categories A, B, C, in declining order of their perceived language skills. Workers in the C category are assigned additional training sessions. Workers who do not fit into any of these categories are flagged.

Voice profiling exercises were often randomly conducted, at times even while the workers were undergoing training. A quasi-scientific form of filtering the willing hordes, the process in itself entailed that trainers train their hearing to listen for mistakes, individual syllables inflected differently, and wait for the pattern to repeat itself. They were guided by a sheet listing parameters such as 'vowel sounds', 'tone', 'sentence structure', and 'clarity'. Trainers graded job applicants on the basis of a five- to ten-minute conversation during the course of which the latter were asked to talk about themselves. Many would state by rote, 'Myself ABC, I am coming from Pune, my hobbies are music and surfing the Internet.'

While management and the sourcing department required that the number of open positions be filled as soon as possible, the paucity of skilled labour often led to a large number of workers making it through the profiling filters even when their performance levels did not match the stated parameters. Trainers and sourcing personnel were in a permanent tussle, negotiating to ensure each of their disparate agendas. In the event that trainers succumbed to pressure from the human resource departments, many more workers than could communicate would make their way to that most coveted of spaces—the call centre floor. There were many instances during my tenure when clients would demand crisis management, because of complaints from customers in the US about the quality of service and workers' inability to communicate in spoken English. Short-term hiring policies, however, allowed for workers to continue being trained even while holding down their positions. As a result, the organization could show the required number of workers on the roster and bill clients accordingly. Also, companies often hedged their bets and hoped that the client would not complain until later in the work cycle during which time the quality of work could ostensibly be addressed. Workers told me, during one of my training sessions, how they had undergone at least four language and voice and accent sessions with different trainers and had yet, continued to be at the receiving end of management and client complaints. Consequently, they were also suitably nervous about losing their jobs. Communication training had become an end in itself, a process repeated sufficient number of times to register marginal change that could then be converted into statistics to prove to the clients that their complaints were being addressed.

New workers underwent anywhere from two weeks to two months of communication training. Often, even when these workers were conversant in English, their speech was inflected and influenced by the local language. Scholars in World Englishes have extensively documented the hybridity of South Asian English in India, especially with reference to literary theory. While such hybridity finds place in questions of language development and change, it becomes a deterrent to transnational communication and its attendant relations of client power. In the call centre, the tendency to Indian English is collectivized under the initialism MTI or 'Mother Tongue Influence'. Alternatively, workers are sometimes seen as 'transliterating'. The latter here refers to a literal translation from the speaker's native tongue into English. Trainers were instructed to work at 'neutralizing' such influence—hence the term 'neutral' accent. Workers were also constantly instructed to pay heed to the structures of English and not indulge in literal translations.[6] To standardize skills and provide appropriate training, workers' voices were profiled as the first step of indoctrination into work. Since the organization was located in Pune in western India and many workers came from Marathi-speaking families, the MTI had been determined by senior managers in the training department to be very specific. Instances of interchange in long and short vowel sounds ('ee' for the shorter 'i' sound and vice versa, i.e., Virgeenia instead of Virginia), and inability to pronounce certain words like 'vision' were very common. Besides issues of pronunciation, a large number of workers had difficulty speaking fluently and constructing thoughts in English. Workers often shared their sense of frustration in trying to render complex thoughts into inchoate tongue. Their vocabularies were limited, and their understanding of grammatical structure unorthodox.

All trainers had two to four weeks to turn a language problem into a communication solution. So we were instructed to break it down into a problem–solution approach. We enumerated bits and parts of sentences, enunciation, and tone. We attempted to define MTI, taught workers nouns and verb forms, intoned long and short vowels, and attempted to prevent them interchanging 'v' and 'w' sounds (bite your Vs and kiss your Ws). Language training became a process of repetition and memorization. After a month, when I observed and listened in on agents taking calls, change was palpable. Agents repeated sentences suggested by the trainers. Words were mispronounced but confidently. Grammar was garbled but without pauses. Agents spoke assertively, their sentences fluid. Language disabilities had metamorphosed into smart communication. The lessons they had learnt well along with the tips on language were on presentation, tone and confidence—in other words, a complete repertoire of 'soft skills'. Indeed, they were talking the talk.

Lest it be misconstrued that call centres are well equipped to impart standard language skills, it is important to know that trainers themselves had varied linguistic and educational backgrounds. Some, like me, had been hired on account of life experiences in the US and UK, others were former agents who had moved up the organizational ladder, still others were former English schoolteachers. The content of training manuals was often configured by the latter in consultation with senior management. As a result, not everybody was uniformly conversant with language teaching as a set of rules. Once, a trainer, recently promoted from her role as an agent, rushed out of a training session in tears. She later reported being terrorized by the rookie workers:

> Bahut badmaash hain, they ask me about grammar. Ab mujhe kya pata ki subject aur object kya hota hai?
> [They are up to no good, they ask me about grammar. Now what do I know what subject and object are?]

The everyday workings of language training are thus quite contrary to accounts that emphasize the tendency to high linguistic discipline in the call centre.

The other side of the story is that workers come in with their own agendas. Many are young students, often just out of high school or in the process of completing their undergraduate education with little idea of Weberian corporate discipline.

While uniformly instructed to speak in English at all times, few complied. As Ravi confessed, 'Kitni der angrezi main bakne ka? Kantal aa jaata hai! [How long can I jabber in English? I get bored after a while!]' Such resistance was, however, neither uniform nor openly rebellious. Workers were clearly aware of the performance parameters and minimal skills needed to keep their jobs. Others, while possessing limited ability to communicate in English, nevertheless worked hard at perfecting their presentation skills to be perceived as competent—not only in the call centre but also in future interviews for other urban service industries, or even graduate school. Many of my trainees were very open about having joined the organization to gain lessons in 'professionalism'. They had entered the call centre in a bid to gain the requisite skills demanded of a professional, English-speaking, transnational worker.[7] Language skills and 'personality training', as imparted in the call centre, could travel to other service industries such as retail, hotel management, and airlines. Workers often join call centres and leave right after undergoing training in communication and being certified as competent speakers. Language invariably forms a part of this agenda. Rohan, a former call centre worker shares, 'My language has improved a lot thanks to you. Since childhood I was studying in an English school, but all Gujaratis around me. Now I try and converse a lot in English.'

English Pasts, Hybrid Presents

While my argument thus far has been to locate English as both fragmented and awkward in its enforcement as a linguistic standard within the call centre, I nevertheless do not intend to take away from attendant relations of power within which the English language continues to thrive in the Indian political milieu. This tendency to power has a long and complex history in India. Since my research is primarily concerned with the call centre industry between the late 1990s and contemporary India, it bears very distinct connections with the ways in which English competence forms a kind of 'cultural capital' (Bourdieu, Harker et al. 1990; Bourdieu and Passeron 1990) in postcolonial India. The English language is considered one of the most prominent legacies of British rule. Rooted in the colonial diktat to create a 'a class who may be interpreters between us and the millions whom we govern—a class of persons Indian in blood and colour, but English in tastes, in opinions, in morals and in intellect'[8] (Macaulay and Young 1967), English language education branched out from its colonial past to find increasing acceptance in an India determined to become global. The language skills that catalysed the rise of the call centre industry are the result of pre- and post-Independence language education policies that privileged English as a medium of education for the middle class as well as for higher education (King 1997; Pennycook 1998; Sonntag 2000). The history of English language policy in India as well as the many political battles won by its supporters through the 1960s and 1970s can be seen as one of the most important reasons for India's success as a call centre hub. Scholarly work on this period and its linguistics gives us several permutations and combinations in this battle for articulation. These can primarily be categorized as Hindi versus English, English versus the vernacular, and English and other vernaculars in complicity against Hindi. This is the English language background that forms the basis of my understanding of language usage in the call centre. I summarize from these literatures to state that English language knowledge is seen as inextricably connected with a class status, mainly middle- to upper-middle class, and, therefore the default language of modernity and upward mobility (Ramanathan 2005). Such knowledge is not just functional but also aesthetic—in Bourdieu's terms, a linguistic marker of distinction (Bourdieu 1984).

Recent investments in the Indian service industry have channelled this history into effective transnational profits. Many upcoming service sectors such as retail, airlines, hospitality, and outsourcing have contributed to this increasing demand for English-speaking workers. As a result, the need for language training and linguistic competence announces itself boldly across urban spaces. Billboards, private lessons, and local experts all claim to mediate access to the English language. Posters, advertorials, and telesale spots attest to a continuing and, in some ways, accelerated concern with the ability to communicate in English. If one were to believe this evidence, then it wouldn't be too far off the mark to suggest that English is the lingua franca of an India seeking to become global. Even as it leaves the corridors of schools and colleges and becomes reconfigured both as commodity as well as service, it now enters the corporation as a skill.

So, I ask, what is the status of English language ability in a matrix comprising additional, and often modular, ways of moulding a productive call centre worker? Although English continues to be a 'link' (Kachru 1983) language in preserving and expanding connections between India and the rest of the world, the ability to be transnational in the instance of the call centre is being coupled with a corporatized self that goes beyond and develops differently from the aesthetics of a distinctly classed English language capability. I argue that English then becomes a modular capacity, more instrumental than its rendition in post-1947 debates on language.

If English is the lingua franca of globalization, and globalization continues in spite of and along with 'bad' English, then I argue that outside of World English and hybridity, it is important to examine the process wherein the appendage of 'bad' disappears into the service of a serviceable language.

English in India has always been political. While a distinct corollary and result of postcoloniality, it is nevertheless not the country's native tongue and yet has been vying for the top spot as unifying tongue, mandatory requirement, and prerequisite for globalization. It is also held up against Hindi, which is only familiar to northern India and is yet the national language. It thus fulfils two functions—the first looking outward to the global stage and the second inward to resolve the problem of linguistic heterogeneity. If one were to believe this evidence, then it would not be too far-fetched to suggest that English has become hegemonic and has won the battle for the voice. At the same time, it continues to be identified as colonial legacy, mark of the comprador class, and sign of highfalutin-ness. The question remains: Who speaks English and how? I pose questions of language in the call centre in an attempt to open the playing field and recover English language ability from its singular, or at best segmented, descriptions. What does Indian English sound like? Who speaks what kind of English, and where?

English, especially in the call centre, is now only one among many skills that need to be mastered in order to be a productive subject of the corporation and the nation. I do not conflate the two carelessly. In 2007, I volunteered to work for a leading government-affiliated civic body in Pune. Since I had already spent some months training at the call centre, I was asked if I could conduct workshops for older government employees in Pune. The workshops were meant to talk about presentation and management skills. I never ended up training for these workshops but did see banners for communication programmes week after week as I rode by the imposing gates to the institute. An institute offering government-recognized call centre training courses in Pune works with young men and women with very little knowledge of English in order that 'our people' are not 'left behind'. According to Sagar Gharpure, a trainer at the institute, their objective is to 'groom up the Marathi people so we can groom them in the coming corporate world'. When I asked if teaching people English was counterintuitive to the projected desire to preserve the vernacular, he responded, 'What the government is doing is okay from the perspective that when you go outside you need certain things. Government knows that it is an international language. If they want to develop their state, they need language.'

Hence, the state preserves its national integrity and identity even as it couples its mandate with the corporate call for globalization and economic liberalization, by creating a separation between a newly created inside and the outside (Chatterjee 1990).

Limits of the Hybrid and the Fluid

The ability to speak fluently and confidently in English is cultural capital. Using a certain mode of speech in English brings people symbolic capital through prestige as well as material rewards (Bourdieu & Thompson 1991). Control over language is perceived as a sign of education, which is a marker of investment in class mobility (Urciuoli 1996). While I have posited language as more fluid and increasingly modular in the instance of the call centre, it reaches its limits soon enough. For example, when I attended the interview of an aspiring worker with ten years of experience in hotel management, he was asked to talk about himself. He responded in halting English, and was promptly sent away. Evaluations of expertise are therefore contingent upon questions of demand and supply, and notions of flexibility (Ong 1999). The worker in this instance was also no doubt judged as too old and hence lacking the flexibility to be trained in English language skills.

When I started working in the call centre, I was initially struck by the discomfort a number of trainees felt with the English language. Most trainers attempted to dispel workers' insecurities by exhorting them to speak in English all the time, insisting that it is ultimately only a matter of practice. Trainers, though themselves possessing varying levels of language skills, did not hesitate to make fun of specific workers in their absence, mimicking inflected pronunciation or language usage. During evaluation sessions, the trainer leading the process would often have to intervene and request the trainers to demonstrate more respect for the workers' sentiments. Evaluation sessions were held collectively for trainers so that they could all be uniformly aware of the parameters by which language skills needed to be inculcated. Such sessions involved six to seven trainers evaluating a set of applicants over a telephonic interview. Trainers gathered in a conference room and clustered around a conference table bearing a phone on an internal line connected to the interview room. Applicants were shepherded into the room and asked to speak to the person at the other end of the line. The session lasted for about three hours and all trainers were required to grade the voice on the phone for clarity, tone, sentence structure, etc. based on a quasi-scientifically worded grade guideline sheet that also defined parameters. Often, interviewees would be asked to pronounce certain words over and over again so trainers could understand if the errors were a normal occurrence (and hence could not be trained) or random occurrences (which could be corrected).

Only a few floors separated the trainers and the interviewees. Sessions often ended with trainers rushing to the interview spot to sneak a glimpse of the face of the voice on the phone. Anahita, the training manager, would be forced to adopt a stern tone, warning them to hold their laughter and avoid leaving the room to spot interviewees. In one such session that I was a part of, we encountered a man who identified himself as Ramoji. He answered the phone and said nothing but hello. When asked as to who was speaking, he said, 'Myself Ramoji'. Clearly the man had not understood anything being said. Subsequent questions, even when enunciated slowly, elicited no response except sounds of acknowledgement. To every question, Ramoji would reply '*haan*', 'okay', 'yes'. Finally, in frustration, Anahita asked him to end the call and usher the next person in. He did so and the room erupted into laughter. Ajay said, '*Pata nahiin kahaan kahaan se aa jate hain, HR paagal ho gaya hai kya?*' (Where do they come from? Has the human resource department lost its mind?) The others speculated that he must have come into the organization along with the walk-in interviewees. A new trainer Reema said, '*Isko laga hoga ki mereko bhi call centre mein kaam karne ka hai. Full khede-gaon*[9] *type lagta hai.*' (He must have thought that even he could work in a call centre; seems like a complete villager.) Anahita dialled again only to find Ramoji back on the line. Apparently, he had hung up but stayed on, not comprehending Anahita's instructions. She then spoke to him in Hindi—only to have the same thing happen again. Finally, someone in the room told him in Marathi to bring the next candidate in. Ramoji finally went offline.

In this instance is also another kind of marking of people that are excluded from the space of the call centre—those that belong to the interior that cannot access globalization or transnational shores, even as they are made nearer through the portal of the call centre. Some language skills can be learnt but clearly Ramoji needed to be sent back.

Sneaky Subjects, Forked Tongues

This essay is concerned with language usage in Indian call centres. I contend that understanding everyday communication around the call centre is an important window into the globalization of English and linguistic hegemony as contradictory processes. Further, such examination of language on a purported transnational and translational site might chart a path to the new English of urban India; to Hinglish, local English, and Indianized English. I use the latter not as markers of perfectly formed alternatives and patois that signify the triumph or resurgence of the 'local', but rather as imperfect, messy clues into an overarching yet unformed and constantly reforming globalization. While outsourcing as an industry has been made possible by the influx of global capital, its terms have had to be negotiated within the specificity of the locale, which in turn also becomes indelibly transformed in its wake. It is therefore not my intention to posit an authentic locality or even Indianness that subverts globalization. Instead, this essay contends that these meanderings between and across linguistic codes are contingent and specific to the time and place of use. More importantly, I argue that they redefine, over the longer term, the realm of the normative in language, communication, and forms of linguistic identity.

Furtive tongues are thus furtive, not in their sneaking in a word of Hindi and a phrase of Marathi, or in the refusal to speak English, but in the ways in which they have slowly and furtively redefined the norms of language in the call centre. At the same time, what are also furtive are the ways in which flexible capital schools new labour populations. While borrowing from a past that created English-speaking populations, new service economies nevertheless allow for an increasing cache of labour forces by relaxing the norms of the linguistic aesthete and reconfiguring ways of attaining communicative efficiency and corporate subjecthood. Where then does agency lie and what pray is the status of language? In conclusion, I disavow the question of Hinglish and insist that while naming is an important practice of asserting as well as questioning power, what matters more are the boundaries of flexible speech. By noticing changing boundaries of good English, we can chart a path to understanding how globalization configures commodities and selves. I seek to open the debate to ask if the current moment of language can be read not in terms of its status as one linguistic code or the other, but as a symptom of times to come.

I argue that in the case of the call centre, the politics of English has been defanged in the service of a language that, minimally, gets by and, maximally, can be used in tandem and enhanced by a corporate selfhood. To what extent then does this also expose the messy nature of globalization that seeks to create a universally recognizable, communicable worker yet often ends up with a particular local/global subject—impure, mixed up, crafty? I conclude by stating that this selfhood is linguistically impure and local, yet stylistically global and communicable. I locate and dislocate in the same instance.

In conclusion, I also offer an anecdote. As I was leaving India to return to Austin, Texas, I visited a new privatized bank in my hometown Rasayani, a semi-urban industrial estate in western India. I needed to transfer my salary account, which had been created when I started working at the call centre. In chatting with the bank officer Akash, who was helping me with procedures, we discovered that we had attended the same high school and had common friends. I updated him on my whereabouts in the US, and we chatted about people and caught up on our life paths. While glancing at my paperwork, he noticed that I had worked with a call centre for a few months. So now, Akash had two pieces of information to help map me. One, I was working on a doctoral degree in the US; two, I had worked in the outsourcing industry. He remarked, 'Oh you worked at a call centre, that is why your English is too good!'

TOWARDS A POLITICAL ECONOMY
OF HINGLISH TV

Daya Kishan Thussu

As one of the world's largest television markets, India offers fascinating possibilities for exploring how the global (read Western) interacts with the national and the national with the myriad variations of the local, given its multilingual and multilayered media scene. This essay examines the exponential growth of the Indian TV market in the past two decades—from the once-ubiquitous Doordarshan, the notoriously monotonous and unimaginative state monopoly, to the current array of over 300 digital channels, covering most genres from soap operas to sports to comedy to children's programming to news and documentaries, catering to a huge Indian market as well as a large Indian (indeed South Asian) diaspora, estimated to be 24 million strong.

The rapid liberalization of media and cultural industries in India, along with the increasing availability of new and sophisticated communication technologies, has created a new market in the increasingly Westernized and culturally hybridized audience. Their growing purchasing power and aspirations to a consumerist lifestyle have, in turn, attracted transnational media corporations into India. After initial successes, the largely Hollywood-based programming did not prove profitable—it was being watched only by a tiny English-speaking minority. Recognizing the limitations of this strategy, transnational networks first Indianized and then localized their programming to suit the range and variety of cultural and linguistic tastes constituting the Indian market.

Focusing on the example of global media magnate Rupert Murdoch's TV channels in India, this essay argues that his dominant position has been achieved largely through localization strategies that skilfully prioritized the local over the global. This included content localization and adoption/adaptation of Indian languages, such as mixing Hindi with English to provide a hybridized media language, Hinglish. This tendency of transnational media corporations to 'go native' with active support from local subsidiaries, as well as increasingly vocal Indian media companies, helps them present themselves as an acceptable, even nationalist, face of globalization. However, in the name of defending national interest, are these channels propagating dominant neoliberal ideology, and helping legitimize a media marketplace in which global corporate clients can consolidate and expand, while the rural poor move further to the margins of a rapidly globalizing India?

Introduction

TV in India has contributed significantly in chutnefying the English language. Despite the extraordinary growth in global online media, TV remains the primary mass medium, particularly important in a country where even in 2009 nearly 40 per cent of the population was illiterate—a figure translating into 400 million people, the world's largest group of unlettered individuals. The rapid globalization of TV and the resultant impact of Western (read American) media culture on Indian TV has led to the appropriation of Western, or specifically American, formats and their Indianization to suit local tastes and languages, thus creating a new model of hybridization between the West and the South. One outcome of this media marriage is the development of Hinglish, a mixture of English (the language of international media) and Hindi (the most widely used language in India).

Language purists may disapprove of the popularity of this hybrid language, and critical political economists may view it as another example of cultural imperialism that the West, led by the US, exercises over the rest of the world. Yet the presence of Hinglish in our public discourse and private conversations is here to stay, if not flourish in coming decades. There is already an overwhelming presence of Hinglish in India's bourgeoning popular culture—Bollywood film songs and dialogues, TV, FM radio, newspapers, and advertising[1] (Baldauf 2004; Kachru 2006).

TV Language in India

In a multi-ethnic, multi-religious, multilingual country like India, language is a crucial element of cultural self-expression. Given its well-established oral tradition, 400 languages are spoken across India, though the Constitution recognizes eighteen.[2] In India, multilingualism is the norm; most citizens speak at least two languages, some speak three. English remains the link language—of higher courts, bureaucracy, higher education—while Hindi, with its regional variations, is the most widely spoken language. It is also the language of India's film industry, which annually produces more films than Hollywood. (In 2009, India produced 1,288 feature films as against 677 produced by Hollywood, according to *Screen Digest*.)

TV has been an important factor in popularizing languages. The role of the state broadcaster was to promote national integration and a unified language was seen as a crucial element of that strategy. Though Doordarshan attempted to cater to regional feelings through its regional centres (broadcasting in regional languages), its 'National Programme', aimed at a pan-Indian viewership and launched in the mid-1980s, was in Hindi and English only. The telecasts were not universally liked, seen as being Delhi-centric and privileging Hindi over the other languages only because of the sheer number of its speakers. This sentiment was strongest in the southern state of Tamil Nadu, which saw Doordarshan as imposing Hindi on a people whose mother tongue, Tamil (a Dravidian language), had little in common with the language of the north. In other parts of India, such as West Bengal, Hindi was seen as an aesthetically inferior language to Bengali, known for its rich literary tradition. Moreover, resentment arose even within Hindi-speaking areas about the *kind* of Hindi used by the national broadcaster—pure and literary, it alienated the masses who thrived on speaking a mixture of 'bazaar' Hindi. Similarly, the English used on TV was elitist, the so-called 'Queen's English'.

Creating a Hinglish TV Market

The liberalization of the Indian TV industry revolutionized broadcasting in what used to be one of the world's most protected media markets (Kohli-Khandekar 2006; Mehta 2008). TV's gradual deregulation and privatization transformed the nation's media landscape—evident in the exponential growth in the number of TV channels, from one state-controlled network till 1991 to over 300 in 2009, including some joint ventures with international broadcasters (Thussu 2007a). Of these, many are in Hindi or English—and therefore national in reach—while others cater to regional audiences in their languages. Much of this has been possible because of media globalization and the resultant expansion of mainly Western transnational media players into India, potentially one of the world's biggest English-language TV markets. As the industry grew, so did the realization that a hybridization of media culture is what sells best.

The use of a hybrid media language was pioneered and popularized by Zee TV, India's first private Hindi-language and most successful satellite channel. Launched in 1992 by entrepreneur Subhash Chandra Goel's Essel Group and targeted to reach the mass market by pioneering Bollywood-based TV entertainment, Zee TV broke new ground in domestically produced entertainment. The Zee network, which made broadcasting history by earning a profit within its first year of operations, demonstrates how national media can indigenize global TV products by adapting and developing derivatives of programme formats and languages. However, Zee would not have climbed these peaks if it had not been for the doyen of the global media market—Australian-born, US-based septuagenarian Rupert Murdoch, chairman and chief executive officer of News Corporation, one the world's largest media conglomerates with 2008 revenues at nearly $33 billion (News Corp. 2008).

The Murdochization of Media in India

As in many other countries of Asia, the greatest contribution to the trend towards hybridized media in India has been that of Rupert Murdoch, whose pan-Asian network STAR (Satellite TV Asia Region), launched in 1991, pioneered satellite TV in Asia, transforming TV news and entertainment (Butcher 2003). Murdoch was responsible for introducing the first music TV channel in India (Channel V), the first 24/7 news network (Star News), the first successful adaptation of an international game show (*Who Wants To Be A Millionaire?*), and the first reality TV series (*Lakme Fashion Show*) (Thussu 2007a). Today, the Star network entertains 60 million Indians daily.

Murdoch's extensive control of both information software (programme content) and hardware (delivery systems) has made him a hugely powerful player in global media. As News Corporation's 2008 Annual Report notes, 'the world's most international media company' operates on six continents in over 100 countries in thirty languages. Before many others could do so, Murdoch realized the potential of media in the world's largest continent, home to some of its fastest growing economies, and invested heavily in Asia's media scene. By 2008, Star was operating across fifty-three countries in Asia, offering sixty-three channels in ten languages and reaching approximately 300 million Asians (News Corp. 2008).

As elsewhere in Asia, in India too, Murdoch started out with Hollywood-based programming aimed at the affluent but tiny English-speaking minority (less than 5 per cent of India's population). He soon recognized the limitations of this strategy and rapidly Indianized his TV operations. Though Murdoch's business interests in India are wider than TV, his investment in TV has been the most important feature of his India strategy. The flagship of his India operations, the Hindi-language general entertainment channel Star Plus, is India's highest-rated private entertainment network (Butcher 2003).

Promoting Hinglish

More than most, Murdoch has contributed to the popularization of Hinglish on TV, as seen in the way he marketed Star Plus in its initial years with slogans like *Aapki Boli—Aapka Plus Point* ('Your language is your plus point'). He realized that to make a dent in India's notoriously diverse TV marketplace, his networks had to chutnefy the language of its programmes. The all-music network Channel V, for instance, originally provided English music presented by Western-born Indian video jockeys speaking in Americanized English. Few outside India's metropolitan youth clusters could identify with them, forcing Channel V to start offering English programming peppered with Hindi words and Hindi songs to reach a wider audience—70 per cent of India's 1 billion people are aged below thirty-five years.

News Corporation's interests in Indian media are wide and growing. By 2009, Murdoch controlled a great deal of TV in India, directly or through joint ventures. These included wholly owned channels (Star Plus, Star One, Star Gold, Star World, Channel V, Star Movies, Star Utsav, Star Vijay); joint ventures (ESPN Star Sports, National Geographic, Fox History, Star News, Star Ananda); distribution (Disney channel; cable distributor Hathway; DTH Tata-Sky); and programming (until recently Balaji Telefilms, one of India's most prolific TV serial makers).

The inclusion of the southern Tamil language entertainment channel Vijay TV and the twenty-four-hour Bengali news service Star Ananda into the Star family demonstrates Murdoch's interest in going beyond the Hindi-speaking parts of India, aiming at a mass audience and reflecting growing localization strategies. Right from his entry into the volatile Indian broadcasting market in 1992, the localization of his operations was a unique characteristic of Murdoch's strategy. Unlike Disney or AOL-Time Warner, Murdoch did not see India as 'another syndication opportunity'; instead, he invested in local programming and cooperation with local TV companies. His control of the Zee network between 1993 and 2000 gave Murdoch a crucial insight into the Bollywood-driven Indian popular culture (Thussu 2007a). Having resourceful local partners is crucial for media conglomerates and Murdoch has shown an uncanny knack for choosing these. One of the most significant joint ventures Star signed in India was with Tata on DTH (direct-to-home) TV for Tata-Sky, a pan-Indian, state-of-the-art digital infrastructure for pay TV (Kohli-Khandekar 2006).

Partly as a result of media's Murdochization, Indian TV has been transformed. Via exponential growth in the number of TV channels, India has emerged as one of the world's biggest TV markets (Kohli-Khandekar 2006; Mehta 2008). This unprecedented growth has been spurred on by massive increases in advertising revenue as Western-based conglomerates tap into the growing market of 300 million increasingly Westernized, educated middle-class Indians with enhanced purchasing power and media-induced aspirations to consumerist lifestyles (Ganguly-Scrase & Scrase 2008). Cable and satellite TV have consolidated substantially since their introduction in 1992, when only 1.2 million Indian homes had access to these facilities; growing annually at the rate of 10 per cent, TV connectivity was set to touch 134 million households by 2010, of which 85 million were expected to be cable and satellite households. In 2009, there were 400 million TV viewers in India. The media and entertainment business, one of India's fastest growing industries, was projected to reach nearly 23 billion dollars by 2011, according to the 2007 report *Indian Entertainment and Media Industry: A Growth Story Unfolds*, prepared by PricewaterhouseCoopers (PwC) for the Federation of Indian Chambers of Commerce and Industry (FICCI). The Indian TV broadcasting market was projected to be worth 11.8 billion dollars by 2011. In addition, TV accounted for 46 per cent of the total advertising industry worth nearly 3.5 billion dollars (FICCI 2007).

Indian media has also benefited from media outsourcing industries in such areas as animation and post-production services for Hollywood and other industries. The marriage between Hollywood and Bollywood, already on the global media agenda, has contributed to the globalization of Hinglish (Trivedi 2008). The globalization of Bollywood—Hindi films are shown in over seventy countries—has also ensured that Indian films are increasingly watched by an international audience as well as a wider diasporic one. Indian film exports witnessed a twenty-fold increase in the period 1989–99 and, by 2005, exports accounted for nearly 30 per cent of the industry earnings. This has made it imperative for producers to invest in subtitling to widen the reach of films, as well as privileging scripts that would interest overseas audiences. The Indian government's decision, announced in 2000, to allow foreign companies to invest in the film industry imparted immense momentum for joint ventures between Indian film producers and Hollywood production houses.

A Credit Suisse (2006) report, *Opportunities of Hollywood in Bollywood*, noted that the Indian media market offered global conglomerates possibilities to develop new streams of income, attracted by the progressive easing of foreign ownership rules. Also benefiting from relaxation of cross-media ownership rules are such non-media groups as Tata (India's largest industrial house), Adlabs, and Bharti, which have invested heavily in DTH. Large companies are increasingly visible across various segments of the media and entertainment world—new 'media conglomerates', inspired by the US model, are in the making. The emerging political economy of what has been termed as 'the multiplex paradigm' contributes to a seamless corporatized distribution of 'symbolic culture' (Athique 2009).

The expansion of the TV industry has demanded new programme content, from news to game and chat shows, from soap operas to reality TV, which have been provided by a burgeoning TV industry, catering to a huge Indian market as well as a large South Asian diaspora (Thussu 2007a). The availability of new delivery and distribution mechanisms, as well as the growing corporatization of its film factories and TV industry, have ensured that Indian TV has entered the global media sphere, and has the potential of reaching out in new directions, towards further horizons.

As India integrates further with the globalized free-market economy, the Indian version of the English language is likely to have a transnational reach, attracting new viewers beyond its traditional South Asian diasporic constituency. This interest has partly been generated by the growing visibility of Indian enterprise and its cultural products around the world.

Hinglish in the Diaspora

A contributing factor to the growth of Hinglish TV is the availability of Indian media products to the 'global' Indian, thanks to technological transformation in production, distribution, and delivery of cultural products. Indian film and TV companies have striven to increase their presence in such hubs of global media as London—home to a sizeable South Asian diaspora. Hinglish is more acceptable to the members of this linguistically diverse group; most of them, especially from the second or third generations, converse in a language that bends and blends, often in innovative ways, English words with Punjabi, Urdu, or Hindi. This linguistic affinity is also reflected in programmes like the BBC's popular comic series *Goodness Gracious Me* and spoof shows like *The Kumars At Number 42* where Hinglish words are used routinely, often for comic effect. So widespread is its use in the diaspora that, in 2005, the word 'Hinglish' entered the *Collins English Dictionary*, even as a dictionary of this new hybrid language, *The Queen's Hinglish*, was compiled by a British teacher of Indian origin (Mahal 2006).

Tamasha TV, in Hinglish?

Is Hinglish TV a democratizing influence or does it defile public culture? Has Hinglish become the language of tamasha on TV?

Elsewhere, I have argued how the three Cs (cinema, crime, cricket) have contributed to the 'Bollywoodization' of TV culture that is increasingly becoming hostage to infotainment (Thussu 2007b). The growing tabloidization of TV indicates the 'Murdochization' effect that I have characterized as 'a process which involves the shift of media power from the public to privately owned, transnational, multimedia corporations controlling both delivery systems and the content of global information networks' (Thussu 1998: 7). It can be argued that the ideological imperatives of such a TV culture debase the quality of public deliberations in the world's largest democracy. By overwhelming public discourse with the three Cs, national and transnational conglomerates—in concert or in competition—are taking over India's airwaves at a time when it is integrating with the US-led neoliberal economic and political system, both as a producer and consumer of commodity capitalism.

Where does such commercialism leave public broadcasting? Despite severe competition from private networks, the state broadcaster still retains the highest audience figures in India; Doordarshan's main national channel, DD-1, reaches about 400 million viewers. In 2008, it was operating twenty-seven channels, including DD News, the country's first and only terrestrial news channel with the highest reach into TV households in India. However, in the affluent urban cable and satellite homes the share of DD News was a mere 7 per cent.

The 'public' aspects of India's social reality seem to have been taken over by private corporate interests, which thrive on what a new study has called 'celebrity ecology' that ensures that 'celebrity culture is the new cool of our lives' (Nayar 2009: 181). The alarming absence of rural/developmental issues on Hinglish TV demonstrates that such themes do not translate into ratings for urban, Westernized Hinglish-speaking viewers and are displaced by the diversion of infotainment. The lack of concern among TV networks for India's majority population is at once tragic and ironic in a country that was the first in the world to use satellite TV for educational and developmental purposes, through its 1975 SITE (Satellite Instructional TV Experiment) programme. Scribes who were intellectually rooted in the secular, socialist ideals of the Nehruvian era have given way to younger, brasher journalists, in the 'business' of broadcast news. Concern for the poor and the dispossessed and for the broader questions of global equality and social justice appear to have been replaced by an admiration for smooth-talking Hinglish-fluent business tycoons, charismatic CEOs, and American/Americanized celebrities.

Implications of a Hinglish TV Culture

Does a TV culture that celebrates hybridity erode cultural authenticity? Are Indian languages—prose, poetry, critical commentary—undermined by the multinational media onslaught? Do such chart-topping Bollywood songs as *'Pappu can't dance saala,' 'Zara zara touch me,' 'You're my lucky boy'* or *'Small town girl'* indicate our popular culture in a film industry that has produced poets of the calibre of Shailendra, Sahir, Shakeel, Hasrat, and Majrooh? Is Indian popular culture poorer or more globalized (read Americanized)?

The concern that the global spread of English is hastening language 'decay' and 'death' has a long, complicated history (Kachru & Smith 2008). Despite its imperial legacy, it can be argued that English is an Indian language—some of the finest novelists writing in the language today belong to South Asia. However, there is a deeper consideration. Has the ascendance of a chutneyfied media language lulled the capacity for critical engagement in audiences—have they become merely consumers? French situationist Guy DeBord (1977) theorized about what he called the 'Society of the Spectacle', defining the spectacle as 'the existing order's uninterrupted discourse about itself, its laudatory monologue'. He claimed that the imagery devised by TV and advertising masks social reality—'the spectacle is capital to such a degree of accumulation that it becomes an image'.

TV, with its semiotic and symbolic power, is a crucial element in promoting such a spectacle. Elsewhere, I have discussed how strong the US presence is in the world's visual landscape, despite steady increase in volume and value of media 'contra-flow' from countries like India, Japan, and Brazil (Thussu 2007c). It could be argued that the notion of 'the culture industry', enunciated by Max Horkheimer and Theodor Adorno (Adorno 1991), has been globalized and heightened in the era of global branding under neoliberalism, resulting in a 'global culture industry' (Lash & Lury 2007). Though hybridized programming—inspired by successful American/European formats and indigenized by local clones of transnational conglomerates—dominates TV schedules, the Indian government is not particularly perturbed by its growth, as it can keep the masses diverted with various versions of 'reality TV' and consumerist and entertaining information, displacing serious news and documentaries, which might focus on the excesses of neoliberalism (Thussu 2007b). In this context, it is important to understand the role of the national elites—part of a transnational class that largely benefits from neoliberal economic activities— in the establishment and popularization of a hybridized media culture. As Sklair (2002: 156) suggests,

> The transnational capitalist class is not identified with any foreign country in particular, or even necessarily with the First World, or the White world, or the Western world. Its members identify with the capitalist globalization and re-conceptualize their several local and other interests in terms of the capitalist global system. Their political project is to transform the imagined national interests of their countrymen and women in terms of capitalist globalization.

The Indian chapter of this transnational capitalist class is susceptible to the charms of neoliberalism, as it benefits from closer ties with the powerful core of this tiny minority, largely based in the West, as the annual Fortune 500 listings attest to. In this sense, the Gramscian idea of hegemony can be deployed in a wider context to assess how far neoliberalism has been embraced, almost universalized, by dominant sections of the Indian elite, who have come to regard its basic tenets—private (efficient, therefore preferable) versus public (corrupt, inefficient); individualism (to be applauded) versus community (to be decried); market (good) versus state (bad)—as undisputed opposites within the rubric of 'common sense'.

It is no coincidence that the contestants on the Indian mirror version of the reality TV show *Big Brother* belong mostly to Hinglish-speaking urban India, exposed to Western, reality-TV culture. The success of Murdoch's TV channels in India has primarily been predicated on infotainment, blending the Hollywood-style, Bollywood-generated spectacle in ways that reconfigure neoliberal ideology in Indianized forms (Thussu 2007a, 2007b). The growing presence of 'glocal Americana' is feeding and creating a media culture where neoliberalism is taking deep roots. And the US, the fount of such an ideology, is receiving acceptance bordering on admiration—a 2005 survey by the Pew Global Attitudes Project found that US image was strongest in India, with 71 per cent of Indians expressing a positive opinion of the US, compared with 54 per cent in 2002 (PRC 2005). A 2009 survey put the figure at 76 per cent (PRC 2009).

There is little dispute that the Hinglish-oriented TV has forgotten the rural poor—remarkably absent from dramas and serials on Murdoch's channels and indeed on most market-driven, ratings-conscious networks. A socially relevant TV agenda does not fit well with such networks as they are primarily interested in the demographically desirable, Hinglish-speaking urban middle class, which possesses the disposable income to purchase the goods advertised on their channels. With increasing competition from private channels—as these proliferate while audiences fragment—the tendency to maximize advertisement-friendly programming at the cost of socially relevant shows is likely to intensify while the public-service role of TV continues to be undermined.

As TV is increasingly driven by ratings wars and advertisers' demand for consumers, and given that visuals can be a powerful instrument for propagating dominant ideology, is it possible that the electronic media is being exploited as a vehicle to promote free-market capitalism that enables corporate clients to consolidate and expand? Rather than toeing the government line, as was the case when Doordarshan in *shuddh* Hindi or pure English ruled the roost, are Hinglish TV channels now mouthing corporate propaganda?

In recent years, much has been written about cultural hybridization (Appadurai 1990; Garcia Canclini 1995; Kraidy 2005; etc.). More often than not, the discourse has a celebratory feel. The argument is that in a globalized media culture there is no single identifiable centre of cultural production—though I still await the first Indian reality TV show, or indeed any other TV show, to be adopted by a European/American network. I can list at least half a dozen instances demonstrating the reverse trend.

The increasing emphasis on entertainment-led Hinglish TV may be a cause of celebration among those that subscribe to a 'postmodern' view of a culturally hybrid, globalized world. However, the linguistic and intellectual confusion it may cause could contribute to the trivialization of vital public concerns. Crucially, the subservience to corporate power, nationally and globally, on which Hinglish hegemony is ultimately based, does undermine the public-service ethos and the empowering potential of TV in a country that is still home to the largest segment of the world's poorest people.

ENGLISH *AAJKAL*: HINGLISH IN HINDI CINEMA

Rita Kothari

> *Dhrubo exhaled richly out of the window, and said, 'I've a feeling, August you're going to get hazaar fucked in Madna . . . Amazing mix, the English we speak. Hazaar fucked. Urdu and American.' Agastya laughed, 'A thousand fucked, really fucked. I'm sure nowhere else could languages be mixed and spoken with such ease.'*
>
> —Upamanyu Chatterjee,
> *English, August: An Indian Story*, 1988

The encounter with Hinglish in most parts of urban India is impossible to escape. In the city of Ahmedabad, which does not represent the 'Hindi-speaking belt' of India, my day begins with substantial doses of Hinglish. As I tune in to the FM radio channels to listen to music, I am subjected first to a radio jockey's cheerful assault: '*Aaj aap apne* boyfriend *se ek naya* gift *maangein* and *uske* love *ko* test *karein!*' This is followed by Hinglish songs like '*Zara zara* touch me . . .' and statements such as 'Pappu can't dance *saala*', surprising, because he has a 'Rado watch and Nike shoes'. If this typifies the aural experience, the visual signs of 'pure *bhi poora bhi*' advertising cooking oil or posters of *Love Aaj Kal* outside multiplexes are equally code-switched.

This essay examines the social meanings surrounding English and Hinglish in Hindi cinema and the continuities and discontinuities running through them in post-Independence Hindi cinema. I argue that during this period Hindi cinema used English with connotations of cultural alienation such as Westernization and class elitism, giving way in the last two decades to a less anxious use of Hinglish—creolized, constructed, and promoted as a language of fun-on-Indian-terms. While the association with class persists, it moves from signifiers of exclusivity to aspiration, as more people are now able to access that class. If the class theme represents continuity, the discontinuity lies in the shift of perception of English from being a language 'outside' the sphere of everyday Indianness (1950s–1980s) to Hinglish as simultaneously Indian-and-global, embracing *des* and *pardes*, nation and diaspora in cinema after the 1990s. Thus the essay runs as a narrative from English to Hinglish, and traces the journey of English from the past to the present, shedding some legacies and acquiring new social meanings. While the part on 'English' refers to the insertion of English words or phrases in the Hindi text of cinema from the 1950s to the 1980s, Hinglish is the code-switched language of mainstream Hindi cinema after the 1990s. The two are not watertight, discrete phenomena; they flow into each other, differentiated here by the social meanings they generate.

The 1990s may be described as a convenient marker to contextualize India's transition from a socialist to a consumerist (and globalized) economy. Among the many subsequent changes, the shift in attitude towards English is perhaps profound. At the same time, such overemphatic periodization runs the risk of a ruptured historiography—too neat a separation of categories before and after the 1990s. The present essay employs this marker but also attempts to diffuse neat categorizations by demonstrating the legacies of class and superiority that continue to be associated with English before and after liberalization, along with a simultaneous increase in comfort at indigenizing English and mixing it with Indian languages.

The first half of this essay focuses on the anxieties surrounding

English in Hindi cinema in the first four decades after Independence. It demonstrates the various, but not mutually exclusive, positions of English as the language of an anglicized elite, of villains and buffoons, and of people who created divisions in homes, communities, nations. These patterns are constructed not so much in terms of a linear history but conjured as forms of signification (at least in my mind). Mapped as a series of dominant patterns associated with English in Hindi cinema, this section is an evocative, non-linear narrative extracted from my memories as a viewer.

The second half discusses, through Hindi cinema, the cultural construction of 'Hinglish' as a language shaped by and shaping the post-1990s generations in contemporary India. In a liberalized India, the media, youth, the middle class, and Hinglish form not just intersecting but constitutive ways of being modern.

It is important to clarify what is meant by the 'Hindi' of Hindi cinema. Sifting through various positions on whether the language of Hindi cinema is 'Hindi' at all, if not Urdu and/or Hindustani, Trivedi (2007: 52) underscores the continuity of the linguistic spectrum that renders the classification of Hindi, Urdu, and Hindustani somewhat tenuous. The linguistic signs in Hindi cinema may point to multiple forms of signification but are identified by the popular notion of 'Hindi'. Whether this Hindi is closer to Persian or to Sanskrit is not critical to this discussion, but suffice it to say that it occupies 'the middle ground of wide intelligibility' (Trivedi 2007: 58). Hereafter, the label 'Hindi' stands for the widely intelligible language of Hindi cinema.

I

During the sultry months of June–July 2007, when I first began to examine the phenomenon of Hinglish, a high point of conversations in India was the appointment of Pratibha Patil as President. The subject was discussed hotly, and arguments thrown back and forth—on talk shows, at *paan* shops, on blogs, at dining tables—on whether Patil deserved to hold that office.

The moral, ethical, and political contexts of such arguments are not germane to what I want to say. However, one of the oft-raised objections expressed by the very young and the old alike was: 'She can't even speak proper English.' The irony of subjecting the nation's President to such a test was lost on Midnight's great-grandchildren who see English as nothing but a *naturally* desirable, Indian language.

This minimum qualification for being Indian and, more important, for representing Indianness, was hardly articulated in so many words. However, it came as something of a fresh development to those of us who have been witnessing the process of English-in-the-making-of-an-Indian-language. We expect our presidents and prime ministers to know English, yet few had understood Jawaharlal Nehru's English address to a newly independent India in 1947. It would appear then, that from 1947 to 2007, our relationship with and competence in English has changed drastically. However, the intervening decades show that it was not really so drastic. English continued to be a part of India's public culture, especially cinema, the primary arena of concern in this essay.

But as in cinema, so in real life, the journey of English was chequered. Elsewhere, I have discussed India's ambivalent relationship with English with regard to language policies; the silence around the subject of the exclusion of English from the official languages of the nation and implicit hope that the postcolonial state would somehow work its way around this problem (Kothari 2006). Cinema, like several other institutions until the 1980s, also reflects this ambivalence and anxiety. I illustrate below the multiple embodiments of English in Hindi cinema—its position, variously, as a language of another nation, class, and people. Manifest variously as an element of divisiveness, collaborator with urbanization and gentrification, and sometimes a source of comedy, English had an uneasy relationship with Hindi cinema.

Growing up, as I did through the 1970s and 1980s, on a heavy diet of Hindi cinema, led me to some inevitable conclusions about the use of English in the films of that period. The cinema of the 1970s and early 1980s presented English as the language of such 'Westernized' and anglicized minorities as Christians, Anglo-Indians, and Parsis. When the Anglo-Indian Julie (in *Julie*, 1975) strummed the guitar and sang '*My heart is beating, keeps on repeating, I'm waiting for you ...*' it seemed that Anglo-Indians always spoke English, and that you could 'romance' only in English. It was a new way of being in love, and even if we couldn't or didn't want to be Anglo-Indians, English could take us some distance. Anglo-Indians could be substituted by Christians or Parsis, yet the perception persisted that some communities were 'free'—their women could wear short skirts, bring boyfriends home, and sing songs in English.[1] While the component of English in the actual dialogues may have been negligible, English got stereotyped as the language of the anglicized minorities, with its accompanying signifiers of Westernization such as the guitar and frocks, which lingered on in viewers' minds.

To a lesser extent, it also portrayed English as the language of romance. For instance, note the character of Vikram who declares his love for Julie in the popular song:

Bhool gaya sab kuchh, yaad nahiin ab kuchh
Ek yahi baat na bhooli, Julie, I love you.

It was not clear then (nor is it now) whether Vikram professed his love in English because Julie is what she is, or because he needed to express his feelings in a language outside the feudal orbit of his upper-caste Bengali Hindu community.[2] What is important is to see that the two strands—English as a language of certain 'Westernized' minorities, and English as a language of romance—intertwined to form a stereotype. A synonymy between English and particular forms of identity, mostly away from everyday Indian experience, persisted at overt and subtle levels.

Among the films that go into the folklore of families, such as mine, was the famous Raj Kapoor starrer *Shree 420* (1955). The characters of Raju (or Raj) and Vidya belong to the lower middle class, which values education and continuously strives to improve its living conditions. All conversations between Raj and Vidya or her father, also an educated person and a retired teacher, are in Hindi. English appears as a language of the casino which Raj visits—significantly, through impersonation. Finding himself amidst pretentious millionaires, Raj speaks a mix of Hindustani and English. Meanwhile, the English-speaking stereotype is grafted on to the rich and decadent; a woman with a cigarette greets everybody in a phoney accent—'Hello! You naughty boy'—while another character with French beard, stick, and cigar makes generous use of the stock phrase 'Not a bad idea.' In such films, English assumed a disruptive role by being portrayed as the language of the 'bad' Westernized elite, insensitive to the predicaments of the working class. In the socialist frame of the film, this also indicated the common man's disillusionment with the decadence of the elite.

In the 1970s when I was watching these films, I was also the first of six children in my family to have studied in an English-medium school. Each time I was aloof and stayed away from social gatherings, it was attributed to my English-medium education, a source of some pride, some disapproval. English was a language of divisions, creating wedges between people, families, and nations—a pattern we see across an array of films. The divisiveness of English was at times through the language, at times through characters who spoke the language, making it difficult to separate the agent from the identity of disruption. For instance, the view of English as a disruptive force was extended to 'foreign-returned' relatives in *Purab Aur Paschim* (1970). The 'solution' offered was the taming of such 'outsiders', integrating them into the community, by making them shed cigarettes, dressing more fully and, of course, speaking Hindi. In fact the non-resident Indian's language as well as accent, whether in *PAP* or, almost forty years later, in *Namastey London* (2007) served as a fertile site for certifying 'Indianness'. The difference between Saira Banu's alienation from India in *PAP* and that of Katrina Kaif in *NL* is constructed through the same set of 'Indian' and 'foreign' signifiers.

Noted filmmaker Mahesh Bhatt mentions (in this volume)

that when he joined the industry in the late 1970s, only villains and comedians used English, pointing thereby to yet another pattern. From the most quoted 'villain' Ajit (whose English dialogues pass around now as jokes) to Bob Christo (*Mard*, 1985), English in the late 1970s and 1980s was strongly associated with villains who spoke more English than Hindi. Even their vamp girlfriends, with names such as Rita and Mona, used more English than Hindi—when they *did* speak at all. Their accents, clothes and even backdrops had a touch of exaggeration, marking them as 'outsiders'. If by being villains or vamps, they could not be taken seriously and absorbed into the moral universe of the audience, the comic and light-hearted use of English also ensured their non-seriousness in the narrative.

The comic use is complex, as it entails elements of parody as well as reverence. Songs about teaching and learning English (Kishore Kumar's famous '*C-A-T cat, cat maane billi*') or frivolous references to high life, '*Mera naam Chin Chin Choo ... Hello mister, how do you do?*' in the 1950s or Veeru's inebriation in *Sholay* that leads him to turn Hindi words into 'English' by suffixing '-ing' are non-serious. In such instances, both the English language and the comic speakers who murder it are simultaneously portrayed as objects of ridicule.

This subtext of comedy directed at the English language is particularly pronounced when English appears as a jumble of polysyllabic, pretentious words thrown by the working class in the face of 'English'-knowing people. An example is *Namak Halaal* (1982) where Arjun, on being asked by his sly and villainous employer whether he can speak English, replies that he 'speaks better English than the Angrez themselves'. He demonstrates this through the gibberish: 'I can talk English, I can walk English, I can laugh English, because English is a very funny language. Bhairon becomes Baron and Baron becomes Bhairon because their minds are very narrow.'

If part of the joke is directed at the way Indian names are mutilated in English, some of it is also directed at Bhairon, a villager turned into a meek and pathetic character in a city, a far cry from 'Baron'. English in Hindi cinema often collaborated with urbanization and contributed to a view that the city has a debilitating influence on those who come from villages.

This joke is followed by a breathless and incomprehensible account of what is essentially a cricket commentary—committed to memory and rendered rapidly with impeccable pronunciation—a subaltern's nonsense thrown at the powerful:

> In the year 1929 when India was playing Australia at the Melbourne stadium Vijay Hazare and Vijay Merchant were at the crease. Vijay Merchant told Vijay Hazare, look Vijay Hazare, this is a very prestigious match and we must consider it very prestigiously. We must take this into consideration, the consideration that this is an important match and ultimately this consideration must end in a run.
>
> In the year 1979 when Pakistan was playing against India at the Wankhede Stadium Wasim Raja and Wasim Bari were at the crease and they took the same consideration. Wasim Raja told Wasim Bari, look Wasim Bari, we must consider this consideration and considering that this is an important match we must put this consideration into action and ultimately score a run. And both of them considered the consideration and ran and both of them got out.

In *Amar Akbar Anthony* (1977), Anthony's song '*My name is Anthony Gonsalves*' is nothing but subversive prattle, an erudite verbosity born out of perhaps an incomprehensible English education: 'You see the coefficient of the linear is juxtaposition by the haemoglobin of the atmospheric pressure in the country. *Jisse meri yaad aaye jab chaahe chali aaye, Rupnagar premgali kholi number 420*. Excuse me please!'

The parody of English robs the 'English machine' of its own historicity, its power (perhaps), its legend, its authority. As a cultural memory of a subjugating race, English is given a nod of acknowledgement but also resented enough to evoke jokes. Thus Hindi cinema evoked several interconnected associations of class, Westernization, pretentiousness, power and parody in the average spectator's mind. However, not all use of English in Hindi cinema draws so much attention to the language; there are instances when English appears without being invested with moral judgement—natural and even with a certain flair.

My enduring memory of such an example is Tariq Ali in *Yaadon Ki Baraat* (1973), who also strums the guitar and calls out, *'E laal kapdon waali memsaab'* in the middle of his song. *'Kaun main?'* replies someone from the audience; with a flourish, Ali says, 'Of course!' A youthful, romantic film, *YKB* circulated an image of being young, being centre stage, and being somewhat audacious in a different language. In fact, we see similarly performative elements in the use of Hinglish later.

II

In the decades when cinema showed English-speaking characters as 'outsiders', publishers did not issue vast lists of Indian English fiction, and writing in English evoked mixed feelings of suspicion and admiration. Until the 1980s, an oft-repeated question that Indians writing fiction and poetry in English had to face was why they wrote in English. They had to explain the choice or compulsion of writing in a language that was not perceived as 'authentic' and carried colonial baggage. In seminars and conferences, writers testified to their 'Indianness' of spirit and content. Some, like Kamala Das, stridently defied their anti-English critics:

> ... *Don't write in English, they said.*
> *English is not your mother tongue. Why not leave*
> *Me alone, critics, friends, visiting cousins,*
> *Every one of you? ...*
> ... *The language I speak*
> *Becomes mine, its distortions, its queernesses,*
> *All mine, mine alone. It is half English, half*
> *Indian, funny perhaps, but it is honest ...*

> —Kamala Das, 'An Introduction',
> *Summer in Calcutta: Fifty Poems*, 1965

Meanwhile 'Hindi', one of the two most used ingredients in 'half Indian', was also moving along a complex trajectory. Pitted as the adversary of a Western language such as English or of an allegedly Muslim language such as Urdu, Hindi became a political tool of nationalism from the late nineteenth century onwards. Its idiom was manipulated and a stilted bureaucratic register that formed official Hindi distanced it woefully from spoken Hindi. *Chupke Chupke* (1975) parodies this Hindi, as also the irrational rejection of English. It is after the 1990s that we see Hindi and English, previously pitted against each other as adversaries in years gone by, cohabiting in the cultural landscape of India, and Hinglish becomes a manifestation of this cohabitation. Hinglish constitutes the possibility of taming English, branding upon the outsider of former years an indigenous mark, and having fun and fulfilment in doing so. In addition, it tends to be used extensively by the global and diasporic Indian, who draws on commonly used Hindi expressions in English conversations with other South Asian constituencies in the diaspora. At home, it evokes associations of money, commodities, and freedom to choose, never mind whether the choices are radical or superficial.

In Zoya Akhtar's debut film *Luck by Chance* (2009), a scriptwriter makes a tragi-comic attempt to teach a beautiful but somewhat linguistically and intellectually challenged heroine to enunciate the word *khoon* properly. Exasperated, the scriptwriter substitutes *khoon* with 'murder'. In a Hindi–Urdu script, a smattering of English solves the problem of an actor's linguistic inadequacy. The scriptwriter can take it for granted that a spectator would be familiar with 'murder'. However, this also shows that the audience's lexicon might accommodate the English word 'murder' more easily than the Sanskritized Hindi word '*hatya*', which is in fact a precise equivalent of 'murder' whereas the literal meaning of *khoon* is 'blood', 'murder' being metaphorical. The opening consonant of *khoon* reflects the educated stylistics of an Urdu register that is beyond the reach of a South Bombay urban character played by the heroine. *Hatya* would not be a part of her lexicon either; indeed it would be a mouthful for a character with a limited linguistic repertoire. Hindi or Urdu, with or without the stylistic enunciation, *khoon* forms a part of common parlance in the vocabulary of Hindi cinema and its patrons, and its quick substitution with an English word shows the easy accessibility of English.

To return to the example from *LBC*, a superficial reading would be to show how the female lead representing elite, urban India suffers from a disconnect with authentic India, by not having bothered to learn the language of the people. However, a judgement of that kind would obfuscate the complex sociological issues surrounding the episode and do injustice to Akhtar's meta-cinematic and ironic comment targeted at the industry of Hindi cinema. The episode points to the people who constitute the upper echelons of Hindi filmdom, who increasingly appear to know less and less Hindi–Urdu. As a generation of scriptwriters and actors fluent in Hindi literary traditions is replaced by English-trained creative personnel, Hindi cannot be taken for granted. Scriptwriter Rekha Nigam mentions how actors in Hindi cinema find it difficult to give interviews, learn dialogues, and read in Hindi. Scriptwriters are reminded to use a mixture of Hindi and English by way of a 'youth lingo' (personal interview, 28 November 2009). The episode also points to another concurrent phenomenon—the familiarity of the audience with certain English words, allowing filmmakers to substitute one language for the other, without worrying about the ideologies that once made English and Hindi adversaries.

The blithe Hindi–English mix in the example from *LBC* does not betray anxieties of the kind we witness in the past, but an accommodation made for the different constituencies that comprise the social reality and market forces driving cinema in contemporary India. The ideologies of colonialism and lack of authenticity that attended English recede in the mix but the ideology of class overlaps with consumerism and is intricately tied in with Hinglish. In her discussion of a new bourgeois public sphere in India, Leela Fernandes (2000) explores a gamut of media messages. She notes that many of them are targeted specifically at the middle class and often characterized 'by a hybridized language, the mix of Hindi and English'. Not only Hindi and English, but mixing English and Indian languages has come to represent a peculiarly Indian way of being urban, and though the period after the liberal reforms has not created this bilingualism, it has contributed to its legitimacy as a cultural expression. It has arrived at a point where we have stopped creating binaries of an 'Indian' language, which could represent our emotions and 'English' that was the language of our 'intellectual make-up' (Kothari 2006). A song from the 1960s, '*Jodi hamari banega kaise jaani, hum to hain Angrezi, tum ladki Hindustani*' (*Aulad*, 1968), which spelt out the impossibility of coupling English and Hindi, would seem a quaint problem in the code-switched universe of media today.

The construction of a happy blend is both visible and visual through Hinglish cultural products—films, advertisements, signboards, short text messages, talk shows, T-shirt slogans, social networking sites—promoting in overt and covert ways a lifestyle that allows you to be *desi* and consumerist simultaneously. The austerity of a generation that grew up in the early decades after Independence has given way to a generation that sees no virtue in thrift and self-denial. Consumerism is not embarrassing, but a celebratory part of being Indian. It is vital to understand this phenomenon in the light of the increasing legitimacy of consumerism, evident in the intergenerational shift in the lyrics from Hindi films below:

> *Zyaada ka nahiin laalach humko*
> *Thode men guzaara hota hai*
> (*Jis Desh Mein Ganga Behti Hai*, 1960)

> *Thoda hai thode kii zaroorat hai*
> *Zindagi yahaan phir bhi khoobsoorat hai*
> (*Khatta Meetha*, 1978)

> If you want my love, sure enough *tumhen mil jaayega. . .*
> If you pay my bill *mera ye dil tera ho jaayega*
> Money show me the money, ha ah
> If you want romance, *nahiin koi* chance

Unless let's do wanna spend . . .
Emotion's out money is in, *yehi hai* latest trend
Money show me the money
If you pay my bill, *mera dil tera ho gaya, yahi hai* latest
trend
Money, show me the money
(*Apna Sapna Money Money*, 2006)

Songs like these circulate through multiple media, old and new—FM channels, downloads, ringtones, caller tunes. They are loud, audacious, and peppy, some pointing to the pleasures of commodities, some to pleasures of the body as a commodity in its own right. Inseparable from the plethora of the post-1990s 'feel good' films, which also celebrate pretty looks, luxury goods, and a monochromatic view of the 'good life', such songs evoke the imagery that all is well with the world. As far as cinema is concerned, the evidence of an aspiring India lay in the restless protagonists of the post-1990s, yearning to redefine their lives. The opening up of the economy in 1991 signalled, among other things, an ease for the youth in crossing socio-economic barriers. This demographic shift and desire for new self-definition is very often captured through a mix of Hindi and English in cinema. Raring to reject the old self-definitions, this India is hungry for more and sees no reason why it should not be possible.

One of the more successful films of the 1990s, Ram Gopal Varma's *Rangeela* (1995), dealt with this restlessness in the middle class. Made during the early years of a liberalized India, *Rangeela* is the story of Milli, a young middle-class girl and her desire to have more, become more. The theme for 'more-ness' is set at the very beginning—the credits begin with Milli's dream in which she is centre stage, dancing with everybody else following her. The song '*Yai re yai re, zor laga ke nache re*' presages her aspirations through '*bade bade naamon pe apna bhi naam ho . . .*' The ambition for distinction and singularity, as the song unfolds, is accompanied with the dilemmas of a child consumer who says:

Cadbury's *bole main meetha hoon*
Amul *bole main meetha hoon*
Chocolate *khaane men* tension *hain*
Doodh peene men tension *hain*

Milli refuses to fit into the middle-class, predetermined role by announcing to her parents: *'Mujhe parh likh kar* clerk *nahiin banna.'* Her invocation of a 'clerk' to connote an unproductive life typical of another generation and another time in India has semiotic similarity with the term 'ticket collector' that Bunty (*Bunty Aur Babli*, 2005) uses to reject his father's lifestyle.

Meanwhile, the names of brands and products that make up the child's verse above continue in many later songs, for instance, in the films *Rock On!!* (2008), *Gulaal* (2009) and *Jaane Tu Ya Jaane Na* (2008). '*Yaaro sun lo zara*', another song from *Rangeela*, is peppered with words such as 'TV', 'video', and 'bank balance'—linking technology and money with what came to be seen as the 'good life' in the 1990s. In fact, objects of middle-class desire, names of products, educational degrees and cuisine form a strong base for the Hinglish lexicon. If Hindi helps communicate to larger numbers, the English element provides the aspiration quotient. One helps relate, the other helps buy dreams and commodities.

Not all linguistic practices under the rubric of Hinglish make overt references to money. In a manner where a certain degree of affluence can be taken for granted, films like *Dil Chahta Hai* (2001), *Pyaar Mein Twist* (2005), *Thoda Pyaar Thoda Magic* (2008), *Sorry Bhai* (2008), or more recently, *Love Aaj Kal* (2009) seek a new epistemology of love. Based on the lives of diasporic, global Indians for whom moving from Delhi to San Francisco and back could be a reality, a host of films in Hinglish speak to audiences that do not have to leave homes, learn English, make money, but have them all. They slide into Hindi with apparent unselfconsciousness.

The current status of Hinglish in cinema—and in today's youth—is perhaps best showcased by Imtiaz Ali's *Jab We Met* (2007), a love story set in contemporary India. The film opens with industrialist Aditya escaping the claustrophobic environment of his boardroom by shedding the trappings of his class—he refuses the services of a chauffeur, abandons his car and even his cellphone, commutes on a local bus, and finally boards a train where he meets Geet, a fellow passenger he later falls in love with.

The film's Hinglish title was the product of an open competition inviting suggestions from the public. Despite the awkward juxtaposition of words, the film deftly constructs Hinglish as the 'natural' language of the girl, Geet, who is nothing if not natural and transparent. Note her choice of words when she relates how she almost missed a train:

> Line cross *karte karte* train *pakdi*
> *Mera* record *hai ki aaj tak meri* train *nahiin chhooti*
> Thank you *babaji*
> *Mujhe* non-A/C *mein zyaada achha lagta hai*
> *Lekin meri* family *kehti hai akeli ladki ko* non-A/C *mein* travel *nahiin karna chaahiye*
> I mean A/C *ka ladki hone se kya matlab hai*
> And most of all *is* train *se, yeh to mera* second home *hai . . .*

Unlike its predecessors in the 1990s, *Jab We Met* does not employ English or Hinglish as a language of upward mobility. Its presence is taken for granted, and the focus is upon the naturalness of a relationship. While there are unmistakable signs of affluence in *Jab We Met*, the train, youth and Hinglish constitute a sense of being ordinary, everyday, and natural in a youthful way. In such a context, Hinglish acquires a justifiably sunny quality. It would also appear that this is how two young cosmopolitan people from different parts of India would connect, though we know from other essays in this volume that such a generalization cannot be made without qualifications. The branding of Hinglish is being perpetuated through homogenization of differences and by catering to only the metropolitan youth. Baffled by the Hindi text of a letter which mentions, '*Maine azaadi se shaadi kar li hai*', a Delhi-based young man in the film *Rang De Basanti* (2006) asks, 'Who talks like this now?' People in non-metropolitan centres in India do, but they are not the ones projected as templates for modernity. The Hindi cinema of contemporary India is looking out for one age group, one market, one language—made out of two. Its chequered relation with English of the past remains buried under a celebratory spell of 'this new big thing'.

VIEWS FROM A DIFFERENT INDIA: NOT HINGLISH BUT NAGAMESE

Rohini Mokashi-Punekar

If Hinglish is the register of the upwardly mobile and aspiring urban middle class of contemporary India that has grown in economic and political strength after liberalization, what about the politics of speech in the underdeveloped, remote, and politically fraught regions of the nation such as the North-East? Long before television shows, advertisements, and Bollywood made Hinglish the swinging lingo of the Indian market, there were All India Radio news broadcasts from Kohima in Nagamese, the pidgin language of Nagaland, born of contact between Assamese and various Naga languages, with Hindi and English loanwords. And Nagamese is not the sole instance of a contact language here; elsewhere in the region, news broadcasts in pidgin languages such as Nefamese in Arunachal Pradesh and Sadani, the language of the tea tribes, have been routine. The lingua franca of the North Cachar Hill region in Assam, an incredibly complex mix of diverse populations, tribal and non-tribal, is a pidgin known as Haflong Hindi.

Diverse even by Indian standards, the North-East is home to some 220 languages from three different language families, namely, Indo-European, Sino-Tibetan, and Austric (Moral 1997: 43). If Khasi spoken in Meghalaya is representative of the Austric family, and Assamese and Bengali of the Indo-European family, the Sino-Tibetan group is represented by the Tibeto-

Burman and Tai languages spoken in Assam as well as in the hill areas of Nagaland, Mizoram, Manipur, and Arunachal Pradesh. Linguistic debates have been intrinsic to the North-East since colonial times: the Assamese struggle against the imposition of Bengali by the British administration or the controversies over the adoption of the Roman script for Khasi are cases in point. The gradual reorganization of the region into seven states after Independence, the growing disenchantment of different groups within these states with the policies of the Indian nation, and their assertion through linguistic and cultural identities has resulted in a mêlée of increasing antagonism amongst linguistic/tribal communities. This is over and above the insurgency against the Indian state which manifests itself in sporadic attacks on Hindi-speaking people in parts of Assam.

The regions flung over large tracts of hilly country bordering Bhutan, Tibet, China, and Burma that today constitute Nagaland and Arunachal Pradesh had remained virtually undisturbed over many centuries. Ahom invasions and later British annexation of undivided Assam had a limited impact on the tribal world. It remained, till Independence, a territory inhabited by myriad ethnic communities whose languages have no scripts and are not understood beyond the immediate set of native speakers. Policy decisions of state governments of these regions have tended to favour English as the medium of instruction in schools. In Nagaland, a state with a large number of tribal communities speaking mutually unintelligible languages, the Naga identity, not language, has been the rallying point of Naga nationalism. The state has declared English as its official language, and not Hindi for obvious reasons. Historically the trade contact between the Assamese in the plains and the Nagas in the hills created Nagamese, which gradually became the medium for inter-tribe communication amongst Nagas themselves—in the absence of a common tribal language. Nagaland's lingua franca today is Nagamese; its categorization as pidgin continues to be debated by linguists, originating as it did in situations atypical of European pidgins. This study focuses on the sociolinguistic dimensions of Nagamese: its origins, the lexical changes it accommodates, its continued absorption of large numbers of Hindi and English loanwords, and its increasing creolization, paradoxically amidst a political and cultural climate which is inimical to its growth.

The paper is divided into three sections: the first attempts a brief account of Nagamese from a socio-historical perspective, tracing the history of the Naga people, their linguistic culture, and the birth and development of Nagamese; the second traces the peculiar position Nagamese occupies in the political, social, and cultural life of contemporary Nagaland; the third offers concluding observations.

I: Nagamese: A Historical Perspective

The Nagas

While historical accounts vary considerably, they agree that the Tibeto-Burman tribes came through Burma and entered the north-eastern region around 1000 BC, perhaps displacing Austric populations that had settled there between 2000 and 2500 BC (Moral 1997: 44). The Khasis were pushed into the hills of Meghalaya, as the Tibeto-Burmans settled in Assam and the Brahmaputra valley. The tribes now identified as Naga may have moved into Nagaland after the first waves of migration had already entered Assam (Bhattacharjya 2001: 69). The latest wave of invader-settlers into the Brahmaputra valley were the Tai-Ahom tribes, who entered through Nagaland and conquered the erstwhile undivided Assam in the early thirteenth century, ruling it till the British annexed it in 1826.

The initial Naga–Ahom encounter during the early decades of Ahom rule around the thirteenth century was brutal and its memory, preserved in local Naga traditions, has set the tone of their mutual relationship. The Nagas rebelled by conducting continual raids on the plains, plundering produce and killing people or carrying them off as slaves. The Ahoms' historical chronicles, known as Buranjis, refer to the punitive expeditions sent to curb them, which also enabled the Ahoms to capture salt wells in Naga territory (Bhattacharjya 2001: 81). The later

Ahoms, however, adopted a policy of conciliation with the Nagas, partly for reasons of trade and partly because their villages were positioned in strategically sensitive areas. Alternating bouts of hostility and friendship marked the Assamese–Naga relationship.

The British assumed control of the entire undivided Assam in 1826, after repulsing the Burmese invaders and signing the Treaty of Yandabo. Towards the initial part of their rule in the North-East in the mid-ninteenth century, the British seem to have adopted a mode of non-interference as far as the Nagas were concerned. Interested primarily in pursuing economic gains, the British, like the Ahoms, had no policy to absorb the Naga Hills area. They encouraged trade with the Assamese but withdrew the privilege when the Nagas plundered the plains. When the raids intensified, leaving the plains populace defenceless, the British did establish a police station in the Naga Hills in 1866 and instructed its officers to 'endeavour to maintain conciliatory intercourse with the Nagas' (Mackenzie, cited in Bhattacharjya 2001). This indeed was the first step in occupying Nagaland and taking over the area's administration, a process completed by 1878. The Nagas, as was expected, rebelled against British rule in numerous bloody uprisings, which were ruthlessly put down (Bhattacharjya 2001: 93). The advent of the missionaries accomplished what mere politics could not; conversions to Christianity and access to schools opened by the church brought the Nagas out of their isolation. Practices of head-hunting, raiding, intra-tribe feuds, and slave trade were gradually abandoned, though there are records of punitive parties sent to punish tribes accused of taking heads as late as the early decades of the twentieth century. Then, the two world wars transformed Naga society; improved transport and communication ensured their emergence into modernity, though the political strife, as we shall find out, had only just begun.

Naga Languages and Nagamese

The first significant ethnographic studies of Naga culture and languages by Baptist missionaries and British officers were made several decades after the British took over the Naga Hills region. The bewildering diversity of customs, political systems, arts, and languages in the hundreds of isolated villages defeated attempts at classification. It was a while before administrative needs and processes together 'created' relatively fixed Naga groups with distinctive social organization and language (Bhattacharjya 2001: 72). The fact is that while there are as many as twenty-three Naga languages, there is no one common language or dialect—a unique predicament for a people who share racial and cultural features and have lived in close proximity for centuries. The nearly continual internecine tribal wars have probably caused this isolation. It is also quite evident that no Naga language has exhibited a tendency to assimilate or borrow loanwords from another Naga language even after free contact has been established among tribes. 'If a language is a way of life,' in Temsula Ao's words, then 'the Naga languages have remained in general as distinctly individualistic as before' (Ao 1993: 152).

Nagamese has borne the functional load of communication not only with the immediate world outside in the North-East, but also within the Naga world. The first full-length study of Nagamese was, appropriately enough, a multilingual dictionary titled *Nagamese Into Anglo-Hindi-Ao* by Dharani Baruah in 1969. The author developed twelve lessons in Nagamese to teach the language to Indian army officers posted in Nagaland. Besides providing substantial data on syntactic structures, it offers a historical account of the origin and development of Nagamese. Baruah identifies three varieties of Nagamese spoken by different classes of Nagas—a Nagamese with more Assamese words, one with more Hindi words, and one with more English words used by the educated Nagas. These variations tend to be noted by most studies on Nagamese and this paper too will address the question in the next section.

Perhaps the most systematic work on Nagamese from the linguistic perspective has been done by M.V. Sreedhar from the Central Institute of Indian Languages, Mysore. His several works on the subject focus on the linguistic structure of the language, by scrutinizing the evolving morpho-syntactic and phonological features. More relevant to this paper, Sreedhar examines the socio-linguistic background of the development and continued use of this language. In a political environment antithetical to its growth, Nagamese seems to flourish despite the opposition set up by Naga politicians, leaders, and litterateurs who see in this pidgin tongue both the history of Assamese domination and exploitation and a future impediment to the growth of indigenous Naga languages.

II: A Socio-political Perspective

Nagaland and the Indian Nation

Perhaps the oldest continuing insurgency against the Indian state, the Naga movement began with the consolidation of the different congeries of Naga tribes in the early part of the twentieth century. The Naga Club was formed in 1919, the members of which were educated, English-speaking, Christian government officials. When the Simon Commission came to Kohima in 1929, the Naga Club submitted a memorandum signed by 200 Nagas of various tribes praying that the British government would place their country directly under its rule and not include it in the Reformed Scheme designed for India. During the Second World War, Nagaland was thrust into the centre stage of world politics when the Japanese invaded India in 1944, making Naga Hills a battlefield between the British and Axis forces. Recognizing their considerable contribution to the war, the British brought a detachment of the Nagas to participate in the victory celebration at Delhi in 1946. The Naga National Council (NNC) was formed, and that led to increased solidarity amongst the diverse ethno-linguistic groups. Standing for the unity of all Nagas and their self-determination, the NNC gradually became the most significant political organization of Nagaland. Led by middle-class intellectuals whose ideas were propagated in *The Naga Nation*, there was a nationalist movement active in a region not even remotely touched by the Indian national movement. However, 'self-determination' can assume multiple interpretations; very soon, there were passionate debates within the NNC about the future of Nagaland and the directions it had to take. The Angami Nagas, who had a history of fighting all outsiders including the British, wanted sovereignty and were supported by both the British and the Church; the moderate Aos argued for autonomy within the Indian state, a status that Nehru had already assured to them. In June 1947, the NNC issued a declaration that Nagaland should not be a part of independent India, even as a delegation met the Governor of Assam to discuss the terms by which the Nagas could join India. Meanwhile, another delegation went to Delhi to meet Nehru who again promised autonomy to Nagaland within the Indian state, rejecting their claims for independence. This same delegation also met Mahatma Gandhi, who assured them that they had to exercise their free will and, if they so desired, could declare their independence even before India. No one could force them to join India, Gandhi said, even though he personally felt they belonged to it and that the whole country was theirs. On 14 August 1947, the NNC, led unofficially by Angami Zapu Phizo, declared independence; and though the British later left and India became free, the Nagas are still engaged in their endless struggle for sovereignty.

Decades of violence and bloodshed have ensued since in the relentless conflict between the Indian armed forces and the Naga insurgents, and among different Naga ethno-linguistic/political bodies. The violence has continued despite the declaration of Nagaland as the sixteenth state of India in 1963, separating it from undivided Assam. The national and international borders of this tiny state are still in contention. Its eastern borders are coterminous with the international boundary between India and Myanmar; in fact, there are several Naga villages in Myanmar, not surprisingly giving rise to a feeling that the Nagas are one community, whose territorial sovereignty has been divided by international borders. Almost continuous insurgency and violence has taken its toll on the quality of relations between different groups, some of whom are termed 'over-ground' in the sense of having accepted their political identity as part of India. Others who still struggle for sovereignty call themselves 'underground'. Fratricidal killings between different militant outfits claiming to represent the interests of particular ethnic groups are all too common. In the fraught web of complex political affiliations, minor local issues acquire intense significance and knife-point, trigger-happy confrontation; as a result basic and primary agendas recede into the background and ever-escalating violence spills over and becomes a routine aspect of the public sphere.

Politics of Language

Linguistic issues are part of the political maelstrom and exacerbate the conflict. According to the 1981 census, only about 14 per cent of the population spoke those languages at home that are recognized in the Eighth Schedule, such as Hindi, Assamese, Bengali, Nepali, and Manipuri (Sachdeva 2000: 11). More than 85 per cent of the people of Nagaland speak the twenty-three mutually unintelligible Naga languages, of which seventeen are recognized by the state as mediums of instruction in early schooling. None of these Tibeto-Burman tongues forms a part of the Eighth Schedule for the obvious reason that none is dominant or even understood by a majority. It is not surprising that the Nagas feel they are an ethno-linguistic minority and do not consider themselves a part of the Indian nation. The state has a literacy rate of about 65–70 per cent, spread unevenly across different tribes; tribes such as the Aos, who have had early exposure to the missionaries, have a higher rate of literacy and education.

What is the impact of this political turmoil on Nagamese, the contact language? Naga ethnicity, rather than any particular Naga language, is the basis of Naga nationalism. We must remember that literacy and Christianity, with English in their wake, came to Nagaland only a hundred-odd years ago, while Nagamese has been around for at least two centuries, if not more. It is undeniable that Nagamese has been and is the mode of communication across tribes—it is paradoxically the medium through which the Naga cause has been consolidated. Without Nagamese, it is unthinkable that Naga nationalism could have acquired its strength, its momentum, and its solid base among the people. In contemporary politics, electoral processes and campaigns are couched in this 'bazaar lingo'. A recent news item reports two major parties sloganeering in Nagamese to reach the message to all sections of the public (Kashyap 2008). Even as the Nagas disavow the legitimacy of the pidgin today, its use is extensive and ubiquitous, and among certain communities such as the Dimapur Kacharis it has creolized over a period of several decades now.

Since Independence, All India Radio services in Kohima have used Nagamese as the language of communication, whether for newscasts or programmes for farmers. Mobile telephony services use Nagamese, Hindi, and English for their recorded messages. While the tribal languages are made available to a limited extent in such mass media, it is Nagamese that is more conveniently used as the lingua franca and is predominant in the public sphere, sometimes in addition to English, and this is also true for Assembly proceedings (Talukdar 2003: 84). A survey conducted by the State Council of Educational Research and Training has discovered changing patterns of language usage in Naga society, primarily because of inter-tribe marriages and the lack of textbooks in Naga languages (Dholabhai 2004 b). Morphological and lexical analyses of the development of the language affirm that though Nagamese uses a simplified form of Assamese syntax as its base, its essentially Assamese lexicon is extended in contemporary usage by drawing on English, Hindi, Nepali, and Urdu. 'There is some evidence to suggest that the Assamese lexicon is undergoing limited relexification with loanwords from these languages' (Coupe 2007: 342).

English is Nagaland's official language and a compulsory subject at school from the start. While standard Hindi is the third language at school, it is the Bihari and the Nepali spoken by migrant labourers that have crept into the lexicon of Nagamese. In fact, there is a version of Hindi used by the

Nagaland Armed Police known as NAP Hindi, a unique Hindi with a Roman script that binds the state's 19,000 police personnel. This Hindi has been in use for all official communication since the inception of the force. It follows no rule of grammar such as gender or tense distinction and the police report that the rebels speak it better than them (Dholabhai 2004a). A telling tale of vexed relations of power and a shared discourse of violence whose linguistic code is mutually understood.

Three very marked variations of Nagamese—a feature that B.K. Baruah noted in 1969—are perceptible today to a greater degree. Depending on the speaker's social class and context, there is (1) a Nagamese with a limited Assamese lexicon spoken among uneducated Nagas belonging to different ethnic tribes, (2) a Nagamese with more Hindi/Urdu loanwords spoken in public domains of market and trade circles between Nagas and uneducated non-Nagas, and (3) a Nagamese with more English loanwords spoken by educated Nagas of different tribes and between them and educated non-Nagas, and these are all seen in contemporary Nagaland (Sachdeva 2002). It is also certain that code-switching from Nagamese to Hindi or English takes place in the last two varieties, over and above the incorporation of loanwords. While 'standard' Nagamese does employ a large number of words from English, Hindi, Urdu, and Nepali, these three variations are based quite obviously on the class and educational background of the speakers. As elsewhere, with other languages in urban India, English and Hindi permeate Nagamese, however, in a very different social context and for entirely different political reasons.

III: Conclusions

It may be an old-fashioned truism to say that a language reflects a way of life. If one were to frame the thought to suit contemporary fashions and indicate that language constitutes reality, then what language can be the measure of the Naga way of life at this point of historical time? As a functional language of contact for trade, Nagamese does not reflect Naga culture and its ethos in their deepest sense, beyond certain mannerisms of thought and speech. At the micro level, Nagas feel threatened by the Nagamese invasion into their homes, as children of mixed marriages between Nagas of different tribes seem to communicate more and more in the pidgin, accelerating the loss of their mother tongues. In a news item titled 'Bazaar dialect intrudes Naga homes', a reporter rues the fact that English and Nagamese are diluting Naga dialects (Dholabhai 2004b). At the level of polity, Naga politicians, academics, and litterateurs resist Nagamese on political and cultural grounds. Temsula Ao, perhaps the most well-known Naga writer of contemporary times, bemoans the loss of the Naga cultural tradition (Ao 1993: 153). In an interview with Rajesh Sachdeva, a linguist who has worked extensively on language planning and education in the North-East, Nagaland's former minister of school education I. Imkong says emphatically:

> As a lingua franca Nagamese is okay but it would be unwise to make it into a common written language—I think that's the way in the present situation. Nagas would feel, the situation can change, but it must change with the will of the people, and Nagamese may be difficult to accept. Nagamese is not based on any of our Naga languages, its roots are not 'native', and it is not a Naga language, not a marker of Naga identity. It is a borrowed language and people don't want to give it a place in their culture. Personally, I'd rather speak Hindi, which is much more respectable and useful. (Sachdeva 2001: 13)

Considered unrespectable and illegitimate, Nagamese is unwanted in Nagaland. It is not promoted by the state or the people and yet it thrives, absorbing new words from English and Hindi and expanding its reach. While I was able to source transcripts of news broadcasts in Nagamese as well as short plays in Nagamese meant to educate people about pressing social problems such as alcoholism and drug abuse, it cannot, for the Nagas, serve as a language to express their deepest emotions or their most intuitive thoughts in. Will the Nagas ever use Nagamese for literary purposes? One wonders what Nagaland's literary languages will be in the near future, apart from English? Who will be the readers of these literatures, given the fractured and fragile political being of the state and the continued presence of Nagamese in the public sphere?

On a different note, and connecting this paper to the theme of this volume, one could examine the effects of mainstream media institutions on Naga society and its lingua franca. Satellite television networks like Star, Zee, and Sony have had little use till recently for the North-East as the region did not constitute a viable market; teledensity remained low as did the numbers of cable/satellite TV connections. The impact of Hinglish, a medium spawned by these networks to reach and form urban audiences, seems non-existent. Quite clearly, the peculiar blend of economic, social, and political conditions that mark the emergence of Hinglish in mainland India are simply absent in Nagaland. This writer was told that Korean and Hollywood films are far more popular in Nagaland than standard Bollywood fare; as is Western music in various avatars. While there are no specific studies of media impact on Naga society, it seems safe to assume that Hindi cinema and Hindi film music, the staple of several TV shows, enjoy less popularity amongst the Nagas.

The summer of 2007 saw the unprecedented phenomenon of the reality show *Indian Idol 3* taking the hills of neighbouring states Meghalaya and Sikkim by storm with the entry of Amit Paul and Prashant Tamang, the two finalists from the respective states. In both states, fans set up websites and blogs to generate support; organizations sponsored landline voting booths and distributed prepaid phone cards to ensure votes; and politicians, recognizing the mass base of the phenomenon, joined the fray. The extensive media coverage of the phenomenon focused on the apparent political refashioning of the terrain enabled by this reality show that saw people cast off long-standing separatist identities to mobilize support (Mazumdar 2007). Informed analyses of the changing dynamics of public discourse generated by media technologies in India argue 'that reality television and its plebiscitary logic have enabled new modes of cultural and political expression' in the North-East; they claim that 'convergence between television and various mobile technologies' create shifting and transient publics (Punathambekar 2009). Though transient, and perhaps unreal, these publics may create the possibility of the renewal of everyday forms of interaction that have been in recession under the impact of unfavourable political conditions. It seems ironical to consider that Hinglish may well become the linguistic medium that encodes these new publics in the North-East. Despite separatist aspirations in certain quarters, Meghalaya and Sikkim have a greater degree of political stability, seen for instance in the relatively successful management of the tourism industry in these states, that makes them amenable to market incursions in the form of new media technologies. As for Nagaland, it stares at two possible contending futures amongst a host of others—continued insurgency or relative political stability. The former has seen the entrenchment of Nagamese, the latter may well invite Hinglish.

TAMIL, HINDI, ENGLISH: THE NEW MÉNAGE À TROIS

G.J.V. Prasad

Introduction: Delhi Hinglish, Circa 1960s

The history of Hinglish, whether we define it as a language produced of code-mixing English with Hindi or Hindi with English, is a long one. Mix another Indian language to the brew, adding it to or substituting it for Hindi, and you will have parallel histories of different Hinglishes or Indian Englishes. I grew up in Delhi in the 1960s and 1970s and attended a Tamil school. (The school was initially set up as a school for Madrasis, i.e., people from the state of Madras, run by the Madras Education Association, later renamed as Delhi Tamil Education Association to change the Madrasis to Tamilians; there is a story in that!) We spoke Tamil and English at home, Hindi and English among friends in the residential area for government officers where we lived, and Hindi, Tamil, and English at school. Punjabi was also a strong presence in Delhi then. Our school had Tamil students from all strata of society—children of road workers, construction labourers, and maidservants as well as children of upper-middle-class families. This meant a difference in caste and a difference in the kind of Tamil we spoke, since Tamil is a caste- and region-marked language. Speaking a code-mixed language was imperative to develop bonds between people of such diverse

141

backgrounds. To speak mainly in Tamil was to give in to the hierarchization implicit in the language as well as its tensions and prejudices; to speak in English was to leave out so many who couldn't speak it well (again because of their backgrounds); to speak only in Hindi was to speak a street language, which was what it was perceived to be then, and to give up completely on our ethnic identities or class preferences. Yet, not to speak the street language was to be an outsider, ripe for bullying. Thus the democratic alternative at school was to speak a mix of street Hindi and Tamil (trying, quite unconsciously I concede, to lower the caste distinctions as much as possible), with English thrown in. The proportion of each language would change with time and situation—moving towards a greater proportion of English as we grew older.

Hinglish (in this case, a mixture of three languages, so actually Tamhinglish!) was thus born for us in specific social and historical circumstances. While it could be argued that we did not have enough control over any of the three languages and that this language of our schooldays was not enriched by the commingling of three languages but only showcased our linguistic impoverishment, what I want to assert is that it answered to our specific needs in a specific situation. Obviously, we couldn't use Tamil with non-Tamil-speaking friends from outside school; we would then speak straightforward Hinglish. And in later years, with friends of our own class, even if all Tamilians, we would switch to English completely with a few Hindi words thrown in, while we would always speak Hinglish if we wanted to speak in Hindi to each other. We didn't think of such commingling of languages as creative, only as something we needed to establish a democratic medium of communication—that is, if we thought about it at all.

What this demonstrates is that the influence of languages on each other, to the extent of interpenetrating each other in popular speech, is the result of complex historical, political, and social realities. One doesn't give up the value systems inherent in one's own linguistic culture unless one feels the need to do so. The fact is that languages are as dynamic as people—and as vulnerable. It takes major effort to police and discipline us, to keep us static, in our places. From marriages to other socio-political boundaries, structures of surveillance work overtime to defend the borders. However, this policing cannot stop various incidents at the borders and incursions across them. All borders are permeable and are permeated. Not even academies—and certainly not academics—can keep the border spaces of languages pure from contamination. Just check out the number of American English words that have become part of the French language. Within India, there are a number of disputed boundaries between states, and these are linguistic boundaries as well. Take the case of Maharashtra and Karnataka—Marathi- and Kannada-speakers from the border areas will speak both languages and will have allowed the languages to 'contaminate' each other as would have Kannada- and Tamil-speakers at another border. Purity of language is a chimera—our languages are born and thrive in hybridity.

We know that traders bring forth new terms from alien languages, as do travellers. We will use these terms if we need them, if we need to interact with the people from across linguistic distances. Conquerors have, of course, always imposed their languages, and the languages of power and commerce are magnets that attract most of us. Unless we see profit of some kind in isolation, we will never stick our heads inside our own houses and refuse to learn, speak, or work in other languages. Once we allow ourselves the luxury of embracing the new, the boundaries of our own languages will be broken down sooner rather than later. Languages mix on the verandas of our homes and enter the living rooms. The language of the kitchen and the language of the study and the language of the office are never as pure as people think but as time goes by even these so-called pure languages begin to intermingle. As different cultures and value systems collide, we learn to take the line of least resistance and use words and phrases from other languages because they convey new concepts without setting up clashes or creating confusions in one's own languages. Languages of power, languages of prestige (usually the same but not always—Hindi is the language of power, but English that of prestige; Sanskrit was not always the language of power but always of prestige), and simply languages that afford you a living are languages that will fight your loyalty to your mother tongue, always assuming that your mother tongue is your father's tongue as well. Otherwise, the conflict begins even earlier.

Perhaps this language contact and conflict is a major part of the intellectual and emotional history of every urban Indian. Our 'impure' speech, the ever-increasing hybridization of our languages is a symptom of our conflicted location, our desire to make the best of it in the given circumstances. In India, we claim that the water changes every ten miles and the language changes every forty miles or so. Obviously the claim is that language variation begins within forty miles and that such variation is the norm throughout the country. In the case of language then, we claim that there is an almost imperceptible movement from any one of our multitude of languages to another, a movement that can be plotted from any direction. So, we can move from Punjabi to Tamil almost seamlessly, if we actually take the physical route, one language transforming itself into the other along the way. This is fascinating! One should do the route, taking in the food along the way to see how the savoury *samosa* of the north becomes the sweet *somaasi* of the south. If our languages flow into each other (obviously the travel can be done both ways, or actually in multilinear directions), their impact on each other must be such over centuries that it must be impossible to say where many words come from, in which languages they originate.

Hinglish: Indian English

However, this is not what this paper is about. We Indians seem quite excited about the fact that we have—or are in the process of creating—our own variety of English and that this Indian English will take over the world simply because of the size of our population, because so many of us want to learn and live our lives in English, because we have been busy browning the world with a large diasporic population spread across the globe. Leaving out the diaspora from the discussion, I have argued elsewhere and often that Indian English can only be Indian if the English is said in the plural, Indian Englishes, and that local realities can be translated into English only if the borders of English are left open and the language 'biryanized' (for instance, Prasad 1999a and 1999b) with the specific flavours of the parts of India that are being represented, and that this is what Indian English writers do. English, by itself, cannot represent any of our Indian constituencies; local languages need to be infused into English so that characters can be delineated and differentiated by their language use, located in their specific class and religious matrix, and the interaction between characters be shown in terms of the languages they speak to each other. In literature, this can be and has been done extremely creatively, going to the extent of inventing a language that has all the appearances of a translation without actually being one.

On the other hand, while the fact of commingling of English with the local language is true for almost all Indian languages, and the intrusion of English in Indian language movies is ubiquitous, this occurs to varying degrees of acceptability in newspapers, journals, and literary works. In the case of Indian English writing, there is acceptability—though limited—for the use of Indian words. Words from Hindi seem to receive greater favour than words from other languages, though words used by 'genuine' native English writers have a currency that others are yet to achieve. Indian newspapers have gone from 'cane charge' to '*lathi* charge' ('lathi' being a Hindi word) almost without people noticing the shift, and the Hindi word 'lathi' is used in every edition of the newspapers regardless of the linguistic region they are published in. There are many such words that went into common usage in English during the Raj but 'lathi' and 'dharna' (strike) and 'gherao' (to surround someone) head an honourable list of Hindi words that have been absorbed into Indian English after Independence. While names of food items are region specific and perforce have to enter Indian English, what I want to establish is that if there is a Hindi equivalent, it will have greater acceptability in Indian English; for instance, 'kurta' would be seen as more Indian English than the Tamil (though it may not be of Tamil origin) word 'jibba', which like other region-specific words may be used in the regional variety of Indian English. Suffixes like 'da' or 'di' or words like 'machi' will be used in Tamil English (Tamlish) while 'yaar' would be part of Indian English. The relationship between Hinglish and Tamlish (and any other form of Indian English) is parallel to the relationship between Hindi cinema from Mumbai and other cinemas in India—the Mumbai cinema is Indian, while the rest are regional.

Thus, Hinglish is, in a real sense, pan-Indian, but only if it is English with Hindi mixed in it. A slogan such as '*Yeh dil maange more*' would make very little sense in many parts of India, with the sound of the English word 'more' registering as the Hindi homophone meaning 'peacock' to those knowing only Hindi and as the Tamil homophone meaning 'buttermilk' to those knowing only Tamil. When my novel, *A Clean Breast*, came out in 1993, a major hurdle it had to cross was the mindset of people who couldn't accept Tamil words being used in an English novel that was only half set in Tamil Nadu and was, in any case, intended for a pan-Indian, even potentially worldwide, readership. None of the reviews objected to the Hindi words, most pointed attention to the Tamil words, some saying that they would be unintelligible to many readers. (Yes, you guessed right—these latter reviews were written by Tamilians.)

This is why you find more Hindi than other languages in Indian English fiction, and most writers try to be creative with the English sentence structure or even idioms and phrases to build the sense of regional location. Generations of non-south Indian students in my Indian English literature class at Jawaharlal Nehru University in Delhi have found Raja Rao's *Kanthapura* (set in rural Karnataka and written in an English heavily infused with Kannada rhythms and forms) extremely difficult to appreciate when compared to Mulk Raj Anand's *Untouchable* (similarly infused by the Punjabi language). You realize that both writers, like all Indian English writers, undertake a translatorial task—and their results can be uneven as any translation, including in the reception from readers.

R.K. Narayan and Vikram Seth come to mind when one thinks of how Indian English writers have managed to represent Indian characters using nothing but English. Seth has needed to do this in only one novel but Narayan did this throughout his career. However, a close reading of Narayan reveals that he had to face every dilemma of every translator. Narayan is aware of the challenge posed by his choice of language and said of his generation of Indian English writers that 'often the writing seemed . . . an awkward translation of a vernacular rhetoric, mode or idiom. But occasionally, it was brilliant' (1979: 22). This process of transmutation of English, he says, has served his 'purpose admirably, of conveying unambiguously the thoughts and acts of a set of personalities, who flourish in a small town named Malgudi (supposed to be) located in a corner of South India'. This transmutation is brought about by a careful consideration of how to pollinate and bend English to an Indian and a Tamil reality. The referential world of these novels in terms of notions of kinship, respect, politeness, family structure, religious (and social) ceremonies, and belief system is Tamilian, specifically the world of Tamil Brahmins. But it is also a world altered in various ways by the colonial experience. Hence, Narayan's English is a language born in and constantly recreating itself in the interface of cultures—a rough interface, where language slips as much as it sticks. One of the few instances where Narayan allows Tamil to come in marked as Tamil (and he has quite a few stories where the clash of languages and cultures is explored, quite hilariously I must add) is the short story 'Annamalai'. It features a gardener speaking in Tamil to show not that he is empowered by the language but that he lacks basic knowledge of his profession:

> If I asked, 'What is this?'—'This?' he said, stooping close to it, 'this is a *poon chedi* (flowering plant),' and after a second look at it declared what I myself was able to observe, 'Yellow flowers.' . . . If he liked a plant

> he called it '*poon chedi*' and allowed it to flourish. If it
> appeared suspicious, thorny or awry in any manner he
> just declared, 'This is a *poondu* (weed),' and, before I
> had a chance to observe, would pull it off and throw it
> over the wall with a curse. (Narayan 1970: 80–81)

Otherwise Narayan has a straightforward strategy—try to use
English as far as possible. When that doesn't work out, go for
pan-Indian intelligibility by using Hindi words that have currency
even in Tamil country. And only when that fails the test of
people like him understanding without difficulty, does he decide
to move to Tamil. Take this instance:

> He opened a small wooden box and took out a dry
> *dhoti* and towel, a box containing ingredients for
> marking his forehead, and a rosary. (Narayan 1949:
> 10)

The Tamil *veshti* becomes the Hindi *dhoti*, and there is an
English towel along with it. We are not told how or with what
Srinivas, the old man, is marking his forehead (in the very next
sentence, he proceeds to 'mark his forehead with a symbol'!)
but even more intriguingly the traditional Hindu has a rosary in
his hand.

The *veshti* is always *dhoti* in Narayan's works, for *veshti*
wouldn't be intelligible to his other Indian readers, while *dhoti*
would be intelligible to all Indians, perhaps even to Western
readers. But the upper garment worn with the *dhoti* creates a
problem and Narayan nearly always uses the Tamil term for it,
as in this instance:

> He wore a loose *jibba* over his *dhoti* . . . (Narayan 1967:
> 9)

The following example illustrates Narayan's difficulties even
more clearly:

> At his tea-shop he had been bare-headed; now he had
> donned a white khaddar cap, a long mull jibba and a

dhoti, and had a lace upper cloth over his shoulder—he had dressed himself to come to town, I suppose. (Narayan 1961: 111)

Look at the way he switches code—*khaddar cap*, *mull jibba*, *dhoti*, and a *lace upper cloth*. He eschews the Tamil *kulla* for the English *cap*, though in conjunction with the Hindi *khaddar* (which would have been intelligible across India), the Hindi *mulmul* or muslin, the Tamil *jibba*, the Hindi *dhoti*, and the most curious 'lace upper cloth'. The last item is, of course, the *angavastram*, known as such across Brahmin India, but Narayan thinks upper cloth would be intelligible to all. What about lace though? He is not talking of an *angavastram* made of lace but one with a golden, *zarigai*, border. It is worth noting that Narayan isn't consistent with italicizing Indian words—sometimes he does, and sometimes he doesn't. This inconsistency is a symptom of the fact that Indian Englishes are always evolving and one is never too sure if an Indian word has become acceptable or not. In any case, even R.K. Narayan wrote Tamhinglish—an English which was laced with Tamil and Hindi, an English that was always under the pressure of the Tamil language.

This is largely true of all Englishes spoken on the subcontinent—that the sound system and vocabulary and the grammar of local languages have a great impact on them. Most north Indians have a 'good name', for instance. And many Tamilians do things simply—the Tamil *chumma* translates into English as 'simply', an answer you will get only in Tamil Nadu to questions about intent, as in answer to 'why are you throwing stones at the street light?' While on the word *chumma*, one must remember that the Hindi homophone means 'kiss' and could cause misunderstanding between Hindi- and Tamil-speakers if used as such in Hinglish! Tamlish has a long history, and one only has to look to theatre to see a wonderful combo word—*rajapart*, which meant the role of the king in historical plays, and therefore designated the lead actor. Since these plays were performed by all male companies, some of the men had to play *streeparts* as well.

While the term *machi* is used in Tamlish, when a male addresses another male friend, it would be quite unintelligible to a Hinglish-speaker who would wonder why he is being addressed as a fish—the Hindi homophone strikes again. And while *machi* can translate into 'brother-in-law', it doesn't quite work like the Hindi *saala*, being more a term of friendship like *yaar*. *Saala* is also a term of abuse, calling into question the honour of a family where girls sleep around and at least one has with the speaker, while *machi* isn't. Thus, what one sees is that Indian languages are always under and above the surface of English in India, and that Hinglish is but a natural outcome of this. Indian English writers give the best examples of this kind of pressure and the resultant hybridity of their language.

In his latest work, *Sea of Poppies* (2008), Amitav Ghosh gives different kinds of Englishes to his characters, but the Bhojpuri that bursts through, that cannot be contained by the necessities of an English narrative, is translated into English due to the very necessities that it is fighting against. Interestingly, the Bhojpuri songs come largely from the works of Western ethnographers! One must remember that the comingling of languages is often perceived as leading to a comedic or parodic narrative and to accusations of incompetent bilingualism (see Dyson 1993 for instance). In any case, it seems clear that the more Hinglish you get in English, that is, the more marked your regional linguistic nuances, the more unintelligible your text will be.

Tamil: Reluctant Hybridity

Our languages and cultures are so locally rooted, so specifically nuanced that they are marked not just by region, but also by religion, caste, and gender. Two Tamilians meeting outside Tamil Nadu are more likely to speak in English or Hindi or whatever than Tamil—outside their land, they want to create a bond of fellow feeling, and to speak in Tamil is to give all old caste prejudices a chance to play, so caste-marked is the language. But because now people cross the caste divide through the affiliations of class, and accept regional locations as valid (though not hermetically sealed or permanent), we need to look at what happens to the language at certain locations at specific moments. Tamil is so heavily inflected by English and other languages that it is difficult to think of a pure Tamil. It is commonly felt that Tamil has transformed because of the bilingual education that Tamilians have received. People believe that the language of unlettered people does not undergo the same change, and that dictionaries should not depend only on the written word for it is usually the product of a bilingual. This ignores the fact that one doesn't have to be literate to be bilingual.

It also sidesteps the history of Tamil, a language that has always been under tremendous pressure from other languages— Sanskrit and Prakrit, Urdu and Marathi, then English and French, just to name a few that have had a relationship of power with Tamil at various times. Tamil has been influenced by all these languages, been hybridized to the extent of having texts written in different scripts to accommodate the sounds and words from these different languages. The most famous instance of this is the literary style *manipravalam* of the thirteenth century, when Tamil texts were written in the Grantham script to accommodate Sanskrit, which formed part of the same texts. There are also texts from Tanjore, during the Maratha rule there, where you can find Tamil, Marathi, Sanskrit, and Urdu—all in the same text. It can be argued that this written representation was still that of the elite, but this does not take into account the fact that the common man is the one who is forced to learn languages for a living, neither the language nor the life being anything to write home about.

Coming to contemporary times, no one can argue that unlettered people are less open to influences of media than educated people. They are as subject to the world of consumerist wants as anyone else. They are as moved by political stars of the Tamil world and as addicted to the dialogues and songs of movies. And anyone who has watched Tamil movies and TV channels or heard Tamil songs and FM radio (the tagline of a channel is 'Radio Mirchi, semai hottu', where only one word, semai, is from Tamil) will know how hybridized their Tamil is, how much English and Hindi influence them (even more than the other major south Indian languages). Thus, the language of the common Tamilian is not immune from the influences of the big bad other language worlds. This has always been so. The ordinary Tamilian who is a *killadi* (*khiladi* is a Hindi word meaning 'player') has been a smart guy, a player, from the years of Muslim rule. The legal language of the Persian court is part of Tamil spoken by all people—ordinary Tamilians talk of *vakalat* and *dastavej*, the first term meaning 'one authorized to argue on behalf of a client' and the second meaning 'a legal document'. A Tamil rowdy is a KD, derived from the very English 'known dacoit'. Many Tamilians look for OC things in Tamil, living their lives in the very English 'on credit'. One can list many such examples of impact of various languages and cultures on spoken Tamil, none more startling than the way Dravidian politicians address people in their public speeches— *rattattin rattame*—the very Christian 'blood of my blood'. Even as Tamilians absorb items from other languages due to contact, they also aspire to and absorb cultural terms and items accessed through media contact, like the playing of Holi in Tamil movies; what a god-given, unsubtle way of getting heroines into wet dresses!

While Tamil has long resisted the hegemony of other languages, starting with the northern Sanskrit, the anti-Hindi agitation of the mid-1960s is a thing of the past now. Tamil magazines have involved jokes about godmen afraid of the north Indian custom of tying *rakhi*. The joke is, of course, dependent on your knowing what *rakhi* is as much as the fact that many so-called celibate godmen have been arrested for molesting their women devotees. However, as already stated, Urdu, Hindustani, and Hindi have loaned many words and concepts to Tamil. The Madras dialect (as well as that of North Arcot) is heavily inflected and pollinated by these other tongues, as also by English. *Bimani* is a good Madras Tamil word derived from Urdu/Hindustani/Hindi and meaning a person without scruples. *Jor* is another such common word from the north, though it has an additional connotation of 'wonderful'. Madras Tamilians begin their day with *naasta*, the Hindi breakfast. People who irritate them are quite *bejaar* and nincompoops are *bekku(s)*. The provenance of the first word is debatable though it does seem that Dakhani Urdu may have something to do with it, while the second seems to have been derived from the Urdu *bevakoof*. A *vastatu* will do his *kasrattu* (*ustad* and the word for exercise, *kasrat*), and then go out to show off his *dillu* (the Hindi *dil*, the heart standing in for Tamil guts). Chennai autorickshaw drivers (the original speakers of Madras Tamil) drive *feeda* (at great speed) and if you don't want them to turn at that *feed* they will go *staita* (straight ahead). *Rightu* and *leftu* are of course Tamil words of long standing as is *rights*, the shouted instruction from the conductor to the bus driver to tell him that all is okay and that he can drive on. At some point, the autorickshaw driver or bus conductor may ask you to *adjist* (this English word has a pan-Indian presence for we are very adjusting people, like that only).

It is interesting to note that while some English words have made their way into spoken Tamil, they don't carry the same charge when used in English. The word 'colour' for instance, used to refer to girls by young men doesn't quite translate back into English, nor does the other term 'figure'. Ogling at girls is manifested as the combo phrase *sight adikkaradu*, literally, 'sight hitting'. 'Cutting' refers to an intersection when used by Tamil speakers, and for a generation or two 'slacks' meant shirt and not trousers! 'Super' is a wonderful Tamil word, which means, well, super as in fantastic, great, wonderful! *Bittu* is what we used to hide about our persons in school to copy from during exams, but it also means short strips of pornographic films added to censored films during certain shows.

Tamil Magazines and Language Promiscuity

When you look at contemporary Tamil magazines, you realize that it is presumed that most are read by English-literate, upwardly mobile consumerist readers. Of course, there is also a slotting of readers in terms of the magazines themselves. Take a community-based magazine like *Thambraas*, which caters to Tamil Brahmins. An advertisement for a catering service (in Tamil Nadu, these services take care of the entire function, let us say a marriage) has the name Thanjai Catering Services in Roman script. It is said, supposedly by a person in a conversation that when given charge of his daughter's wedding, the caterers took it over completely: 'A–Z *pattunda*.' The address is also in English—if you need caterers, you know English! (*Thambraas*, December 2008, p. 11) In the same issue, another catering service calls itself a 'marriage catering service' in the Tamil script with a punchline in the Roman script: 'Best Catering in Tambaram' (p. 21). The rest of the advertisement is in Tamil except that the three generations of chefs are called 'Master of Cook' in English!

Yet another catering service has the entire copy of its advertisement in the Roman script, mostly in English, but promises 'Seer for Bride and Grooms' (now didn't know polyandry was a common practice, and can you make out the first word? It stands for all the gifts and dowry items) and *Beetle* Leaves and, even worse, Beetle Nuts after having assured us of 'Quality & Delicious Veg Food' (p. 17). The language mélange can be seen in advertisements for clothes; Ramraj Cotton (written in Tamil) promises us *Veshtigal*, *Shirttugal*, *Baniyangal* (written in Roman script, main issue, inner front cover). The advertisement lets us know in Tamil where the 'showrooms' are. The showroom obviously comes from a different marketing culture. The need for different languages is felt in terms of who your target audience is. So an advertisement completely in Roman script in the same Tamil magazine is for 'Navagraha Darshan! Temple Tours!' (p. 60) Brahmin pilgrims don't need Tamil. Another agency advertises its '*Srardham* Special' in Tamil (p. 53).

In another magazine, the copy of an ad for Shri Kumaran Tanga Maligai reads '*Yeralamana* Design*kalil* .../ Diamond, Antique Jewels, Real Stones, Polki Diamond *Nagaigal*'—all in the Tamil script (*Kumudam Bhakti*, 1–15 December 2008, inner front cover). It also advertises its '*Visalamana* [large] Car Parking'. What is the reason for this hybridity in an advertisement that also has the Tamil *vaira nagai* (diamond jewellery) in its copy? The English part of the copy is about the quality of diamonds, which cannot (obviously) be expressed in Tamil! In the same issue, Hrishi Pain Killer has a money back offer, with the clincher 'Money Back' written in both Roman script as well as transliterated into the Tamil script! The magazine also advertises an issue of a sister magazine, *Kumudam Snekiti*. One of the features it highlights in Tamil is '*palapala* kitchen! / *ungal veettu* kichen*ai* clean / *seyya sila* super tips!' How can readers of this Tamil magazine have a room called *samayalarai*, it has to be the kitchen and then it has to be cleaned only in English and therefore you need 'super tips'! As we have seen, 'super' is a much-valued, much-used Tamil word which means, well, 'super' or 'superb'. This special issue of *Bhakti* has a gift for us, a New Year daily calendar, *puttandu tinasari calendar* written in Tamil script—calendar is, of course, now a pan-Indian word.

This publication group has another niche Tamil publication, *Kumudam Health*—'health' has to be a Western concept coming to India through the grace of English. Obviously, the issue (16–30 November 2008) has recipes from outside India and inevitably includes words completely alien to Tamil—for instance, '5 *vagai* mushroom recipes'. The five types of mushroom recipes are 'Yummy Mushroom Balls', 'Mushroomballs and Tofu*parotta*', 'Noodles Mushroom *theekha masala*' (notice the entry of Hindi), 'Japanese Mushroom and Red Cabbage Salad', and 'South American Mushroom Meals' (all written as such in both Roman and Tamil scripts, though one has the balls missing in Tamil!). Another issue (1–15 December 2008) has 'baby corn soya *paal* gravy' (written in Tamil; the only concession to the Tamil reader being *paal*, Tamil for milk), and 'babycorn soya balls *in* Chinese sauce' (in Tamil), which becomes 'Soya Balls in Chinese Sauce' in Roman script. The Tamil states that the Chinese sauce belongs to the babycorn balls! Another recipe is 'microwave baby corn' (in Tamil) and 'baby corn *aanda*' (written till here in Tamil). 'Flax Meal Sauce' (in Roman)—a startlingly hybrid title that says that Flax Meal Sauce was ruled by baby corn. In the same issue, they have a 'fitness' column (so titled in Tamil) featuring actor Ria Sen. The caption reads (in Tamil), 'slim, fit, Ria'. She wears a top that advertises the magazine in English: 'Read Kumudam Health'. It is quite fitting!

An astrologer advertises himself as a '*jotidar*' (Tamil for astrologer), and a 'Philanthropist' (in English), as if we cannot be both in the same language! *Kumudam Snekiti* has a feature in its 1–15 November 2008 issue, which tells its presumably women readers, '*aankalai* handle *seivatu yeppidi*', how to handle men for you have to handle them only in English. A well-known sari shop, Kumaran, has an advertisement almost completely in English in this issue—it gives the dictionary definition of the word 'sparkle' and then says, 'This Diwali, its your turn to/ Sparkle.' Pothys, another sari shop, has a 'Deepavali Release' (films released near the time of the Deepavali festival) in English. Beneath four models is the text 'Starring One Minute Dew Drop, One Minute Golden Pleats, One Minute Sparkle, and One Minute Black Beauty'. In Tamil, in much smaller font, it reads, '*ivay anaittum* One Minute ready made *selai ragangalakum*', meaning all these are kinds of readymade saris that can be donned in a minute. This ad is placed in *Aval Vikadan*, 10 October 2008, which says on the cover that it is a 'Mega *sirappitazh*', a mega special issue! No wonder one of the features is 'Fastfood *Mela*' (in Tamil; but note that 'mela' is a Hindi word). You can learn about north Indian *tikka*s and *palak samosa*s along with Western dishes.

Language and Kollywood

Hindi and north Indian cultural practices and landscapes and Punjabi bhangra connect Tamilian films to the world of globalization and the exotic other as well. They provide new paradigms for exploring man–woman relations; they provide visual and aural differences. This role could be played by foreign locales, white (or even light-complexioned) extras, and rap music. However, apart from Singapore and Malaysia, other foreign locales seem too distant from Tamil culture, while Southeast Asia is one's own backyard. The aspirational possible, one that is sufficiently different at the same time, is the world of north India, extending from Mumbai to Delhi to Rajasthan—especially Rajasthan with its exotic desert colours. Hence, many Tamil songs are set in 'exotic' north India, which is also at the same time the gateway to global culture through bhangra rap. Now you have English rap and hip-hop also playing a role in Tamil songs, almost in the remix mode practised in Hindi as well, where English lyrics with its singers take up a separate space within the song. However, the Hindi lyrics are not so clearly segregated in Tamil songs. 'Mukkala muqabla O Laila' (from Kadhalan, 1994) is an old favourite; the same film featured a very popular song that went 'Urvasi, Urvasi, take it easy Urvasi'. However, take a song like 'Major penna, minor penna, kandu pidida, saiva penna, asaiva penna, kandu pidida' (those two English words are part of Tamil now) from Pasupathi c/o Rasakkapalayam (2007), where the chorus goes on to sing the Hindi line asking for the heart to be stolen: '. . . leja re leja re, dil mera leja re'. Of course, this is a popular Tamil song. English too enters Tamil film songs as blatantly. In Indian films, the English-speaking girl has always been the proud one who must be tamed but English is now fashionable and shows how savvy you are. Hence you can have Tamil film songs comparing a girl's laughter to the ringing of a telephone, 'telephone mani pol sirippaval ivala' (Indian, 1996) and another likening a girl's eyes to strawberries, 'strawberry kanne' (Minsara Kanavu, 1997), and this in a straightforward, non-comical manner.

One of the things to have changed in our advertisements and movies is the recognition that people speak various languages (and various dialects of the same language) in our country. This means that we have characters who do speak in other languages and are not figures of fun. The Tamil hero in Ek Duje Ke Liye (1981) famously sang 'I don't know what you say' to his Hindi-speaking heroine. And you have characters speaking Hindi in *Roja* (1992) or *Mouna Raagam* (1986), which are set in Kashmir and Delhi. You also have a lovely advertisement from this century for a brand of plywood; a Sikh boy suddenly screams in Tamil to stop the bus he is on, *'Bussai niruthungo'* (interestingly there is a Tamil word for bus but not in popular use). The bewildered parents and viewers accompany him into an old mansion where he recognizes his desk and wife from an earlier birth. Such ads of cross-cultural humour are quite common now and gained prominence during the first edition of the Indian Premier League Cricket tournament in 2008.

We must also consider a Hindi film like *Hum Hain Rahi Pyar Ke* (1993) where the heroine belongs to a Tamil family and her family is located not only by the fact that she and her father converse in Tamil (which is not subtitled, or translated by the characters themselves, so far as I remember) but also by the Tamil Brahmin accents in which they speak English. Take the recent hit *Abhiyum Naanum* (2008), *Abhi And Me*, a movie about a father–daughter relationship, where the daughter's boyfriend turns out to be a Sikh from Delhi (the real 'other' for Tamilians). English can mark the Tamilian, but Hindi/Punjabi marks the outsider! Thus, English can become a marker of regional identity while Hindi becomes the global marker of the metropolitan or national identity.

Conclusion

One of the issues of interest is the pressure of English on Tamil, one that is obvious in the language of Tamil VJs and DJs (who of course speak Tamil from the tip of their tongues, as they say in Tamil!), and is equally obvious in how language has evolved and is evolving in popular usage. (A strange phrase *avan phoninan* is now used in crime novels, meaning 'he telephoned; while phone itself is a loanword, the replacement of 'phone *panninan*' by '*phoninan*' shows the pressure of English sentence structure on Tamil—the Tamil structure would be 'he made a phone call'). This can be nuanced further if we look at the use of English in Tamil advertisements. After all, English comes with lifestyle, progress, vertical mobility . . . How can you be the best if it is not said in English? So the Tamil advert for a Tamil magazine *Kungumam* has this tagline: 'Best *Kannaa* Best' (*kannaa* is the Tamil term of endearment for a child). An advertisement for an amusement park realizes that it is the English-speaking child who will plead to go to such parks again and again: 'Once more *polaamaa* daddy?' (Can we go once again daddy?) Notice also the change in the use of the kinship term; parents are daddy and mummy now, almost all over India, in almost all languages.

What seems clear is that the use of English, the anglicization of Tamil, and the use of Hindi all show the pressures that Tamil is under. There is an aspiration for other lifestyles, other cultural practices; there are also diasporic influences, and caste/ community practices (there is a large Muslim population in Tamil Nadu) and affinities to other languages—all of which influence the hybridization of Tamil as any other language. It is not as if there is clarity of protocol in such hybridization. One can never be sure which words will be accepted as Tamil, which sentence structures will make it, which words will be just slang to pass away soon into history. We have seen that 'colour' is used to signify girls in Tamil as does 'figure'—when someone talks about lack of colour in an audience or in a class, or talks about figures, he (usually he) is talking about women. How else can you talk about the attractiveness of the other sex except in English? The modern language of love comes to us in English; Indians have 'girlfriends' or 'boyfriends' regardless of the language they speak. They fall in love in English (and even in translation as the new Tamil *'kadalil vizhunden'*—I fell in love— shows; incidentally this new phrase is the title of a recent Tamil movie), and declare it in English, have their wedding reception in English, get pregnant in English, and divorce in English (even though Tamil has a word for it). The English word 'jolly' is now a bona fide Tamil word that means having a good time with its associations of happiness. We roamed around in a jolly manner would be a rough equivalent of one of the common sentences where you will find the word in a jolly manner!

This hybridization may be a symptom and product of democratization, and of changes in values and cultural practices. However, a group of students who studied in school with me have recently got in touch with each other after a gap of thirty-odd years. What we find is that the success stories are all those who have competence in English (the others are not part of the rediscovered group, not being Google-able) and also that while we value our Tamhinglish as a way of re-establishing our bonds, our translingual punning and other humour is born of an increased and visible confidence in our creative skills in the languages at our command.

Thus, while languages collide, commingle, beget newer expressions, it is also possible that this may be a marking of privilege rather than an opening out of a democratic space. Linguistic creativity is the preserve of people who have mastered languages and not been mastered by them. Also, an underprivileged Indian who is trying to learn English to be an equal participant in globalization and its benefits may be taught a localized version of Hinglish, which ensures continued disenfranchisement. This is an extremely interesting situation where Hinglishes are works in process, as languages always are. Watch this space after ten years to see if we are like that only.

HINGLISH AND YOUTH: A CAMPUS PERSPECTIVE

Soumik Pal and Siddharth Mishra

The authors bring an everyday and ethnographic perspective on Hinglish, based on their experiences at an elite Indian institution of higher learning. The views expressed are their responses to the conference on Hinglish which formed a strong basis for this book. The conference discussions as well as the journalistic discourse on Hinglish lean heavily towards a synonymy of Hinglish and the 'youth' of India, homogenizing the two in disturbing ways.

This essay interrogates this homogenization and elicits a very necessary debate. The authors are speakers of several languages, including a code-switched Hinglish. Their reflection is caught here in 'speaking' voices to provide a minimally edited and unmediated view on this subject.

The authors are also professionals, who at the time of the conference were in the process of completing graduate studies in communications management at Mudra Institute of Communications Ahmedabad (MICA), the institution that pioneered the discussion on Hinglish in an academics–practitioners forum. Its student profile embraces all the linguistic regions of India. The authors situate Hinglish in their learning at MICA and its relationship with the seductive power of brands and the interpellation of human subjects through brands. Through voices that suggest resistance as well as acknowledgement of the branded value of Hinglish, they provide profound insights and an 'on-ground' view of Hinglish.

—Rita Kothari, Rupert Snell

Siddharth Mishra

English in modern India has always been associated with the middle class, from which have also emanated most modifications to the language. Belonging to that class myself, I have carried its genes since childhood. Born into a family totally into academics, the obsession with 'purity' of language has been of great significance in my life. Academics usually frown upon anything 'adulterating' mode of communication. In a state like Bihar, where speaking 'good' English has always been considered important, they try hard to maintain the purity of the language. My family was no exception.

Hailing from a small city, Patna, but having spent almost ten years of my life in other, diverse parts of the country, I can divide my experiences into three periods. The first, my childhood in my hometown; the second, the period spent studying engineering in Punjab, followed by a three-year stint in the corporate world; and the third, my life at MICA.

Although I was reared in an essentially Hindi-speaking place, my schooling was mainly in English—that too in a hardcore missionary school. Communication was usually in English, to the extent that it was a school rule to speak in that language even during the daily recess. It is a different matter that we usually gave this rule a pass and carried on most of our conversations in Hindi (sometimes featuring certain colloquial 'adjectives', ours being a boys' school). Generally I find that missionary institutions try to maintain 'purity' in everything, including language. Even in elocution or poetry recitation contests, whether in Hindi or English, any language mixing was strongly discouraged. On one occasion in class VIII, I decided to recite a poem by the renowned satirist Ashok Chakradhar. His poems, very contemporary in nature, are written in common *bolchaal ki bhaasha,* the colloquial language that includes non-Hindi words. Despite tremendous response from the audience and even some teachers, the head of the panel announced that I did not win because the poem had many English words and did not qualify as a good piece of verse. I was taken aback but was too naive to understand the politics of language.

Despite all this, language mixing continued. My city had its own style: *'Aap kyun nervousa rahe hain?'* (Why are you getting nervous?); *'Aap humko bahut* taken for granted *le rahe hain!'* (You are taking me too much for granted); and so on. English has always been viewed as the language of the elite, well-educated, affluent class found in all parts of the country, but our part of India has a peculiarity. Lacking any one particular language, and with a variety of languages (or dialects) used across the state, language mixing happens frequently. When any language is spoken in its original form, it is considered elegant and worthy of respect, be it pure Hindi or pure English.

From childhood, my sister and I were encouraged to read English newspapers and magazines. Interestingly, the readership of English newspapers has always been significantly high despite the generally low levels of literacy in the language. Although we were never restricted from watching TV (essentially Doordarshan, the government channel), we were supposed to watch the 8 p.m. English news every day. The advertisements we saw in the late 1980s and early 1990s had a great influence on us. Until this time, most electronic media was controlled by the government or by a culture inspired or promoted by the government; and though I am not complaining, anything new or different came like a breath of fresh air. I was perhaps in class IV then, and was amazed to see the Pepsi campaign with its famous punchline *'Yahi hai right choice baby . . . aha!'* The Remo Fernandes–Juhi Chawla campaign created a flutter among Indian audiences, especially teenagers. We used this punchline in day-to-day conversations, especially at school, just to show off. Such campaigns, I feel, had a tremendous impact on the behaviour and language of teenage Indians and urban audiences with easy access to TV.

At first sight, the population of a small city like Patna seems socially and economically almost homogeneous, as most people work in either the government sector or small businesses. This is, however, deceptive. Even at school, we came from homes with varied lifestyles and living standards. For some of us, entertainment meant *Chitrahaar* (a film-songs-based TV show) and the evening Hindi film on TV on Sundays. Others had video recorders/players at home, giving them easy access not only to Hindi films but also the latest Hollywood flicks. This difference had a deep impact on the behaviours of our batchmates, influencing their conversation and vocabulary. It was Hinglish— a slightly high-class variety, which I was not quite comfortable with at that time, but nevertheless found interesting. American and British lingo started making inroads into the vocabulary of our generation. Words like 'baby', 'chap', and 'dude' became part of everyday conversations, and ads like Pepsi's reinforced this cultural change.

The most important phenomenon of the early 1990s was the advent of cable TV and the new liberal economic policies that brought events from across the world to Indian audiences. The good old days of Doordarshan faded away and people gradually started to emulate their neighbours by acquiring cable connections and discussing the latest number on *Close-up Antakshari* or the latest happenings in *Campus*. The phraseology of '*Chitrahaar ke praayojak hain . . .*' was slowly replaced by '*Milte hain* break *ke baad*'. Change was happening, slowly but steadily. With not many film theatres screening English (i.e., Hollywood) films and without a VCR at home, we had to wait for the cable TV revolution to start watching English films regularly. But by the time cable TV reached us, both my sister and I were leaving the city for higher education.

Alongside the changes in the market and the broadcasting system, another silent revolution, in an entirely different segment, would shape the destiny of this part of the world in the years to follow. This was the advent of the personal computer. Started in the mid-1980s by the Rajiv Gandhi government, the revolution gained momentum in the mid-1990s. In addition to technical advantages, computers also had a real impact on the language of Indians, affecting especially the middle class for whom they proved such a boon. The fact that they could be used only in English at that time encouraged the import of English words into Hindi and other Indian languages. I think mine was the first generation of Indians to be drawn into this revolution in a big way. Computer education had just begun and it was magic for us. Phrases like 'data save *kar lena*', 'file *ki* location *kya hai?*', '*yeh* file corrupt *ho chuki hai*' were swiftly added to the vocabulary of Indian youth—understandably the most tech-savvy group. Such terms were not only used in computing but became the new lingo of educated Indian youth.

Next came the Internet revolution, which changed how people communicated in India and across the world, making letter-writing seem a waste of time and effort, reducing the status of post offices to places for form-filling, pushing libraries into history, and making everything real seem 'virtual'. It brought people closer to the rest of the world. But the Internet had the same limitation as computers—even when writing an email in their own language, users had to transliterate everything into the Latin alphabet, and this accelerated the mixed-language culture known as Hinglish. With the Internet came chatting, which (before mobile telephony and messaging) was the most popular and cheapest pastime of young India. I was to experience this drastic change when I embarked on the second important phase of my life, engineering.

Jalandhar, or for that matter Punjab, was a novel experience for me. The USP of any regional engineering college (now rechristened as national institute of technology) in those days was the mix of students it attracted from almost all over the country. And though it gave you excellent exposure to people you might not have even dreamt of meeting, such as students from Lakshadweep, it was really very difficult to communicate with them. Initially, this was a serious problem for all of us, including the professors; and the only solution we could find for this was English. It was fascinating to hear different forms of English from different parts of India. There was Mallu English ('Mallu' being a generic, and mildly disparaging, term for Malayali, a Malayalam-speaker from Kerala), Bong English (from West Bengal), and Punjabi English. At the risk of grossly generalizing, I would say on the basis of my six years in Punjab that there is something unusual about Punjabis, especially the youth, when they speak English. It's a common joke in Punjab that a Punjabi speaks different languages for different moods, especially while conversing with a non-Punjabi—English when he is happy or trying to show off, Hindi when he is just normal, Punjabi when he is pissed off! English in Punjabi or Punjabi in English, they are so mingled with each other now that it is really difficult to filter them out. And the trend is quite understandable. With many of their relatives living in different parts of the world, there is a natural tendency in the younger generation to follow in their footsteps for easy and quick money, or for the sake of lifestyle; and English is considered to be the gateway to these.

MICA was different, albeit a difference I was prepared for. My experience was in a sense similar to that of Soumik's (*see below*) except that my involvement in theatre and related activities gave me some surprising insights into the linguistic behaviour of some students. The ones I would have never imagined in my wildest dreams to speak even a sentence in proper Hindi did well in auditions and rehearsals, and with excellent diction. And yet, once out of the rehearsal room, they hardly seemed the same people. They felt comfortable in English, but their Hindi was much more grammatically correct than their English. When speaking English, they took linguistic liberties that come with confidence. This they usually avoided in Hindi which, for them, had become a ceremonial language to be used selectively and cautiously. This I assert only about the group I interacted with during various plays.

I have always tried to maintain a level of purity in my Hindi. Ample liberty is taken with Hindi in the parts where I belong.

But somehow, since childhood, I had got it into my head that my Hindi had to be impeccable, and always took pride in this fact. At MICA, for the first time, I encountered a hotchpotch of a language being routinely used. It is not as if I always spoke chaste Hindi, but I was not accustomed to the degree of mixing of two different languages that I heard there. Such mixing and matching tickled Soumik and me deeply, and we often laughed over what we thought were examples of extreme ludicrousness.

Soumik Pal

I was born into a Bengali family, living in Bengal. Bengali was the only language I was exposed to in my early years, the only language I spoke before I could write. I do not recall particularly well the media influences on me at that time. So I must, at the outset, make it clear that both Hindi and English are alien languages to me—though the sense in and the extent to which I feel thus vary according to time and place.

Having established my Bengali identity, I must also point out that English was the language I learnt to read and write before I could read the Bangla script. This was because in my hometown, Durgapur, the most desired school for any infant (rather his parents) was St Xavier's, an English-medium convent. My kindergarten education was thus expended on preparing me for the 'ultimate' test—the admission test for St Xavier's School! But this did not, I believe, hamper my reading and writing skills in my mother tongue. Within just two months of being introduced to the Bengali alphabet, I (along with my classmates) was able to write small but complete and grammatically correct sentences in Bengali, much to my parents' surprise. This is pertinent because it proves the extent to which the mother tongue had already become 'natural' for us. From then on, English was the medium of instruction in school—in the classroom and outside. We were encouraged to speak English at all times, on the school premises. But, at least for me, it remained the medium for communication in only the *written* form. When it came to speaking, the mother tongue always dominated.

My introduction to the other 'alien' language, Hindi, was through the popular media, TV being an important part of my growing up. There must have been an organic relationship between our TV set and me—both of us came into our home in 1984! Right from childhood, I was addicted to Hindi films and managed to pick up from that source enough of the language to enable me, as a kid, to speak a 'make-do' Hindi—something that my parents struggle with even now. The other (albeit very minor) influence was the cosmopolitan nature of Durgapur, an industrial township; from a young age, I had some non-Bengali friends, with whom I would converse in Hindi. For all this, my Hindi vocabulary was mostly limited to what I learnt from films. So although I acquired words such as *pyaar*, *mohabbat*, *badla*, *khoon*, *khaandaan*, *rishta*, *kangna*, *dupatta*, I did not know the Hindi names of fruit and vegetables.

This remained the status quo of my language skills from my schooldays (during which time three years of Hindi as a third language taught me its alphabet), right through to college and university in Kolkata. I majored in English literature but even there I had friends who were more into Bengali literature. That three-year stint actually brought me closer to literature in my own language. Interestingly, in my master's in Jadavpur University, where I did postgraduation in film studies, the language of the classroom was mostly English and partly Bengali. Yet, film studies introduced me to cinema from all over the world. Subtitled cine-viewing became a part of my life. Suddenly my daily conversations were peppered with names such as Buñuel, Godard, Eisenstein and terms such as *cinéma vérité* and *mise en scène*.

This infused me with a typical Bengali *bhadralok* characteristic. The quintessential *bhadralok* is a colonial product; in the colonial era, this class of people developed refined European tastes, in turn influencing Bengali art and culture. This class would happily be Bengali and French or Bengali and English or German at the same time. Of course, the species did not disappear after the British left. Such a person would listen to Rabindrasangeet and Beethoven but probably not Urdu ghazals. He had his Jibanananda and Bankim along with Shelley and Keats, but Maithili Sharan Gupt or Hazari Prasad Dwivedi barely existed for him.

This influx of foreign auteurs suddenly brought to the surface the dormant colonial hangover within me. Anything French became classy; anything *desi* not quite so. Strangely, there was nothing in the academic environment of my university to foster such an attitude. I am yet to figure out the reasons for this sudden burst of elitism in me. It was not as extreme, though, as it may sound. The respect for a Munshi Premchand, a Sa'adat Hasan Manto, an M.S. Sathyu, or a Guru Dutt remained intact. But there was the Bengal *high culture* and then there was Europe! As for 'the rest of India', well, it might as well not have existed.

This state of affairs changed significantly when I left Bengal for the first time to study at MICA. But before I recount the language situation I faced there, I must bring in some points from my family background. An important factor in my relationship with languages was the prevailing attitude towards them at home—my parents being the ultimate determinants. English was always considered important because of the firm belief that if I were to become a 'real man' and achieve something in life, I had to master the masters' language. And since education in English came from school and not from TV or Hollywood or sitcoms, it was considered 'safe'. As in any typical middle-class Bengali household, education was always given prominence, with the English medium being taken for granted as the obvious choice. Bengali, on the other hand, was never discouraged at my home—unlike in some households where ignorance of Bengali was a symbol of pride.

The attitude towards Hindi in my home was most interesting; it could almost be equated with the attitude towards Hindi films. Even though my father had been an avid follower of Hindi films in school and college, Hindi cinema was never considered to be serious entertainment. The image of Hindi cinema in my home was that of crass, cheap, and sometimes even vulgar entertainment. Despite being Rafi, Kishore, and Dilip Kumar fans, my parents thought it unhealthy for their son to watch too many Hindi films. This probably also had to do with the fact that they abhorred the Hindi cinema and music of the 1990s, the period of my childhood. Listening to old Hindi film melodies was all right, even encouraged, but Hindi was never considered as sophisticated and 'proper' as English and Bengali. It was the language of Khotuas (a pejorative Bengali term for people from Bihar) and Marwaris. The attitude was not just disrespectful but also a tad racist.

Coming to MICA, I encountered—for the first time in my life—a group of people of whom pretty much none could speak my mother tongue. Initially, I was so starved of Bengali that whenever I called someone back in Bengal and couldn't connect, the pre-recorded voice saying in Bengali, 'the phone number you are trying to reach is currently not available', was music to my ears. Moreover, I found myself with people very different from my earlier friends. These people, it seemed to me then, had no literary or ideological passions. All they enjoyed was clubbing, 'hanging out', going for a movie/pepperoni (the two seemed interchangeable), and 'chilling'. They were what I called the typical 'B-school crowd'. I desperately tried to keep my distance from 'them' and, as a result, I was promptly branded as the 'intellectual from Bengal'. All this disgusted me in the beginning. My initial judgement (admittedly flawed) was that they were frivolous. And this is also where I encountered, for the first time, the mix of Hindi and English as a normal mode of speech. It was my first real experience of Hinglish.

My being so judgemental of my peers may be improper but they did represent a break from the type of company to which I was accustomed. They were all there with the aim of landing plum jobs, to get everything easy in life. It was no different in the case of language. They were well versed in English; those from Hindi-speaking areas were fluent in Hindi too. But there was a notable tendency to take the easy way out. Speaking proper English or Hindi was more trying than speaking Hinglish. The former required adherence to the rules of grammar and syntax, whereas in a hybrid language, syntax can be played with at will, making speech so much easier.

Gradually, I too took to Hinglish. Speaking chaste English all the time was in any case not my cup of tea. I just did not feel at home with that. Nor could I speak proper Hindi all the time. Therefore, the obvious advantages of a hybrid language readily appealed to me. Another factor was that I was 'expected' to speak in Hindi. It was considered impolite to talk to a fellow Bengali in our mother tongue when a non-Bengali was around. This irked me greatly. It still does. But people around were, after all, friends. I had to communicate. Perhaps this is what caused the influx of English, as a more neutral language, into my Hindi.

Another significant change in my life at MICA came when I first encountered the Internet. Whether by design or by chance, I had managed to evade it until then. I did not even have an e-mail ID. I had a phobia of computers. At MICA, I *had* to use a laptop, and this brought about a momentous change—I started to surf the Net and maintain my email inbox but I also got addicted to chatting. I feel that chatting and SMS texting are two phenomena that go a long way in determining the use of Hinglish.

My style of written communication changed considerably with my adoption of chatting and texting. When I talk to someone face to face or over the telephone, there is a sense of immediacy. Anything spoken by either speaker evokes an immediate response that keeps the conversation going. When I write, however (as in examination papers, diary entries, academic notes), this immediacy is lost. Even with letters, the time lag between statement and response is long. Acquaintance with SMS, and more so with chatting, brought this sense of immediacy into my written communication. As in oral communication, each statement carried the implicit possibility of immediate response. This also brought its inherent casualness to my writing. Thus, my written expression began to acquire a Hinglish character.

The true nature of the debate here is not well served by the term 'Hinglish', which glosses over the regional specificities in the relationship between Indian languages and English. In discussing the interaction of the global/colonial and the local/

colonized, Hindi tends to appropriate the whole of the 'local side' but the 'Hindi versus Other Indian Languages' debate is as important as the 'Global versus Local' debate. There have been several instances of transnational or multinational capital trying to connect with local/regional markets without Hindi entering the picture at all. In Bengal, for example, Coca-Cola has sought to play to local sentiments by associating itself with *para* (street) football. Bengali passion for football has a charm and nostalgia attached to it which is entirely Bengal's. Hindi has no role there.

The common take that Siddharth and I have on Hinglish includes many things which, while they emerge from personal experiences, are in fact part of a more widespread phenomenon. But when I talk of my experiences, I talk not only of what I *think* but also of how I *react*. I mentioned my irritation with Hindi's monopoly over the hybridization process. It wasn't that my Bengali identity was being ignored or deliberately suppressed but that all regional specificities (including mine) got somewhat sidelined during daily conversations, without the participants actually intending it. My reaction was not merely about asserting identity but about exercising it. Being a Bengali (among other things) I kept up an image of being a *typical* Bengali, often playing into the stereotype I had despised earlier. But this playacting helped me maintain a balance. As an individual, what I enjoy the most is to sit back and observe. Even with Hinglish, this is what I did. Even though some things I have mentioned above drove me to action, most often I was just a detached observer, taking in what was happening with a touch of mirthful irony.

Conclusion

We do not claim to represent 'youth' at large. But we *belong* to that segment of society and are not just talking *about* it. Our observations are informed by the general trends, anxieties, and dilemmas that most youth face today.

In the last two decades, the world has seen a tremendous growth spurt of the animal called 'brand'. Marketing and advertising have become more vital than ever before. To compete in the market amidst an avalanche of products and brands, it is not enough to address the customer only vis-à-vis the product. The brand must be built—and that is the role of marketing and advertising. The final effect of this branding exercise is not just increased sales and profit, because brands have now spilled over to constitute the culture of our age. Most brands identify youth as their primary target. Thus, youth culture has become the dominant culture.

This is probably a two-way process. Across the world, brands draw upon youth culture, and youth in turn derives its culture from brands. Major brands that seem to define global culture— Coke, Nike, McDonald's, Viacom, etc.—are not all American. But they do share ideological commonalities, operating on some broad, basic common principles. They all propel us towards a certain 'lifestyle'—a product of free-market capitalism. Lifestyle is today's buzzword. Of course not all market activities pursue this goal single-mindedly. There are variations. But they generally reside at the level of the subtext.

But why are we, of all people, pondering on how marketing and advertising influences youth culture? And how is this seemingly global phenomenon related to Hinglish?

To answer the first question, this essay chronicles our personal experiences and opinions. Both of us are now marketing communication professionals and the way brands work lies within the purview of our work interests. More significantly, we have directly experienced the brand–culture nexus. Exercises in branding or case studies on different brands gave us an understanding of how this 'animal' works.

By way of discussing the connection of this to Hinglish, let us take the case of Pepsi's Youngistaan drive—a very successful and influential advertising campaign of our times. It talks about a fictitious country of young people and people young at heart. It is characterized by youthfulness, living carefree, never giving up. What is particularly interesting is that community formation, once a role of religion or of ideologies (including that of the nation), is being appropriated by brands (this is not the first time, though; Marlboro did something similar in the 1950s in the US). Youngistaan is a similar attempt. The concept has nothing to do with the product—sweetened, carbonated water. What keeps it going is not the flavour of the drink but the rhetoric, which includes other brands (MTV, Pizza Hut, PVR, as evident from the Youngistaan website). The medium of expression of this concept is Hinglish. To grab youth attention, Pepsi had to come up with something that could connect with them while retaining neutrality. Hinglish fulfilled this need.

The Youngistaan concept has been very popular since its launch. At MICA, a group of students called itself the Youngistaan Gang! These were new-age people, up to date with everything, always setting the bar for the 'cool' quotient, and also relating closely with Hinglish as characterized earlier. The notable point, however, is that these young people (and others who would qualify as Youngistaan Gang members) all came from affluent families and were comfortable with the concept of 'commodity'. An array of commodities, powered by their affluence, defined their lives. To them, these were not mere commodities but brands—living, talking, moving things with which they engaged in a continual dialogue.

Brands are often conceptualized as human beings, possessing personalities and characteristics. Their assuming human roles is not uncommon. But young people can also don the roles of brands. A sports-oriented person would, thus, be a Nike/Adidas personality; a fashion-conscious person would be a L'Oréal type. It is not just dialogue but a fusion of brands and personalities.

Thus brands infuse their own attributes in youth. A multinational brand, for example, cannot 'belong' to a region. Any brand aspiring to go global has to have a 'floating' existence. It may try to connect with regions but can never 'belong' anywhere. Therefore brand lingo has to be neutral, similar to what is called 'neutral accent' at call centres. This is what young people also imbibe. Brands neutralize and homogenize them. To say this is not to suggest that all start to look and sound alike, but they start to differ less and less. These people have not lost their regional specificities, but they are starting to do so. What reinforces this 'branded' identity in India is Hinglish. It brings together two languages that can lay the largest claim to being pan-Indian. It glosses over a lot of regional specificities. What works for Hinglish is that it is not locale specific. No wonder Pepsi chose such a Hinglish term as Youngistaan for its campaign. And no wonder it had to actually think of a fictitious land for its youth. It probably indicates that the ties of belonging of today's youth have to be severed somewhat.

We do not, however, suggest that Hinglish is a rootless phenomenon that can only be used for the propagation of a global and (more important) branded culture. The Hinglish that we have talked about is mainly that of urban upper-middle-class youth. But there exist other youth who have their own brands of Hinglish. The reasons and mechanisms of their operation may be different.

As of now, we have identified Hinglish not just as a language but also a new lifestyle mantra. Our experiences, converging at MICA, have given us a limited but first-hand view of this. These, however, are not exhaustive experiences. We have elaborated on just one of the several modes that we identify of the existence of Hinglish among youth.

VOICES FROM INDIAN CINEMA I

Mahesh Bhatt

At the outset, let me say that I would rather be stupid than pretend to be intelligent. So when I found out that I was to speak to this audience, I put my mind to this subject and began speaking to my fourteen-year-old daughter.

Two thousand years ago, English did not exist, yet today it is a language of upward mobility in India. But language experts also say that there will come a time when English will no longer be spoken. One has always wondered how languages across the world evolved and developed over the millennia . . . what makes one language flourish and another die? Are some languages more 'advanced' than others? Is English more advanced than Urdu, for instance? And the mother of all such haunting questions is this: when a civilization declines, can its language survive? Did the death of Urdu begin with the end of the Mughal empire and did the language finally reach its lowest point with the partitioning of this country into India and Pakistan?

Everything under the sun has an expiry date. This is true of languages too; they are born, are used for a period, and finally die. There is no denying, however, that there are vast differences between these languages—some are used for a few generations while others exist for millennia; some are spoken only by a handful of people while others are used by hundreds of millions. How languages arise and vanish and why languages have such different destinies are issues that have to do with what happens to the people who use the languages.

Simply put, languages depend on history, and historical events often depend on the question of which languages are spoken in a given context. Take India's outsourcing industry for example. The 1990s marked the rise of Indian information technology companies and our key competitive strength in the global services market has been our teeming force of educated workers who are literate in English. In the business process outsourcing sector, in particular, most jobs are defined by English language proficiency. No wonder then that through the 1990s, potential earnings of Indians skilled in using the English language surged. It should not surprise anyone that every parent in India wants his or her child to acquire an English-medium education: this is a fact that cannot be ignored.

The victors of the Second World War—the US and the Soviet Union—dominated the world by their military might. Hardly surprising then that English and Russian—the languages of these two superpowers—profited immensely. But look what happened to the Russian language after the collapse of the Soviet Union—at what amazing speed it lost its international standing!

English came to India aboard European ships. For much of the seventeenth and eighteenth centuries, it was perceived mainly as a port language—the tongue spoken by merchants. But when the British reached more deeply into our nation and began to rule us, it became a language of instruction, at least for advanced education. Even so many decades after Independence, our school and administration systems have not been able to switch efficiently from English to our national or regional languages. Though English is associated with the old colonial power, it remains more powerful than most regional languages in the context of our schools.

As we come to the end of the first decade of the twenty-first century, English is swiftly gaining ground in India. But what the world is waking up to is this new language called 'Hinglish', which has evolved over the years in our country and is suddenly in the global spotlight as never before. This only proves that we humans possess enormous linguistic creativity that we deploy to construct something entirely novel, when the need arises. All humans have a basic need for a first language that is used with family and intimate friends, and is an important part of their personal identity. Indians have long felt a need to make English belong to them and, over the years, have peppered it with words from Hindi, marking this alien language with their own identity, and thus making it their own. Turn on the television in India and you are likely to hear things like 'Hungry *kya?*' and 'Tension *mat le yaar!*' These and countless other new words and phrases have become a part of India's fastest growing language—Hinglish.

There is no denying that this blend of Hindi and English has become the language of the street and is the lingo of most college campuses. Some say that Hinglish is a bridge between two cultures that has become an island of its own. It is certainly the language of a distinct hybrid culture for people who aspire to make it rich abroad but do not want to sacrifice the sassiness of the mother tongue.

As storytellers, we make a story our own. We want to inject something of ourselves into a story. It has to do with proprietorship. That is what we did with English—and Hinglish is a consequence. The new idiom, represented by 'Hungry *kya?*', was ridiculed in earlier Bollywood films. Westernized characters, villains, and comedians spoke such Hindi, laced with English. They were screen buffoons or villains. I remember a film in which the comedian Mehmood uses Hindi peppered with English words. He was what we would call ABCD, or the American-Born Confused Desi.

Then you had characters like Robert and Julie, clad in tight coats and pants or dresses with low necklines, and they too spoke such a tongue. The purpose was usually parody, symbolizing bad behaviour. Now, of course, the jumble has become hip. A few years ago, the world got a taste of Hinglish through films such as *Bend It Like Beckham* and *Monsoon Wedding*. Today, a Bollywood screenplay writer feels very comfortable mixing a lot of English in his Hindi script. I was shocked to find that the film we just made has more English words than ever before; and that too from a scriptwriter trained in Urdu—she evidently saw Hinglish as her ticket to Bollywood!

Our buddies in the world of advertising say that advertisements were once conceived in English, then just translated into Hindi almost as an afterthought. That method does not work any more. Since most Indians have only a smattering of English, multinational corporations now speak Hinglish in their ads. Pepsi, for instance, gave its global 'Ask for more' campaign a Hinglish flavour with '*Yeh dil maange* more'. Coke too has had its Hinglish slogan: '*Life ho to aisi*'. Domino's Pizza, which offers Indian curiosities such as the 'chicken tikka' pizza, asks its customers 'Hungry *kya?*' None of this would have happened a few years ago.

The young have an urgency to communicate—they would rather be understood than be correct. And since more than 50 per cent of the population of India is under twenty-five years, the power has shifted to them. Everyone wants to talk to them in their language. Hinglish now has a buzz. Using Hindi in an otherwise perfect English sentence is not looked down upon, or inferred as arising from a lack of education. It is, in fact, a huge asset.

Cultural observers say that the turning point that made Hinglish hip was the introduction of cable TV in the mid-1990s. Music channels like MTV and Channel V originally aired only 'English' music, presented by foreign-born Indian video jockeys who spoke only in English. However, since the response outside the metros was not encouraging, they had to rethink, turning to Hinglish to connect with a larger audience. Once they did that, their penetration into the Indian market went from under 10 per cent to over 60 per cent.

We now see two simultaneous trends in India. On the one hand, English continues to be the language of upward mobility; everybody wants to send his or her child to an English-medium school. On the other, a knowledge of Hindi is also useful. English language coaching institutes are burgeoning nationwide. In effect, Indians are trying to have it both ways: what they speak at work is not necessarily what they speak at home, with their friends, or on the bus.

Let's not get too carried away with this idea though. I do believe that English can be alienating—as can Hinglish. Look at the way rural India is not responding to mainstream Hindi cinema because it is too upper class, its language alien to rural audiences. What explains the rise of Bhojpuri cinema? What we are watching in terms of Hinglish represents only metropolitan India. I believe that you can experience and express your genius in the language of your mother. I grew up as an English-speaking boy and rejected Urdu, the language of my Muslim mother. However, it is only when I spoke my mother's tongue and understood the poetry of Kaifi Azmi and Faiz, Iqbal, and Ghalib that I came into my own. So let's not reject that legacy. It is the repository of our creativity, and I would be sad to see it go.

A British linguist projected that at about 350 million, the world's Hinglish speakers may soon outnumber native English speakers. Is this the beginning of the end of English?

—

Mahesh Bhatt's session elicited a very interesting discussion. A young man stood up and said, 'Why are you so contemptuous of our language? What makes me less Indian if I speak in Hinglish? Whether I wear trousers or a dhoti, I feel equally Indian. Why are we being derided in this conference as people who don't know their language? I speak Bengali and Hindi and English and see nothing wrong with it.' The young man also objected to the bracketing of Hinglish with consumerism, saying, 'If I am earning money and buying twenty shampoos, what is wrong with it?'

VOICES FROM INDIAN CINEMA II

An Interview with
Film-maker and Lyricist Gulzar
by Rita Kothari

I first met Gulzarsaab many years ago in New Delhi. Katha, an organization devoted to literature and translation, had hosted a panel discussion on 'Partition'. The panel comprised writers and scholars who had documented experiences of Partition in the Punjab and Bengal. I was part of the audience.

Interviewing Gulzarsaab over the telephone recently, I began by reminding him of our conversation during the panel discussion.

—

RITA: Gulzarsaab, namaste. I met you some years ago at a Katha conference on 'Partition'. I asked you why there had been no mention of the Sindhis who had also undergone the trauma of leaving their homeland—which they did not manage to reclaim—and even losing their language in the process. I remember you responding by saying that Sindhis need to be more active in archiving, translating, and generally disseminating their literature to the wider world. You will be happy to know that, since then, I have undertaken sociological and literary work on this issue.

GULZAR: Well, *you* will be happy to know that, since then, I have brought up the subject of Sindhi language and the trauma of the community in every possible forum. When Urduwallahs lament the death of Urdu in India, I tell them that Urdu has an entire nation to itself. Look at Sindhi on the other hand—it is without a land and bereft of connections to its culture.

RITA: People who bemoan the demise of Urdu also don't acknowledge the dominating influence Urdu has on other languages of Pakistan such as Pashto, Punjabi, Balochi, Sindhi, etc. Anyway, I wish to talk to you today about something else. I recently organized a conference titled 'Chutnefying English' in Mumbai. The forum examined the relationship between Hindi and English, and whether that stood redefined through the combination of the two into what has come to be called 'Hinglish'.

GULZAR: Why did you call it 'chutnefying?'

RITA: I borrowed the phrase from Salman Rushdie to suggest forms of hybridization in the English language in India, with special emphasis on Hindi–English.

GULZAR: There is no such thing as 'Hinglish'. It is an artificial construction borne of distortion of words and languages. It is true that some Hindi words have entered the English vocabulary—just as some English words have gone into the Hindi. How does that matter though? What is the concern? As long as we don't say things like '*tiinon* window*en khol do*' or '*kuchh* player*on ne kaha*'! *Zabaanon ki apni* dignity *hai*. We have to use languages with the respect due to them. Let's not glorify such distortion by calling something 'Hinglish'. And the encounter is not only between Hindi and English; it is also between English and Bengali, or English and Urdu. It's only natural that languages will mix. I am not taking the purist stand that some advocates of Konkani do, who wish to purify Konkani.

Another thing to bear in mind is that mixing happens between our Indian languages also. You should look at the picture in its entirety, instead of viewing it as a phenomenon concerning Hindi and English alone.

RITA: Agreed. However, of all the language mixing that goes on, isn't the Hindi–English type more common than all the others?

GULZAR: Perhaps it is, but I urge you to look at *all* the languages and examine this as a nationwide phenomenon—or it will drag us into the Hindi versus English controversy of years gone by. More important, we should worry about the actual *survival* of languages instead of just the mixtures they become part of.

I would argue that we are witnessing the gradual evolution of 'Indian English', a language that has come to stay. It is not Oxford or Cambridge English but Indian English, an entity in its own right. If there is Italian English and American English, well there can also be Indian English. It is true that English has emerged as a link language among us, and it is also a global language, but give it time to grow in India into a distinct phenomenon.

When Nirad Chaudhuri or Mulk Raj Anand were writing, it was in British English, not Indian English. These days, Indian English writers receive a lot of recognition but we must still wait for English to become a distinct phenomenon. When that happens, its features will not come from Hindi alone but also from Gujarati and Punjabi and Bengali and so on—it will be a truly *Indian* English.

As someone once said, 'Look, don't point at my English. You have inherited it, but I have *learnt* it.' Let's give English that space.

RITA: Gulzarsaab, let me bring up a question—what kind of changes have you seen in your creative expression over the years? Has there been a change in the style of language you use in your lyrics and screenplays? Do you find yourself using more English words?

GULZAR: I don't use more English words. The characters themselves are using more English. I give the characters the mixed language that sounds natural when they speak—but only that particular type of character. If there are Hindi-speaking people, I can't make them speak Bhojpuri. The language that comes into films comes from its use in society—not the other way round! People hold films responsible for popularizing language but films simply reflect the way real people speak.

RITA: Don't you agree though that some English words in a Hindi/Hindustani utterance—and I am not referring to technical words like 'phone' or 'tyre'—make sense simply because they belong conceptually to English? For instance, in the song '*Kajra re*' from *Bunty Aur Babli*, the woman says, '*Aankhein bhi kamaal karti hain, personal se sawal karti hain*' ... Do you think it would have been difficult to say '*Aankhen niji (ya vyaktigat) sawaal karti hain*' because the notion of 'personal' (as opposed to public) is alien to our languages?

GULZAR: I don't agree with you. It is the character that is saying this. The girl is from Kanpur. She says some things in Punjabi, some in English. She mixes them up. And 'personal' is a solid, pure word. It's not slang, like '*oh ya*', it's not a distortion of anything. You don't even realize that 'personal ' is an English word, it's so seamless. *Angrezi aisi istemaal ho ki uske siivan ka pata na lage*, you shouldn't be able to see the stitching. Having said that, I do believe that people should definitely speak at least one Indian language properly.

I call my language 'Hindustani', not Hindi. The Hindustani that Gandhi wanted. In fact, my new book is dedicated to Hindustani. And it's not merely a mix of Urdu, Hindi, and Persian—it also features Punjabi and Bangla words. When you say, '*Tumhein dekhkar dil nihaal ho gaya*', where does '*nihaal*' come from? From Punjabi, of course! When you say, '*Raakh ko faroko, angaaron mein ab bhi aag hogi*', the word *faroko* is from Sindhi. So Hindustani is much broader than any single regional language.

GRAPPLING WITH MULTIPLE LANGUAGES IN CINEMA: THE CASE OF *FIRAAQ*

Shuchi Kothari and Nandita Das

Nandita and Shuchi began their creative collaboration with another screenplay. In teasing out the emotions and impulses behind that project, they arrived at the truth of Firaaq. *Both carry very personal experiences vis-à-vis communal issues. As a social activist, Nandita was already talking to young people, conducting workshops across India on the nature of violence and of prejudice. These conversations with ordinary people compelled her to address this topic in her debut film as a director. Neither Nandita nor Shuchi knew who the producer would be, and whether the film would be made but the latter also shared Nandita's commitment and passion to spotlight these issues. As an academic and screenplay writer, Shuchi's earlier work had grappled with similar issues around identity politics but this was also a very personal journey for her as someone originally from Ahmedabad and married to a secular British Muslim. Writing across countries, across every possible medium, while maintaining their day jobs, they took two and a half years to complete the screenplay. This long gestation period was beneficial. As many world and national events led to global and local discourses on war*

*and violence, their direct and tangential conversations
began to shape the screenplay and chisel out the
emotional truth of their characters.*

The session began with a trailer of Firaaq, *with
English subtitles and a voiceover by one of the characters,
Khan saahab (Naseeruddin Shah): 'Insaan insaan ko
marta hai ... iss baat ka gham hai Karim miyan ...
[Humans slaughter each other, that is what makes me
sad, Karim miyan.]' and 'Sirf saat suron mein itni
qaabliyat kahaan ke aisi nafrat ka saamna kar sakein?
[How can seven musical notes fight against such immense
hatred?]'*

—

NANDITA: *Firaaq* is about the scars left on a population after
the communal carnage that took place in Gujarat in 2002.
Someone in some newspaper mentioned today that it is 'yet
another riot film'. Far from it! The stories unfold a month after
the worst of the pogrom was over. It is set in a period when
most denizens of the city are quick to proclaim that everything
is normal. But *Firaaq* explores the fallacy of that normalcy. It
shows what really happens to people—across gender, class,
community, and age—and what lingers on when the obvious
violence is over—the fear, the anger, the prejudice, the desire
for revenge, the hopelessness, the faith or loss thereof. *Firaaq*
deals with all those emotions and, in the process, raises questions
that we hesitate to ask at times.

This is just by way of background. I know that this session is
meant to focus on the use of language. While I don't know the
academic frameworks within which Hinglish, Tamlish, and so
on have been discussed in earlier sessions, I know that because
we were dealing with stories across class and community, the
choice of language became critical to the writing process. But it
was something that happened organically as we discussed the
'voices' of characters and ways in which to render them credibly.
I will let Shuchi talk about this point, as my partner in crime.

SHUCHI: The multiple linguistic registers of the screenplay were determined by the ensemble structure of *Firaaq*. Rather early on, we had arrived at a decision that this film would not be served best by one single protagonist. This meant that all subsequent conversations about various characters, their voices, and their back stories were caught up in the authenticity of their experiences—socio-economic class, communal or regional affiliations, geographic locations, neighbourhoods, and so on. Though we never mention Ahmedabad in the screenplay, we were very clear that the film was set in that city. So when we ask ourselves as writers, how are the 5 million residents of Ahmedabad dealing with or not dealing with the situation at hand, we have to acknowledge that, linguistically speaking, these residents include all kinds of people—those who primarily speak Gujarati, those who speak Hindi, or Urdu, or English, or a combination of two or three languages, or a dialect thereof. These multiple languages and registers grounded our stories in a real location and the more specific we were, the more universal the emotional truth became.

It was not just the content of the screenplay that was riding across various languages; our own process of working mirrored that. Nandita and I, not unlike other urban speakers, switched between English, Gujarati, and Hinglish while discussing the stories. I was writing in English because the screenwriting software I use limits me to that language, but often I used the dual-dialogue feature to write in English and the agreed upon vernacular transliterated in Roman.

NANDITA: The use of multiple languages was not a matter of style but of necessity. For instance, the lower-middle-class characters of Paresh Rawal and Deepti Naval would, in reality, speak in Gujarati. In fact, if we had made them speak Hindi, it would have become a caricature not unlike some of Paresh Rawal's Hindi-speaking Gujarati characters in commercial Hindi films where the accent is played up for comedy. While our intentions for seeking an emotional honesty that comes through linguistic authenticity were all very honourable, the reality of film production and distribution pulled us in the opposite direction. People warned me that I was going to lose a fair share of the Indian audience if I steered away from Hindi. I am often asked the question, *'Kya yah Hindi film hai?'* [Is this a Hindi film?] I find myself answering, 'Well, it's Hindi, Urdu, English, Gujarati, and a certain dialect that the rickshaw driver and his wife use.' Of course I don't want to lose audiences in India but then again, we hadn't written it in multiple languages just willy-nilly. The minute you see/hear a character speak a certain language, it acts as a window into so many facets. For instance, a certain kind of English expression reveals a certain type of education. There are Indians in India whose only shared language is English. But, as Shuchi said, it was an organic process as we got to know our characters more and more and figured out who would switch between languages and under what circumstances.

SHUCHI: We too had our own switching—Nandita and I expressed affection in Gujarati and arguments in English!

NANDITA: Possibly! When I deliver talks, I speak in Hindi and am very fluent but when I have to think conceptually it becomes difficult. Every time I act in a south Indian language film, it becomes a nightmare and I swear I will never do it again . . . it's so much harder since language is not just rote learning, it's a journey into a different milieu. But I have a fascination with languages; they open up unfamiliar contexts. At times, I find myself keenly observing how reflective of class language actually is.

SHUCHI: Languages are embodied. In an earlier session, someone spoke of nuance, as against task-oriented communication. We have six stories in *Firaaq*, but there was a seventh we had written which we axed from the penultimate draft. Both of us loved this story of a couple once married to each other, now divorced. Shalini, a Kannadiga woman from Bangalore, and Arjun, her former husband from Kanpur, meet in Ahmedabad six months after their divorce. Everything about their lives has changed, as has the city. The tentativeness with which they approach each other, their sense of loss, their bitterness, their familiarity—we could not tell their story in Hindi. We went round and round but it seemed inauthentic in any other language but English—they fell in love in English, their divorce was in English, the affective dimension of their relationship was in English.

NANDITA: In a multilingual country like ours, people not only speak more than a language or two but, depending on their relationships, switch between languages within the same conversation. In *Firaaq*, you see that with Anu (Tisca Chopra) and Sameer (Sanjay Suri). Sameer, a Muslim, speaks Hindustani and English at home, and Gujarati as a transactional language. Anu and her girlfriend Ketki switch between English and Gujarati, whereas Sameer and Ketki's husband switch between Hindi and English. In most lines of dialogue we incorporated the switch in a manner that seemed to flow naturally for us. Sometimes, the actors would flip it around to suit their speech patterns. For Haneef's and Munira's characters, once we had the dialogue in English, I went to a girls' school in Ahmedabad for help to translate it into what was a regionally accurate dialect of Gujarati.

SHUCHI: That was one of the pleasures for me—writing about the city I have known intimately in its myriad registers and then watching it come alive on screen in such a credible fashion.

NANDITA: That's the linguistic contribution to the film's authenticity. Of course, costumes and sets help in creating that credibility but the decision to make a film in multiple languages is primarily responsible for that sense of realism. Linguistic credibility enables regional cinema to maintain its emotional sincerity but the hegemony of Hindi language films continues to marginalize these films.

IS HINGLISH THE LANGUAGE OF INDIA'S FUTURE?

Panel Discussion I

PANELLISTS: *Gurcharan Das (moderator), Prasoon Joshi, Prashant Panday, Rita Kothari, Cyrus Broacha, Rahul Dev*

This panel discussion was the most dramatic and controversial event of the conference on Chutnefying English, featuring participants with not just divergent but ideologically irreconcilable positions on language. Gurcharan Das, the moderator, laid the grounds for a practitioner's view on Hinglish, as opposed to an academic view which, according to him, appeared defeatist. His judgement was based on the conference sessions focusing on the hegemonic role of English and the consequent impoverishment of Indian languages. Representing worlds as apart as advertising, media, management, and academics, the panel engaged in an intense debate underscoring the significance of language as a marker of identity in India.

DISCUSSION EXTRACT

GURCHARAN DAS: Through this panel, I want to move beyond the academic discourse of this morning. The word used repeatedly this morning was *postcolonial*. It struck me that 'postcolonial' is a bizarre way to think of contemporary India. It is also defeatist, suggesting victimhood. India, it seems to me, has moved on . . . well beyond the colonial paradigm.

Let us now move towards the practitioners who represent an antidote in some ways to the morning sessions—who celebrate the use of Hinglish. I prefer the word 'Inglish', because the mixing of English with our mother tongues is taking place in all parts of India.

Our practitioners are quite aware of their historic destiny—that we might, in fact, be creating a new language in this country. English is also an appropriate vehicle for such experimentation because it is comparatively recent. It came up only in the fourteenth century and grew up, like Hinglish, in the bazaar. Unlike the French of the Norman aristocracy or the Latin of the Church, English was a bastard language. But amazingly, within a hundred years it had produced Shakespeare. Shakespeare was promiscuous—he took from German, Latin, French—and made English immensely rich as a consequence. Imagine if he had written only in Anglo-Saxon! Instead of putting down Hinglish, we might ask instead, 'When will *we* produce a Shakespeare of Hinglish?' It is a historic moment—as historic as the moment that Urdu was born in the camps of the Mughal Empire.

We still do not know enough about Hinglish and I hope the academic world will examine it and provide answers to questions such as 'What is the structure of Hinglish? Where does the grammar come from? Earlier was it only a language of upward mobility? How did it become the fashionable language of South Bombay and South Delhi? Also, what will happen to English if this language takes over? Will 'standard English' go away? What will happen to our regional languages? Will it prevent us from becoming truly bilingual? Personally, I do not think regional languages are going away, I don't think English will go away. The point is: What kind of English will it be?

PRASOON JOSHI: I was just looking at these advertisements here, and noticed something—what we see are two different kinds or combinations of English. One is where you twist Hindi words, for instance *chutnefying* or *rakhoed*, and you know English well enough to feel comfortable twisting it. The other way is where you insert a word of Hindi or English in the other—that yields a very different language.

The former is more fun, a more *youthful* kind of language, probably emerging from a certain pride the young Indian has suddenly discovered for the country, for his or her roots. In spicing up the language, the young Indian finds his or her own expression of identity. You could not imagine this to have happened in advertising earlier. Today, people who speak chaste English are extinct, in the world of advertising at least. They are not considered 'with it'.

The other language is the language of survival, a language of work where Hindi and English words are not being twisted, but *used as they are*. The structures are not touched, not contorted. I am going into the craft now. When my driver says, '*Mera baap off ho gaya*,' that is a language of communication. He is trying to communicate. He is not even aware that he is using an English word. That's a different kind of Hinglish.

The former is what I call 'mixing and turning', vis-à-vis the guy from a Hindi-medium background who uses it as is. He is not comfortable twisting—he might go wrong somewhere, he is underconfident. Bollywood and the advertising industry use the former. The latter is everyday parlance. The former is experimentation borne of comfort in twisting it—I call that 'Indi'. The other is Hinglish. Two different kind of patterns are evident.

GURCHARAN DAS: You are saying that, depending on the context, if the person is from an English-medium school, he will throw in Hindi words: '*Arre yaar yeh* dangerous *hai!*'

PRASOON JOSHI: No, in fact, it's more like 'I *rakhoed* my pencil there *yaar.*' *Rakhoed* is a very evolved way of speaking ... Too much liberty has been taken there.

GURCHARAN DAS: The other is the language of Hindi TV, an expression such as '*Aaj* Middle East *mein* peace *ho gaya'.* We all agreed that it sounded very natural. What are your thoughts on this? (*pointing to Prashant Panday*)

PRASHANT PANDAY: Language is the reason we exist, so that we communicate with 30 or 40 million people across the country, mainly in urban areas. We are measured by the reception we get. If we do anything wrong, we don't get a second chance. It's a competitive democracy out there. So we tend to be practical and less academically oriented.

Prasoon raised a good point about how languages get mixed up. Let's just understand what is happening at a fundamental level in India, and it is unique to this country. Since 1991, when liberalization happened, economic policy and progress started to dismantle the caste system—the age-old system where your occupation was pre-decided by the caste and place you were born in. Today, development has become much more egalitarian—which strata you come from doesn't matter. As long as you have the right skill set and the right attitude, you can join any sector. Indian anchors now host shows on CNN-Global. I don't think this existed some years ago.

In India, if you come to any office—and quite obviously the melting pot is Bombay—the composition of the workforce will convey to you exactly what we are talking about. There is no common language. It's silly to ask anyone in Bombay—or increasingly in any urban centre—what his mother tongue is.

Look at Bangalore, another major hub for broadcasters. What language do you speak in Bangalore, which has 56 per cent Kannadigas, 18 per cent Tamilians, 15 per cent Telugu-speakers, and 8 per cent Urdu-speakers? What is the language of broadcasting in Bangalore? My point is that the concept of language for us really is one of communication.

Prasoon coined an interesting slogan for us. When we chose the word *mirchi*, everybody, every intellectual told us that *mirchi* stood for something that is necessarily downmarket. That was where we began. Prasoon added his own magic to it: *Mirchi sunne waale* always *khush*. He insisted that it had to be 'always', not *hamesha*. That added the zing to it. At the end of the day, society is mixed up. The Chinese will use, at most, one or two dialects—Chinese with Mandarin or Cantonese—but, in India, you can make so many combinations. And some of these combinations are quite weird, for they are not always about mixing English into the local language. For instance, in Calcutta, our success formula is 'Bindi'—Bengali meets Hindi. This is partly because the music has been such and partly because the local population is exposed to Hindi cinema and Hindi TV.

GURCHARAN DAS: The spread of Hinglish is a democratizing process. It is a way for the rich and the poor to communicate in the same language for the first time. I wonder why and how Hinglish came up in the 1990s? Is it the reforms that brought it about? Is it part of the mental liberation of the young in the 1990s?

PRASOON JOSHI: It is a language of survival. People have to somehow communicate, which is why they construct it. That was the distinction I made: one is for fun, one for survival.

RITA KOTHARI: Prasoon, as a practitioner, you come from the privilege—or opportunity—of having known at least two or three languages well. You know your Urdu and Hindi. It is clear that there is a substratum of some languages, so when you make a departure from it, it is a creative experiment. It is still taking liberties from within a framework. I wonder what you have to say about generations that are operating out of a linguistic vacuum—who do not know *any* language well. I am adopting what might be perceived as a slightly purist attitude though this morning I was ranting against it. But as an academic, I feel there is something to be said about knowing languages well, about virtuosity and using a text beautifully. What's happening around us is a certain kind of 'dumbing down'. You can't deny that.

PRASOON JOSHI: You must have heard the song *'Masti ki pathshala'* from the film *Rang De Basanti*. It has a line that says: *'Talli hoke girne se, samjhi hamne* gravity . . .'* Now this line has the English *gravity*, Punjabi *talli*, Hindi *samjhi*. Which language is the song set in? It expresses a youth's experience and I consider this no less poetic than '*Dekho os ke*' from *Taare Zameen Par*. Both are equally poetic and I am equally proud of both.

How does a language become potent? For one, you can express nuances, the grey shades. I did this *Thanda matlab* Coca-Cola campaign. It was a very verbose campaign that we were adapting for Indonesia for TV by exploiting body language and blending it with the words. If I play the same commercial in two different languages, the commercials are very similar but one has visibly more body language. I don't know when Hinglish will be able to express minute thoughts and poetic feelings but I am not pessimistic. I think the language will grow its roots, sprout its grammar. The purity will create itself around the language.

RITA KOTHARI: I am not advocating purity. I am just saying that there is a longer, richer linguistic spectrum and hybridization evident in your work.

GURCHARAN DAS: Rita, I would not have those fears. You use words like 'dumbing down' but I think a language is always in a process of evolution.

CYRUS BROACHA: I just want to say that my name is Cyrus and my screen name is Purnima. I suffer from tension deficit or whatever it is and feel distracted but not out of disrespect to anyone. To come to Rita's concern about tradition and conservative thinking and purity, my father is Parsi and my mother Catholic. I am a mongrel, and I want to fight for the bastardization of everything. When you want to communicate with someone, are you going to be the alpha male, and put him down by speaking in chaste language? Or do you want to communicate? In the business of media, or whatever it is I am called here for, you change your language, have a conversation, and *then* think of the rules. Of course, purity is important but we come to the rules later. First, we must have a conversation.

When I go the North-East, I start to hone my singing. When I go to Delhi, I get set to talk like this: 'Oh Cyrus, *kera haal hai?* Wassup, yaar?' I go down south and the tenses change. The wonderful thing about India is that we allow everything, we absorb everything, including the British who couldn't adjust with the climate and left, but now speak Punjabi and Hindi. They learnt something from us, we learnt something from them. What's the problem, *yaar*? The whole idea of being in the media is to *communicate*—not superimpose.

RAHUL DEV: I am not a practitioner of Hinglish. I am a Hindi journalist, a bilingual. I don't worry about English at all. My worry is about our languages, but I am no purist. No one here is a purist. I haven't met anyone who doesn't know that language grows and changes intrinsically. But there are some who worry about language. I don't think it's a subject to be taken lightly. I wonder if Mr Das has read any serious work in anything other than English. To wait for a Shakespeare in Hinglish goes beyond the ridiculous. The Hinglish we seem to be discussing since the morning is the Hinglish that entertains, spoken by our kids. But there's a mixture that people who come from the hinterland speak, people not fortunate enough to be born in Delhi and Bombay, people for whom these are dream cities—inhabited only by those who speak in English. When such urbane, metropolitan people decide to sound native, they speak Hinglish. But for those coming from hinterlands, the English words mark an entry into the world of the upwardly mobile—it's a matter of survival, it's a question of acceptance. The two are not the same thing and let's also think of those.

I was once talking to students at an Indian Institute of Technology, the youth regarded as the cream of India. Most of them were ill at ease and couldn't manage either of the two languages well. In fact, they could not frame a single question in one language alone. I am a student of English literature but I hate the status English is acquiring in India.

Imagine the India of 2050, by which time illiteracy would have largely been removed. Extreme poverty would have gone too; people would not be dying any more of starvation. Also, 50 per cent of India would have been urbanized. Imagine the language *they* would use, for work, for *masti*, for *gaali*, for street talk, for chat shows ... Hinglish perhaps.

What, however, would have happened to other Indian languages? They would not have died but would have become emaciated, impoverished, languages of the very poor. You wouldn't even remember that these were mighty languages that created the civilization called India. I don't know whether you have thought of such dangers ...

PRASHANT PANDAY: I think that the meaning of Hinglish is not determined by only the languages, Hindi and English, but also by the tone—and that tone has an upmarket connotation.

PRASOON JOSHI: That's what I say. Hinglish is an attitude with a certain class. For the people who use certain English words in their Hindi, there is no experimentation or attitude. It's just that there is no other word for them except this: 'Sir, *yeh gaadi aapke liye* comfortable *nahiin hogi.*' They do this unselfconsciously.

PRASHANT PANDAY: Hinglish is a phenomenon of Bombay or Delhi, where it is a premium language. But going back to the conversation between Rahul and Mr Das, it is clear that Hinglish has an age divide. If you speak Hinglish, you are necessarily part of the *youth*.

RAHUL DEV: There is a Hinglish of fun, of aspiration but there is also a Hinglish of inferiority—where you fill the gaps with English words. Are we talking only of Delhi and Bombay? Are we not talking of Patna or Ranchi? Take a look at the Hindi of any newspaper, and see how a policeman or villager speaks. An inspector says, '*Is prakaran kee vivechna ho rahi hai.*' This is normal language for some people, which some people sitting in this room may not understand. Do we want such language to go away, and thank Lord Macaulay for giving us English?

RITA KOTHARI: Rahulji, the person who says '*Is prakaran kee vivechna ...*' also says '*Ek* missed call *hai.*'

GURCHARAN DAS: She has a point. We have to understand that for people who went directly to cellphones and bypassed landlines, it's a different India and a different idiom. They never learnt *shuddh* Hindi. What you see as 'humiliation'—which makes people use English words—I see as 'liberation'. The young Indian who is going directly to the cellphone has a route available to him, and he does not have to go through the Hindi*wallahs*, the Telugu*wallahs,* the Kannada*wallahs.*

RITA KOTHARI: I think we are aware that language is an organic process. I think we need to go beyond metropolitan examples, and ask whether Hindi or Hinglish would be a pan-Indian language indeed. Is it spoken in Mizoram for instance, or the deep south in India? We have not gone into these issues yet, and formed opposing camps of 'academics' versus 'practitioners'. I am also interested in whether Hinglish is ready for serious thought. When my students were preparing posters for this conference, a student wanted to use terrorism as a theme but could not pull it off in Hinglish. There was dissonance . . .

PRASOON JOSHI: Your concern is valid but somewhat premature. We need to give this phenomenon some time.

CYRUS BROACHA: I just want to say that when rock 'n' roll happened, there were enough people who proclaimed the death of music. But music survived, as did rock 'n' roll. Whether you like it or not, in the East or the West, I feel I am safer with a smattering of Hindi and English. I don't think we can change that.

PRASOON JOSHI: I agree. It's an organic process. Nobody is *imposing* it on anybody.

RAHUL DEV: All I am saying is that language is a serious issue and not only communication. There is something extra and we also need to address that.

PRASOON JOSHI: Yes, we can't deny changes and experimentation. When Dushyant Kumar was writing *ghazals* in Hindi, how many people opposed the idea of Hindi *ghazals*? And imagine what would have happened if *he* had not been allowed to write.

IS HINGLISH A UNIFYING FORCE?

Panel Discussion II

PANELLISTS: *Santosh Desai (moderator), Urvashi Butalia, R. Raj Rao, Kandaswamy Bharathan, Devyani Sharma, Rahul Kansal, Atul Tandan*

The subject of this panel discussion was evoked by a view proposed in journalistic articles and informal discussions—that Hinglish is gaining currency in diverse and, sometimes, oppositional constituencies: upper class and lower class, north India and south India, Hindi- and English-support groups. The moderator situated the cultural and political context of English in India, and asked each panellist whether Hinglish had a more equalizing and participatory role in India's linguistic and cultural economy. In other words, is Hinglish a unifying force in India? Do bear in mind that the panel comprised people from different walks of life and with distinct ideological positions.

DISCUSSION EXTRACT

SANTOSH DESAI: Let me point out a couple of things to frame the subject for a focused discussion. First, if Hinglish does unify, what is the context in which this unification occurs? To comprehend this, we need to bring English into the context. As a language in India, English has played a role in exclusion. It has worked to exclude people, to marginalize those that do not speak it. The power of English needs to be considered.

Let me relate an example from the film *Guide,* based on R.K. Narayan's famous novel. When the film opens, the protagonist Raju is just out of jail. Sitting outside a temple, he is mistaken for a spiritual leader. To test him, the priests ask him to interpret a Sanskrit *shloka*. He rattles off something. What he rattles off is some English but it sounds like a *shloka* to the awestruck villagers. For them, one incomprehensible language is substituted by another incomprehensible language. One mystical language is replaced by another mystical language. This is one of the roles that English plays in our consciousness.

One way of perceiving Hinglish is to acknowledge the fact that it allows for an extension—an opening up of the boundaries that generally separate English from other languages. It is not like this rigid barrier that English creates between itself and other languages/classes. Think of an English-medium school. Or the 'convent-educated' girl you read about in the matrimonial ads. The film *Oye Lucky, Lucky Oye!* talks of this phenomenon—symbolized through this girl in the window. Without the power of English by your side, she remains mysterious and unattainable to a certain class—because the aspiration she represents is an inaccessible aspiration.

So Hinglish allows us, in some ways, to loosen the idea of English, especially around the margins; that's how you create a space that allows for the inclusion of a larger number of people. In doing so, does Hinglish make the conversation flatter? We need to ask whether this unification is with a narrow purview, and accompanied by a flattening of conversation.

Another crucial question: Do we see Hinglish as a way for Market India to communicate to itself, and others, in a market economy? Is Hinglish an instrument of the market? On the other hand, is Hinglish a sign of vibrant, inventive, novel ways in which languages grow and interact? Are we talking about new sets of meanings and, to articulate them, a new language? If so, is that a powerful kind of strength or a marginal one? Similarly, is Hinglish a language constructed through commercial systems or organic processes?

URVASHI BUTALIA: There is no doubt in my mind that it would help enormously if we had a language in common, across India. However 'a language in common' does not have to be just one language. It can be a pan-Indian language, made of many. That would be both interesting and useful. Such a language doesn't have to rule out existing languages. Also, it would help if we replaced the word 'flattening' with 'democratization'. It would allay some of our fears. Let me cite examples from two areas closest to my heart.

The first, from the feminist perspective. One of the things feminists have struggled with is their invisibility in language and with the hierarchies of languages. The resistances that they have met in making their presence felt in language have taken all kinds of forms. So there are questions such as: What will happen to the richness of language? Why are you flattening things out—doesn't the word 'man' include 'woman'? Why are you insisting on changing things that are part of the acceptable norm?

This dilemma has manifested itself in various ways. It has meant changing and redefining language in particular ways. This exercise is one of resistance to hegemony through language. And though I am on the side of the classicists in terms of maintaining a rich repertoire of language, I do think that there are solidarities to be formed for democratizing language. This can provide an interesting and nuanced way of looking at Hinglish.

My second position is that of a publisher. One of the changes that have taken place in the last decade, in English-language writing and publishing, has been the entry of Hinglish—starting with Salman Rushdie's use of Indian words in *Midnight's Children* (and his refusal to italicize them) to the influx of a bunch of Indian authors who write with Indian words, drawing from their mother languages. It has created lots of problems for us and for editors; we are schooled in old English and suddenly people are writing in what appears to be 'bad' English. But it has also opened up the market to new writers, new readers, and buyers who are comfortable buying authors such as Anurag

Mathur and Chetan Bhagat, whose books are selling in large numbers. They are defeating our old, elite notions of what good writing is. If such changes create a sense of commonality, they need serious attention. I don't know if these changes signify a possible unification, however. I think 'unification' is not the apt word. But yes, to see a set of commonalities and democratization emerge through Hinglish is well worth the cost.

RAJ RAO: For me, the word 'Hinglish' is metaphoric. I would use it to dismantle hegemonic language structures. There are two constructs that came across in this conference—purity and authenticity. Hinglish lacks both. It does not have the authenticity of *shuddh* Hindi or the purity of pure English. That is interesting. It enables me to effect disruptions and I'm concerned with disruptions of all kinds.

I grew up in a neighbourhood in Bombay sandwiched between the Metro and Liberty theatres, that street called Cinema Road and Barrack Road. We were enveloped by the magic world of Bollywood—actors arriving in Impala cars and attending premieres. The kind of Bambaiya Hindi spoken there was already a first step in the direction of Hinglish. But, like Urvashi, I will also speak from two identities—one as an Indian writer in English (the only language I can write in) and the other as a gay man.

As Indian writers in English, we were frequently told by critics, including distinguished ones like the late Meenakshi Mukherjee, that we had not been able to do to the English language what the Caribbeans or Africans had done. We had not creolized English and made it native. Our English was not a living language so we had to abandon writing in English. I worked on Nissim Ezekiel's biography, and the poor man was a victim of this. But I think Hinglish is the way, it is the answer. It is tantamount to creolizing English. In 2004, my novel *The Boyfriend* was being translated into French and I was asked to provide the meanings of three pages of Hindi words for the glossary. Simple things like *chai* or *chapatti*, which I had not realized had made their way into the text. It's only when you translate into a foreign language that you realize how unconsciously this happens—three pages of Hindi words! But I think that's a good thing—an answer to the charge made against English authors. I was reading U.R. Ananthamurthy who says English for us is a language without a memory. But I think you *can* connect to your past through Hinglish.

My other stance has to do with class and sexuality. In this conference, it seems to me there's been a lot of 'us-ing' and 'them-ing' going on. References galore have been made to autorickshaw drivers, car drivers, peons, maidservants . . . Hinglish is seen as *their* language while pure English is *our* language. That is a very bourgeois and hetero-normative way of looking at it. What if there are transgressive relationships? What if there are non-hetero-normative, cross-class, intergenerational relationships? My fiction is full of such relationships. What if I have a relationship with a driver? What do I do? Hinglish is a language that sustains such a relationship. If any of you have read *The Boyfriend,* that is what happens— Hinglish becomes a language of love, of survival. It allows you to connect to people of a different class. Hinglish is a language of compromise.

Transgression must be seen as a defining moment. As I said, hetero-normativity and middle-class values seem to be the constructs for this entire discourse. Once you transcend these constructs, whether we should use Hinglish or not becomes a superfluous and redundant question, indeed something of a luxury. It has to do with privilege. Both parties have to make a compromise. Hinglish enables that compromise. And thus, for me, Hinglish is a language of unification.

SANTOSH DESAI: I have one question to augment the question that is proposed in the topic. Is Hinglish a single force? Just *one* idea? Or is it a combination of several ideas—a word that captures multitudes of different strands or strategies but used under the larger label of 'Hinglish'? Are there different intentions at work here?

KANDASWAMY BHARATHAN: I'd like to deal with the use of language in the movies. I don't understand structures or linguistics. Movies are all about how we communicate and tell a story. The whole point is one of effective communication. It is not about wordplay. If we get the message across, we have achieved our purpose.

The film *Roja*, first made in Tamil, would never have become a pan-Indian film. In this film, we had to evoke the uncertainty of Kashmir. In the early days, when we were building up the action phase of the film, we had this actor playing 'Maadhoo', a tourist in Kashmir. He doesn't know a word of Hindi. He is asked in English, 'Are you a tourist or a terrorist?' These words captured the uncertainty of the environment in Kashmir so pithily but they could not have been effective in Tamil. They had to be used in English. So we didn't translate them into Tamil in the Tamil version.

The film was dubbed in several languages. I saw the Hindi, Bengali, Telugu, and Malayalam versions. Interestingly, none of these films had translated those six words. The presence of English or Hinglish or Tamlish—when added to films—makes for effective communication. As filmmakers, we want to be effective and also blur the south–north divide. So, in that sense, Hinglish is a unifying force. I would say it is *particularly* so in films because 'language' is only one aspect of the movie.

DEVYANI SHARMA: Hinglish does have a unifying function, especially in the complex linguascape of a country like India, where you often face a diversity of interlocutors. More often than not, you do not know what the dominant language of each member in a group is. Hinglish allows you to demote the position of each language in the hierarchy and, by mixing it, downplays the imposition of one over another. For instance, Nishant Shah who made a presentation on the Hinglish in digital media talked about examples of political transgression and other hybridities that parallel this effect of Hinglish. In terms of linguistic structure, we saw evidence that Hinglish is a complex combination of skills available to bilinguals. So I wouldn't agree that Hinglish is only a 'commodification' or artificial construction through commerce and market, and therefore not an organic phenomenon.

But I also wish to diverge from media-oriented definitions of language as a tool/medium of communication. In sociolinguistic terms, a language is a mechanism for social participation. It bears traces of your social group. This makes Hinglish a paradox. For the past two days in this conference, we have been referring to Hinglish at times as a language of privileged speakers, and at others as that of underprivileged speakers. The reason is that different varieties of Hinglish index different locations of class.

If you use fluent Hinglish, particularly mixing standard urban Hindi and English that you have been exposed to, it may be seen as a metropolitan privilege. In other kinds of Hinglish, there are indications of reduced competence and aspirations of upward mobility. So the crucial question is not only that of a speaker but the one receiving it, hearing it, and locating the speaker in a particular class. This will always make Hinglish a part of a stratified context and it *cannot* become, in totality, a unifying force.

On the issue of language change, when changes take place, what are the gains and losses? Although we gain playfulness, political transgression, and social connectivity, are we also losing out with respect to Hinglish? Rupert raised this concern yesterday, by asking whether this is actually change in progress, or simply an added style.

If Hinglish replaces some domains of Hindi in use, this can be seen as a loss of some rich registers. If, however, it is an additional bilingual ability, there is no loss. The concern about loss of registers is real but even here you may argue that rich and literary registers of a language were accessible to some speakers and not all, in any case. Their absence allows the inclusion of speakers who need not pass that test. So there is always a certain interplay in language mixing and change. They are unifying locally but they will never be *totally* unifying.

RAHUL KANSAL: Much of the debate has focused on geographical unification. I feel 'social' unification between classes is far more interesting. I work with both *The Times Of India* and *Navbharat Times*—two newspapers that experiment the most with hybridization of language. And I say that Hinglish is a unifying force, largely as a result of the 'ketchupization' of Hindi rather than the 'chutnefication' of English. Hindi has been like a sponge, soaking as much English as possible.

English has not been a mass language but a language of the elite few. On the other hand, Hindi had mass appeal but no brand. Hindi also had more flexible cultural roots compared to Bengali, Tamil, or Malayalam. Quite a nomadic language, Hindi has actively sought the inclusion of English. It is in that sense a *lower* cultural cache language. Our Hindi editors are told to use as many English words as the readers are used to—and it helps.

When I was in school, there were EMTs and HMTs: English-medium types and Hindi-medium types. The EMTs never revealed their secret love for Mohammed Rafi, citing The Beatles instead. The HMTs, with oiled hair and badly tailored clothes, would not be included in the EMT world. It's wonderful how these boundaries are now blurring, how odd phrases and even sentences are used from English in Hindi and vice versa. 'Democratization' is the right word. It is a great coming together.

ATUL TANDAN: I claim neither intellectual inquiry nor commercial success. I cannot understand why we are discussing whether Hinglish will unify India. This suggests that India is *not* unified and now there is suddenly a magical language that will unify us. I do not buy this, and quote:

> . . . *Chhote chhote shehron se*
> *khali bore dopehron se*
> *hum to jhola uthake chale*
> *barish kam kam lagti hain*
> *nadiya madham lagti hain*
> *hum samundar ke andar chale*
> (Song from Hindi film *Bunty Aur Babli*, 2005)

This aspiration of India cannot be wished away, no matter what the discourses, the registers, the languages. The only India we can talk about is the India of tomorrow. If we are talking about the India of the past, why haven't we talked about Pali, which doesn't exist now? Or Sanskrit, which is not spoken any more? We have talked about Urdu, which still survives; Hindi, which does exist; and, of course, English, which we all aspire to. Why are we so concerned with that English word that we know? How are we to know if 'mummy 'and 'daddy' are English words? Each community will find its own measure of how to be relevant. Is there a new discourse, a new relevance, a new aspiration?

ACKNOWLEDGEMENTS

The editors are grateful to the Mudra Institute of Communications Ahmedabad for supporting this project through its various stages. It provided the financial and intellectual resources, as the Chutnefying English project graduated from the idea of a small seminar to a large conference and eventually, a book. Thanks are also due to the contributors and panellists, and the editoral team at Penguin India.

NOTES

Foreword

1. Delivered as the keynote address, and edited and revised by the author from a transcript.

Return of the Native: Hindi in British English

1. Extracted from a speech by the Prince of Wales at a dinner hosted for the British Asian Community at Windsor Castle (transcript online at www.princeofwales.gov.uk/ speechesandarticles, last accessed on 12 December 2008). In this article, I use 'Hindi–English mixing' or Hinglish to refer to any degree of explicit mixing of Hindi and English in a single utterance. I do not use this term to encompass Indian English, whereby Hindi and other South Asian languages affect the grammar and phonology of the variety of English spoken by Indians. Transliteration of Hindi in the colonial Hinglish examples is faithful to the original published spellings; transliteration of Hindi and Punjabi in contemporary examples is standardized.

2. I adopt Cannadine's focus on class rather than race, but not his relative weighting of racial and class concerns, namely, that 'the British Empire was first and foremost a class act, where individual social ordering often took precedence over collective racial ordering' (2001: 10).

3. British language and culture in colonial India is sometimes described as 'Anglo-Indian' in the literature (e.g., Yule & Burnell 1886), a use distinct from the use of 'Anglo-Indian' to refer to individuals of mixed British-Indian ancestry. To avoid confusion,

I use the phrase 'British Indian' here. I am indebted to Shazia Sadaf for bringing to my attention many of the British Indian extracts discussed here (Sadaf 2007).

4. Definitions in (1a) are from Yule & Burnell (1994 [1886]) and the Oxford English Dictionary.

5. See, for instance, www.encyclopedia.com/doc/1029-COCKNEY.html; some words like *mufti* now appear in more general British usage but initially entered via military registers.

6. Lewis (1991: 25–26) suggests that writers such as Scott and Thackeray were entirely focused on the 'princes, newaubs, nizams', to the complete neglect of other portions of the Indian population which held far greater interest for Orientalist scholars.

7. Note that the presence of British working-class syntax and phonology reminds us of the importance of the middle and working classes of British society as conduits for colonial language mixing.

8. Indeed, such was the prevalence and prestige of British speech that members of the Indian upper classes or higher ranks of the military who were in close contact with the British adopted anglicized pronunciations as well, such as naizam for nizam. Here again we see mutual linguistic influence crossing the ethnic divide but respecting class rank.

9. Rampton (1995) finds predominantly vari-directional uses of stylized Asian English by British Asians. Unidirectional uses of Hindi and Punjabi by the same community suggest a recognized and exploited difference in the relative prestige of non-native and native speech.

10. *Rasmalai* (attractive, usually Asian, girls) and *besti* (shame, embarrassment) in (3b.i) constitute a separate category of lexical innovation to mark local subcultural concepts.

11. I am indebted to the UK Economic and Social Research Council for funding for this project. Transcription conventions: **bold+italic**: Punjabi speech. CAPS: loud speech. =: no pause in uptake of turn. ': glottal stop.

Hindi: Its Threatened Ecology and Natural Genius

1. Not to mention a sixth, the more recently arrived English loan *bat* ('but'), which now features so prominently in the speech of many Hindi speakers.

2. This is in contrast to the situation in pre-modern Hindi, when *jo*

(despite being busy with its other work as a relative pronoun and as a conjunction meaning 'if') had this additional function.

3. Nineteenth-century institutions had to go to extreme lengths to avoid using the word 'Hindi' in their titles—as for example in the 'Nagari Pracharini Sabha' of Banaras (in which Hindi is represented by the name of its script).

4. Colin Masica (1991), *The Indo-Aryan Languages*. Cambridge: Cambridge University Press, p. 73.

5. It is not clear to me where *shuddh* Hindi purists keep or kept their possessions, if not in an *almaari*.

6. V.R. Jagannathan (1981), *Prayog aur prayog*. Delhi: Oxford University Press, p. 63.

7. An interesting case is that of *surakshit*, used to translate the concept 'safe'; its literal meaning 'protected' allows it to work well in such contexts as 'safe areas' (those defended against threats from outside), but not in such contexts as 'safe medicines' (those unlikely to cause harm).

8. Raghuvir Sahay, *Pratinidhi kavitaen*. Delhi: Rajkamal, 1994, p. 159.

9. *Shorter Oxford English Dictionary*, sixth edition, 2007.

10. It is presumably a mere coincidence that the closing two syllables approximate to 'cool it' so neatly.

11. There is a particular irony in the fact that the name 'India', though obviously cognate with 'Indus', 'Hindi', etc., has picked up retroflex consonants during its passage to England.

12. This is the very quality that tends to make translations such pale reflections of their originals.

13. Vinod Kumar Shukla, *Atirikt nahin*. Delhi: Vani Prakashan, 2000, p. 13.

14. Rupert Snell (1990), 'The Hidden Hand: English Lexis, Syntax and Idiom as Determinants of Modern Hindi Usage'. *South Asia Research* 10, pp. 53–68.

15. The matter of idiom would merit research. Hindi assimilates many English idioms (*Taang khiinchna*, to pull someone's leg), while losing many of its own. A collection such as S.W. Fallon's 1886 *A Dictionary of Hindustani Proverbs* (ed. and rev. Capt. R.C. Temple and Lala Faqir Chand, Banaras, Medical Hall Press) shows the great wealth of idiom that once existed in Hindi, and which is perhaps no longer so richly current; but much of it was agrarian and/or misogynistic in reference, and may not be either missed or lamented today.

More Than the Sum of Its Parts: Hinglish as an Additional Communicative Resource

1. The example is from http://www.csmonitor.com/2004/1123/p01s03-wosc.html

2. **Transcription Conventions:**

word, *shabd*	Transcribed English and Hindi items
'word'	English gloss
word, *shabd*	Items of interest
.	Declarative, falling intonation
?	Interrogative, rising intonation
,	Continuing intonation
(.)	Brief, unmeasured pause
(..)	Longer, unmeasured pause
Hin-	Speech halted with a glottal stop
((sound))	Contextual information or comment
A Is ⌈he?	Speaker overlap
B ⌊no.	
(?word)	Uncertain transcription
(??)	Inaudible or incomprehensible utterance

3. See Muysken (2000) on 'doubling' in Finnish/Greek and Popoloca/Spanish; Tsitsipis (1998) on 'coupling' in Albanian/Greek; Myers-Scotton (1993) on 'redundancy' in Swahili/English; Gumperz (1982) on 'reiteration' in Hindi/English and Spanish/English; and Pizer (2008: Personal communication) on 'emphasis' in American Sign Language/English.

4. See Woolard (2004) for an excellent review of research on code-switching.

5. Radio Mirchi is a set of private FM radio stations that started operating soon after the media deregulation of the late 1990s to early 2000s in India. It has been a leader in promoting Hinglish broadcasting.

6. In my research, I do not exclude speech that makes reference to or displays a conscious awareness of the recording device or situation. Such talk is still 'natural conversation'—produced spontaneously by the participants in a particular context. I am not convinced that the researcher or analyst can accurately judge some speech to be more 'authentic' than other speech. All discourse, even in reference to the research setting, has a reality and authenticity for the participants in the interaction. The talk

produced is still 'real' speech. Discussion of the research setting is therefore considered legitimate data for the purposes of my study.

7. Foreign Language and Area Studies fellowship.

The Vernacularization of Online Protests: A Case Study from India

1. Recent work by theorists and media scholars (Charnigo & Barnett-Ellis 2007; Goodings, Locke, & Brown 2007; Boyd & Ellison 2007; Beer 2008; Livingstone 2008; Miller 2008) has focused on the formation of community and the sense of belonging in SNSes.

2. The pink ribbon is, incidentally, the symbol of the international breast awareness campaign. On pink and gender identity (specifically feminine identity), see, among others, Pomerleau, Bolduc, et al. (1990).

Furtive Tongues: Language Politics in the Indian Call Centre

1. Keywords extracted from respondents' own descriptions of the ways in which language training is expected to produce results.

2. My dissertation fieldwork was supported by the American Association of University Women, the National Science Foundation, the South Asia Institute at the University of Texas at Austin, and the Department of Asian Studies at the University of Texas at Austin. All names have been changed to maintain anonymity of participants, respondents, and informants.

3. I refer here to customer service or business-to-customer (B2C) communication. Often, technical support, and business-to-business (B2B) communication demands longer call times and conversations.

4. Soft skills, in themselves a term variously analysed in terms of attendant connotations for the gendering of labour, refer here to modes of speech, presentation, and workers' attitudes ostensibly manifest in their interactions with peers and customers. They cover both the emotional aspects of speaking on the phone as well as the affective and people-specific skills the worker brings in dealing with colleagues, subordinates, and supervisors.

5. At the beginning of 2007, the National Association of Software and Service Companies (NASSCOM), India, predicted a demand

for 1.4 million ITES-BPO professionals by 2010. It also estimated that this meant attracting an additional 500,000 workers into the BPO sector given the decreasing caches of skilled labour populations.

6. 'What is your good name?' as translated from '*Aap ka shubh naam?*' or 'Close the computer', which I imagine is self-explanatory except that it is rendered from the Hinglish '*Computer band karo.*'

7. The paradoxical politics of the need to be fluent in English has been widely documented by scholars in South Asian studies. For a historical analysis of the politics of language education in Maharashtra, see Bénéï (2005); for a case study of how multiple language markets subvert the Indian government's language policies, see LaDousa (2008); also see LaDousa (2007) for ways in which language ideology can be seen to construct particular notions of the Indian state.

8. *Macaulay Minute*, 2 February 1835; for the history of British colonial language policy and the rise of English language dominance, see Brutt-Griffler (2002).

9. The meaning of *khede-gaon* is more specific than just *gaon*, which means 'village'. *Khede-gaon*, in slang, seems to indicate an emphasis on village-ness or lack of knowledge of the city and its ways.

Towards a Political Economy of Hinglish TV

1. Among prominent examples of Hinglish in advertising, one might include Pepsi's campaign *Yeh dil maange more* (The heart wants more); Coke's slogan *Life ho to aisi* (Life should be like this); Domino's Pizza poser *Hungry kya?* (Are you hungry?) and McDonald's campaign spoofs *What your bahana is?* (What is your excuse?). In recent years, numerous successful Bollywood films have had Hinglish titles, such as *Singh Is Kinng*, *Jab We Met*, *Bheja Fry*, and *Love Aaj Kal*. The title of Shyam Benegal's 2008 film set in rural India was changed, reportedly under pressure from the marketing department, to the Hinglish *Welcome To Sajjanpur*; the film was officially registered as *Mahadev Ka Sajjanpur*.

2. Of the 400 languages spoken in India, the Census of India publishes details of 114 (which have 10,000 or more speakers). Of these 114 languages, nineteen are included in the Eighth Schedule of the Constitution while ninety-six are not. Speakers

covered by the scheduled languages constitute just over 96 per cent of India's population and the remaining 4 per cent is accounted for by the non-scheduled languages.

English *Aajkal*: Hinglish in Hindi Cinema

1. For instance, the Parsi family in *Khatta Meetha* (1978) and the Christian family in *Baaton Baaton Mein* (1979).
2. Using the example of the film *Roja*, Madhav Prasad (1998) argues how the arranged marriage had to be sealed with an individual stamp, by the hero's words 'I love you' and thereby create a discourse of the individual, away from the feudal state.

REFERENCES

Foreword

Anand, Dev. 2007. *Romancing With Life: An Autobiography*. New Delhi: Penguin/Viking.

Anklesaria, Havovi (ed.), 2008. *Nissim Ezekiel Remembered*. New Delhi: Sahitya Akademi.

Ezekiel, Nissim. 1988. *Collected Poems 1952–1988*. New Delhi: Oxford University Press.

Khatri, Ayodhya Prasad. [1887] 1960. 'Khari Boli ka Padya'. In Shiv Pujan Sahay and Nalin Vilochan Sharma (eds.), *Ayodhya Prasad Khatri Smarak Granth*. Patna: Bihar Rashtrabhasha Parishad.

Prasad, G.J.V. 2008. 'Always in the Poet's Eye: Nissim Ezekiel's India'. In Havovi Anklesaria (ed.), *Nissim Ezekiel Remembered*, pp. 499–508. New Delhi: Sahitya Akademi.

Trivedi, Harish. 2008. 'From Bollywood to Hollywood: The Globalization of Hindi Cinema'. In Revathy Krishnaswamy and John C. Hawley (eds.), *The Postcolonial and the Global*. Minnesota: University of Minnesota Press.

Trivedi, Harish. 2003. 'The Progress of Hindi: Hindi and the Nation'. In Sheldon Pollock (ed.), *Literary Cultures in History: Reconstructions from South Asia*, pp. 958–1022. Berkeley: University of California Press.

Trivedi, Harish. 1999. 'Salman the Funtoosh: Magic Bilingualism in *Midnight's Children*'. In Meenakshi Mukherjee (ed.), *Rushdie's* Midnight's Children: *A Book of Readings*. Delhi: Pencraft International.

Yule, Henry and A.C. Burnell. 1986 [orig. ed. 1886]. *Hobson-Jobson: A Glossary of Colloquial Anglo-Indian Words and Phrases*. Calcutta: Rupa & Co.

Return of the Native: Hindi in British English

Apache Indian. 1993. 'Arranged Marriage', *No Reservations*. Island Records.

Allen, Charles. 1975. *Plain Tales from the Raj*. London: Deutsch.

Bakhtin, Mikhail M. 1981. In *The Dialogic Imagination: Four Essays by M.M. Bakhtin* (ed. Michael Holquist). Austin, Texas: University of Texas Press.

Brown, P. and S. Levinson. 1987. *Politeness: Some Universals in Language Usage*. Cambridge: Cambridge University Press.

Bourdieu, Pierre. 1977. 'The Economics of Linguistic Exchanges'. *Social Science Information* XVI(6): 645–68.

Cannadine, David. 2001. *Ornamentalism: How the British Saw Their Empire*. New York: Oxford University Press.

Goffman, Erving. 1967. 'On Face Work'. *Interaction Ritual*. New York: Doubleday.

Goodness Gracious Me. BBC comedy series. 1998.

Hill, Jane. 1993. 'Hasta la Vista, Baby: Anglo Spanish in the American Southwest'. *Critique of Anthropology* 13: 145–76.

Lewis, Ivor. 1991. *Sahibs, Nabobs and Boxwallahs; A Dictionary of the Words of Anglo-India*. Bombay: Oxford University Press.

Mahal, Baljinder. 2006. *The Queen's Hinglish: How to Speak Pukka*. Glasgow: HarperCollins.

Malkani, Gautam. 2006. *Londonstani*. London: Harper Perennial.

Myers-Scotton, Carol. 1993. *Duelling Languages*. Oxford: Clarendon Press.

Rampton, Ben. 1995. 'Language Crossing and the Problematization of Ethnicity and Socialization'. *Pragmatics* 5(4): 485–514.

Ronkin, Maggie and Helen E. Karn. 1999. 'Mock Ebonics: Linguistic Racism in Parodies of Ebonics on the Internet'. *Journal of Sociolinguistics* 3(3): 360–80.

Sachdev, Itesh and Howard Giles. 2004. 'Bilingual Accommodation'. In T.K. Bhatia and W.C. Ritchie (eds.), *The Handbook of Bilingualism*, pp. 353–78. Oxford: Blackwell.

Sadaf, Shazia. 2007. 'Sahib's English: A Study of the Peculiarities in the Use of Indian Loan Vocabulary amongst the British Ruling Class in India'. Ph.D. thesis, Senate House, London (and University of Peshawar).

Steele, Flora Annie. 1900. *Voices in the Night.* Montana: Kessinger.

Yule, Henry and A.C. Burnell. 1994 (1886). *Hobson-Jobson: Glossary of Colloquial Anglo-Indian Words and Phrases.* Kent: Linguasia.

The Multilingual Mind, Optimization Theory, and Hinglish

Bhatia, Tej K. and William C. Ritchie. 2009. 'Language Mixing, Universal Grammar and Second Language Acquisition'. *The New Handbook of Second Language Acquisition*, pp. 591–622. Bingley, UK: Emerald Group Publishing.

Bhatia, Tej K. and William C. Ritchie. 2004. 'Bilingualism in the Global Media and Advertising'. *Handbook of Bilingualism*, Chapter 20, pp. 513–46. Oxford: Blackwell.

Bhatia, Tej K., and William C. Ritchie. 2001. 'Language Mixing, Typology, and Second Language Acquisition'. *The Yearbook of South Asian Languages and Linguistics 2001*, *Tokyo Symposium on South Asian Languages: Contact, Convergence and Typology*, pp. 37–62. London/ Delhi: Sage.

Bhatia, Tej K. and William C. Ritchie. 1996. 'Bilingual Language Mixing, Universal Grammar, and Second Language Acquisition'. *Handbook of Second Language Acquisition*, pp. 627–82. San Diego: Academic Press.

Bhatia, Tej K. 2007. *Advertising and Marketing in Rural India.* Delhi: Macmillan.

Bhatia, Tej K. 2006. 'Super-heros to Super Languages: American Popular Culture through South Asian Language Comics'. *World Englishes* 25(2): 279–97.

Bhatia, Tej K. 2000. *Advertising in Rural India.* Tokyo: Tokyo Press.

Bhatia, Tej K. 1989. 'Bilinguals' Creativity and Syntactic Theory: Evidence from Emerging Grammar'. *World Englishes* 8(3): 265–76.

Chomsky, Noam. 1988. *Language and Problems of Knowledge: The Managua Lectures.* Cambridge, Mass./London, England: MIT Press (Current Studies in Linguistics Series 16).

Giles, H. 1984. 'The Dynamics of Speech Accommodation.' *International Journal of the Sociology of Language* 46: 1–55.

Kachru, Yamuna. 2006. 'Mixers Lyricing in Hinglish: Blending and Fusion in Indian Pop Culture'. *World Englishes* 25(2): 223–33.

Khubchandani, L.M. 1997. *Revisualizing Boundaries: A Plurilingual Ethos.* New Delhi: Sage Publications.

Myers-Scotton, C.M. 1993. *Duelling Languages: Grammatical Structure in Code-Switching.* Oxford: Clarendon Press.

Ritchie, William C. and Tej K. Bhatia. 2004. 'Social and Psychological Factors in Language Mixing'. *Handbook of Bilingualism*, Chapter 13, pp. 336–52. Oxford: Blackwell.

Romaine, S. 1989. *Bilingualism.* Oxford: Basil Blackwell.

More Than the Sum of Its Parts: Hinglish as an Additional Communicative Resource

Abutalebi, Jubin, Simona M. Brambati, Jean-Marie Annoni, Andrea Moro, Stefano F. Cappa, and Daniela Perani. 2007. 'The Neural Cost of the Auditory Perception of Language Switches: An Event-related Functional Magnetic Resonance Imaging Study in Bilinguals'. *Journal of Neuroscience* 27(50): 13762–69.

Auer, Peter. 1984. *Bilingual Conversation.* Amsterdam and Philadelphia: John Benjamins Publishing Company.

Auer, Peter. 1995. 'The Pragmatics of Code-switching'. In Lesley, Milroy and Pieter Muysken (eds.), *One Speaker, Two Languages: Cross-disciplinary Perspectives on Code-switching*, pp. 115–35. Cambridge: Cambridge University Press.

Auer, Peter (ed.). 1998. *Code-switching in Conversation: Language, Interaction and Identity.* London; New York: Routledge.

Bhatia, Tej K. and William C. Ritchie. 2008. 'The Bilingual Mind and Linguistic Creativity'. *Journal of Creative Communications* 3(1): 5–21.

Blom, Jan-Peter and John J. Gumperz. 1972. 'Social Meaning in Linguistic Structures: Codeswitching in Norway'. In John J. Gumperz and Dell Hymes (eds.), *Directions in Sociolinguistics*, pp. 407–34. New York: Holt, Rinehart and Winston.

Bucholz, Mary and Kira Hall. 2005. 'Identity and Interaction'. *Discourse Studies* 7(4–5): 585–614.

Finch, Shannon. 2005. 'Repetition in Hindi–English Bilingual Conversation'. MA thesis, The University of Texas at Austin.

Gumperz, John. 1982. *Discourse Strategies*. Cambridge: Cambridge University Press.

Halliday, M.A.K. 1994. *Introduction to Functional Grammar*, 2nd edn. London: Edward Arnold.

Kachru, Braj B. 1978. 'Toward Structuring Code-mixing: An Indian Perspective'. *International Journal of the Sociology of Language* 16: 28–46.

Labov, William. 1974. 'Language Change as a Form of Communication'. In Albert Silverstein (ed.), *Human Communication*, pp. 221–56. Hillsdale, NJ: Erlbaum.

Lambrecht, Knud. 1994. *Information Structure and Sentence Form: Topic, Focus, and the Mental Representation of Discourse Referents.* Cambridge: Cambridge University Press.

Muysken, Pieter. 2000. *Bilingual Speech*. Cambridge: Cambridge University Press.

Myers-Scotton, Carol. 1993. *Social Motivations for Code-switching*. Oxford: Oxford University Press.

Rodriguez-Fornells, A., M. Rotte, H.J. Heinze, T. Noesselt, and T.F. Münte. 2002. 'Brain Potential and Functional MRI Evidence for How to Handle Two Languages with One Brain'. *Nature* 415: 1026–29.

Schiffrin, Deborah. 1987. *Discourse Markers*. Cambridge: Cambridge University Press.

Tsitsipis, Lukas. 1998. *A Linguistic Anthropology of Praxis and Language Shift*. Oxford: Clarendon Press.

Woolard, Kathryn. 2004. 'Codeswitching'. In Alessandro Duranti (ed.), *A Companion to Linguistic Anthropology*, pp. 73–94. Oxford: Blackwell.

Woolard, Kathryn. 1998. 'Simultaneity and Bivalency as Strategies in Bilingualism'. *Journal of Linguistic Anthropology* 8(1): 3–29.

The Vernacularization of Online Protests: A Case Study from India

Beer, David. 2008. 'Social Network(ing) Sites . . . Revisiting the Story So Far: A Response to Dana Boyd and Nichole Ellison'. *Journal of Computer-Mediated Communication* 13: 516–29.

Boyd, Dana M. and Nichole B. Ellison. 2007. 'Social Network Sites: Definition, History, and Scholarship'. *Journal of Computer-Mediated Communication* 13(1), available online at http://jcmc.indiana.edu/vol13/issue1, last accessed on 18 July 2008.

Byrne, Dara N. 2007. 'Public Discourse, Community Concerns, and Civic Engagement: Exploring Black Social Networking Traditions on BlackPlanet.com'. *Journal of Computer-Mediated Communication* 13(1), available online at http://jcmc.indiana.edu/vol13/issue1/, last accessed on 18 July 2008.

Castells, Manuel. 2001. *The Internet Galaxy: Reflections on the Internet, Business, and Society*. Oxford: Oxford University Press.

Charnigo, Laurie and Paula Barnett-Ellis. 2007. 'Checking Out Facebook.com: The Impact of a Digital Trend on Academic Libraries'. *Information Technology and Libraries* 26(1): 23–24.

Crystal, David. 2004. 'The World'll Speak in Hinglish'. http://timesofindia.indiatimes.com/articleshow/msid-880272,prtpage-1.cms, dated 10 October, last accessed on 8 March 2009.

Everett, Anna. 2003. 'Digitextuality and Click Theory: Theses on Convergence in the Digital Age'. In Anna Everett and John T. Caldwell (eds.), *New Media: Theories and Practices of Digitextuality*, pp. 3–28. London; New York: Routledge.

Goodings, Lewis, Abigail Locke, and Steven D. Brown. 2007. 'Social Networking Technology: Place and Identity Mediated Communities'. *Journal of Community and Applied Social Psychology* 17: 463–76.

Jordan, Tim. 2002. *Activism! Direct Action, Hacktivism and the Future of Society*. London: Reaktion.

Livingstone, Sonia. 2008. 'Taking Risky Opportunities in Youthful Content Creation: Teenagers' Use of Social Networking Sites for Intimacy, Privacy and Selfexpression'. *New Media and Society* 10(3): 393–411.

Lovink, Geert. 2002. *Dark Fiber: Tracking Critical Internet Culture*. Cambridge: Massachusetts Institute of Technology.

Manovich, Lev. 2001. *The Language of New Media*. Cambridge: Massachusetts Institute of Technology.

McNay, Lois. 2000. *Gender and Agency: Reconfiguring the Subject in Feminist and Social Theory*. Cambridge: Polity.

Miller, Vincent. 2008. 'New Media, Networking and Phatic Culture'. *Convergence* 14(4): 387–400.

Nayar, Pramod K. 2008. 'New Media, Digitextuality and Public Space: Reading "Cybermohalla"'. *Postcolonial Text* 4(1), available online at http://journals.sfu.ca/pocol/index.php/pct/article/view/786/521.

Nayar, Pramod K. 2010. *An Introduction to Cybercultures.* Cambridge, Malden: Wiley-Blackwell.

Pomerleau, Andrée, Daniel Bolduc, Gérard Malcuit, and Louise Cossette. 1990. 'Pink or Blue: Environmental Gender Stereotypes in the First Two Years of Life'. *Sex Roles* 22(5–6): 359–67.

Shah, Nishant. 2007. 'Subject to Technology: Internet Pornography, Cyber-terrorism and the Indian State'. *Inter-Asia Cultural Studies* 8(3): 349–66.

Shildrick, Margrit. 1997. *Leaky Bodies and Boundaries: Feminism, Postmodernism and (Bio)ethics.* London; New York: Routledge.

Susan, Nisha. 2009. 'Why We Said Pants to India's Bigots'. *The Observer,* dated 15 February 2009, available online at http://www.guardian.co.uk/commentisfree/2009/feb/15/india-gender, last accessed on 29 May 2009.

Thomas, Douglas. 2002. *Hacker Culture.* Minneapolis; London: Minnesota University Press.

Werbner, Pnina. 2006. 'Vernacular Cosmopolitanism'. *Theory, Culture and Society* 23(2–3): 496–98.

Wittel, Andreas. 2001. 'Toward a Network Sociality'. *Theory, Culture and Society* 18(6): 51–76.

Furtive Tongues: Language Politics in the Indian Call Centre

Bénéï, V. 2005. 'Of Languages, Passions and Interests: Education, Regionalism and Globalization in Maharashtra, 1800-2000'. In J.A.C.F. Assayag (ed.), *Globalizing India: Perspectives from Below*, pp. 141–62. London: Anthem.

Bourdieu, P. 1984. *Distinction: A Social Critique of the Judgement of Taste.* London: Routledge.

Bourdieu, P., R.K. Harker, C. Mahar, and C. Wilkes. 1990. *An Introduction to the Work of Pierre Bourdieu: The Practice of Theory.* New York: St Martin's Press.

Bourdieu, P. and J.C. Passeron. 1990. *Reproduction in Education, Society, and Culture.* London: Newbury Park, Calif., Sage in association with

Theory, Culture & Society, Dept. of Administrative and Social Studies, Teesside Polytechnic.

Bourdieu, P. and J.B. Thompson. 1991. *Language and Symbolic Power*. Cambridge: Harvard University Press.

Brutt-Griffler, J. 2002. *World English: A Study of Its Development*. Clevedon, England: Multilingual Matters Press.

Chatterjee, P. 1990. 'The Nationalist Resolution of the Women's Question'. In K.S.A.S. Vaid (ed.), *Recasting Women: Essays in Indian Colonial History*, pp. 233–53. New Brunswick: Rutgers University Press.

Cowie, C. 2007. 'The Accents of Outsourcing: The Meanings of "Neutral" in the Indian Call Centre Industry'. *World Englishes* 26(3): 316–30.

Fernandes, L. 2006. *India's New Middle Class: Democratic Politics in an Era of Economic Reform*. Minneapolis: University of Minnesota Press.

Kachru, B.B. 1983. *The Indianization of English: The English Language in India*. Delhi: Oxford University Press.

King, R.D. 1997. *Nehru and the Language Politics of India*. Delhi; New York: Oxford University Press.

LaDousa, C. 2008. 'Disparate Markets: Language, Nation and Education in North India'. *American Ethnologist* 32(3): 460–78.

LaDousa, C. 2007. 'Of Nation and State: Language, School, and the Reproduction of Disparity in a North Indian City'. *Anthropological Quarterly* 80(4): 925–59.

Macaulay, T.B.M. and G.M. Young. 1967. *Macaulay, Prose and Poetry*. Cambridge: Harvard University Press.

Ong, A. 1999. *Flexible Citizenship: The Cultural Logics of Transnationality*. Durham: Duke University Press.

Pennycook, A. 1998. *English and the Discourses of Colonialism*. London; New York: Routledge.

Ramanathan, V. 2005. *The English–Vernacular Divide: Postcolonial Language Politics and Practice*. Clevedon; Buffalo: Multilingual Matters.

Sharpe, J. 1995. 'Figures of Colonial Resistance'. In G.G. Bill Ashcroft and Helen Tiffin (eds), *The Post-colonial Studies Reader*, pp. 99–116. London; New York: Routledge.

Sonntag, S. 2000. 'Ideology and Policy in the Politics of the English Language in North India'. In T. Ricento (ed.), *Ideology, Politics and Language Policies: Focus on English*, pp. 133–50. Amsterdam; Philadelphia: John Benjamins Publishing Company.

Urciuoli, B. 1996. *Exposing Prejudice: Puerto Rican Experiences of Language, Race, and Class*. Boulder: Westview Press.

Towards a Political Economy of Hinglish TV

Adorno, Theodor. 1991. *The Cultural Industry: Selected Essays on Mass Culture*. London: Routledge.

Appadurai, Arjun. 1990. 'Disjuncture and Difference in the Global Cultural Economy'. *Public Culture* 2(2): 1–24.

Athique, Adrian. 2009. 'Leisure Capital in the New Economy: The Rapid Rise of the Multiplex in India'. *Contemporary South Asia* 17(2): 123–40.

Baldauf, Scott. 2004. 'A Hindi–English Jumble, Spoken by 350 Million'. *The Christian Science Monitor*, 23 November.

Butcher, Melissa. 2003. *Transnational TV, Cultural Identity and Change: When STAR Came to India*. New Delhi: Sage.

Credit Suisse. 2006. *Opportunities for Hollywood in Bollywood: India Media and Entertainment Tour*. Equity Research, 1 December.

DeBord, Guy. 1977. *The Society of the Spectacle*. Detroit: Red and Black (First published in 1967 as *La societe du spetacle* by Buchet-Chastel, Paris.)

FICCI (Federation of Indian Chambers of Commerce and Industry). 2007. *Indian Entertainment and Media Industry: A Growth Story Unfolds*. Mumbai: FICCI and PricewaterhouseCoopers.

Ganguly-Scrase, Ruchira and Timothy Scrase. 2008. *Globalization and the Middle Classes in India: The Social and Cultural Impact of Neoliberal Reforms*. London: Routledge.

Garcia Canclini, Nestor. 1995. *Hybrid Cultures: Strategies for Entering and Leaving Modernity*. Minneapolis: University of Minnesota Press.

Kohli-Khandekar, Vanita. 2006. *The Indian Media Business*, 2nd edn. New Delhi: Sage.

Kachru, Yamuna. 2006. 'Mixers Lyricing in Hinglish: Blending and Fusion in Indian Pop Culture'. *World Englishes*, 25(2): 223–33.

Kachru, Yamuna and Larry Smith. 2008. *Cultures, Contexts and World Englishes*. New York: Routledge.

Kraidy, Marwan. 2005. *Hybridity, or the Cultural Logic of Globalization*. Philadelphia: Temple University Press.

Lash, Scott and Celia Lury. 2007. *Global Culture Industry*. Oxford: Polity.

Mahal, Baljinder. 2006. *The Queen's Hinglish: How to Speak Pukka*. London: Collins.

Mehta, Nalin. 2008. *India on TV: How Satellite News Channels Have Changed the Way We Think and Act*. New Delhi: HarperCollins.

Nayar, Pramod. 2009. *Seeing Stars: Spectacle, Society and Celebrity Culture*. New Delhi: Sage.

News Corp. 2008. *News Corp. 2008 Annual Report: Across the Globe: A Billion Times a Day*. New York: News Corp.

PRC (Pew Research Centre). 2009. *Confidence in Obama Lifts US Image Around the World: Most Muslim Publics Not So Easily Moved*. Pew Global Attitudes Project, PRC for the People and the Press, Washington. Released 23 July 2009. Available online at pewglobal.org/reports/display.php?ReportID=264, 12 December.

PRC (Pew Research Centre). 2005. *US Image Up Slightly, But Still Negative: American Character Gets Mixed Reviews*. Pew Global Attitudes Project, PRC for the People and the Press, Washington. Released 23 June 2005. Available online at pewglobal.org/reports/display.php?ReportID=247, 12 December.

Sklair, Leslie. 2002. *Globalization: Capitalism and its Alternatives*. Oxford: Oxford University Press.

Thussu, Daya Kishan. 2007a. 'The "Murdochization" of News? The Case of Star TV in India'. *Media, Culture and Society* 29(3): 593–611.

Thussu, Daya Kishan. 2007b. *News as Entertainment: The Rise of Global Infotainment*. London: Sage.

Thussu, Daya Kishan. 2007c. 'Mapping Global Media Flow and Contra-Flow'. n Daya Kishan Thussu (ed.), *Media on the Move: Global Flow and Contra-Flow*. London: Routledge.

Thussu, Daya Kishan (ed.). 1998. *Electronic Empires—Global Media and Local Resistance*. London: Arnold.

Trivedi, Harish. 2008. 'From Bollywood to Hollywood: The Globalization of Hindi Cinema'. In Revathi Krishnaswamy and John Hawley (eds.), *Post-colonial and the Global*. Minneapolis: University of Minnesota Press.

English *Aajkal*: Hinglish in Hindi Cinema

Fernandes, Leela. 2000. 'Nationalizing the "Global": Media Images, Cultural Politics and the Middle Class in India'. *Media, Culture and Society* 22: 611–28.

Kothari, Rita. 2006. *Translating India: The Cultural Politics of English* (rev. edn). New Delhi: Foundation Books and Cambridge University Press.

Trivedi, Harish. 2007. 'All Kinds of Hindi: The Evolving Language of Hindi Cinema'. In Vinay Lal and Ashis Nandy (eds.), pp. 51–86, *Fingerprinting Popular Culture: The Mythic and the Iconic in Indian Cinema*. New Delhi: Oxford University Press.

Prasad, M. Madhava. 1998. *Ideology of the Hindi Film: A Historical Construction*. New Delhi: Oxford University Press.

Views from a Different India: Not Hinglish but Nagamese

Ao, Temsula. 1993. 'Some Reflections on the Linguistic Diversity of Nagaland'. In B.B. Kumar (ed.), *Modernization in Naga Society*, pp. 149–155. New Delhi: Omsons.

Baruah, Dharani. 1969. *Nagamese into Anglo-Hindi-Ao.* Mokukchang, Nagaland: Nabajiban Press.

Bhattacharjya, Dwijen. 2001. 'The Genesis and Development of Nagamese: Its Social History and Linguistic Structure'. Ph.D. dissertation, The City University of New York, New York.

Coupe, A.R. 2007. 'Converging Patterns of Clause Linkage in Nagaland'. In Miestamo Matti and Bernard Walchili (eds), *New Challenges in Typology: Broadening the Horizons and Redefining the Foundations*, pp. 339–61. Berlin; New York: Mouton de Gruyter.

Dholabhai, Nishit. 2004a. 'Hindi with a Twist for Naga Police'. *The Telegraph*, 15 March.

Dholabhai, Nishit. 2004b. 'Bazaar Dialect Intrudes Naga Homes'. *The Telegraph*, 26 June.

Hutton, J.H. 1921. *The Angami Nagas.* London: Macmillan and Co.

Kashyap, Samudra Gupta. 2008. 'Poll Managers Adopt Naga "Bastard Language"'. *The Indian Express*, 4 March.

Mackenzie. A. 1979. *The North-East Frontier of India.* Delhi: Mittal Publications.

Mazumdar, Jaideep. 2007. 'The Hills Are Alive: A Local Lad on National TV Unites a State'. *Outlook*, 1 October.

Punathambekar, Aswin. 2009. 'Reality Television and the Making of Mobile Publics: The Case of "Indian Idol"'. Available online at www-personal umich.edu/~aswinp/Aswin MobilePublics.doc, last accessed on 25 June 2009.

Moral, Dipankar. 1997. 'North-east as a Linguistic Area'. *Mon-Khmer Studies* 27: 43–53.

Sachdeva, Rajesh. 2002. 'Exploring Ground Conditions for Code Production in Multilingual Settings'. In *Linguistic Landscaping in India with Particular Reference to the New States*, Seminar Proceedings, Mysore: CIIL.

Sachdeva, Rajesh. 2001. 'A View-point from the Top: A Dialogue with Shri I. Imkong, Ex-minister of School Education, Government of Nagaland'. In Rajesh Sachdeva (ed.), *Language Education in Nagaland: Sociolinguistic Dimensions*, pp. 10–18. New Delhi: Regency Publications.

Sachdeva, Rajesh. 2000. 'Towards an Explicit Language Policy in Education for Nagaland'. *Vartavaha* 6.

Talukdar, B.N. 2003. 'Language Problem in the North-East region'. In Mrinal Miri (ed.), *Linguistic Situation in North-East India*, pp. 83–88. New Delhi: Concept Publishing Company.

Tamil, Hindi, English: The New Ménage à Trois

Bassnett, Susan and Harish Trivedi (eds). 1999. *Post-colonial Translation: Theory and Practice.* London; New York: Routledge.

Dyson, Ketaki Kushari. 1993. 'Forging a Bilingual Identity: A Writer's Testimony'. In Pauline Burton, Ketaki Kushari Dyson, and Shirley Ardener (eds.), *Bilingual Women: Anthropological Approaches to Second Language Use.* Minneapolis: University of Minnesota Press.

Gupta, R.S. (ed.). 1999. *Literary Translation.* New Delhi: Creative Books.

Narayan, R.K. 1949. *Mr. Sampath.* Mysore: Indian Thought Publications.

Narayan, R.K. 1961. *The Man-Eater of Malgudi.* Chennai: Indian Thought Publications.

Narayan, R.K. 1967. *The Vendor of Sweets.* Chennai: Indian Thought Publications.

Narayan, R.K. 1970. *A Horse and Two Goats*. Mysore: Indian Thought Publications.

Narayan, R.K. 1979. 'English in India: Some Notes on Indian English Writing'. In M.K. Naik (ed.), *Aspects of Indian Writing in English: Essays in Honour of Professor K.R. Srinivasa Iyengar*. Madras: Macmillan.

Prasad, G.J.V. 1999a. 'The Untranslatable Other: The Language of Indian English Fiction'. In R.S. Gupta (ed.), *Literary Translation*.

Prasad, G.J.V. 1999b. 'Writing Translation: The Strange Case of the Indian English Novel'. In Susan Bassnett and Harish Trivedi (eds.), *Post-colonial Translation*.

NOTES ON CONTRIBUTORS

Gulzar started out as a poet with the Progressive Writers' Association. He turned lyricist with Bimal Roy's *Bandini* (1963). While working as Roy's full-time assistant, he wrote scripts, dialogues and lyrics for several film-makers before directing his first feature film, *Mere Apne*, in 1971. Over the next decade and a half he made some of the enduring classics of Hindi cinema like *Parichay*, *Mausam*, *Aandhi*, *Angoor* and *Ijaazat*, remembered not only for their storytelling but also their unforgettable songs. He also directed the TV series *Mirza Ghalib*, a much-lauded biopic of the poet. He continues to be one of the most popular lyricists in mainstream Hindi cinema with several chartbusters to his credit in recent years. He lives and works in Mumbai.

Shannon Anderson-Finch received her PhD in linguistics from the University of Texas at Austin in 2009. In addition to Hinglish and Hindi–English code-switching, her interests include bilingualism, second-language acquisition, foreign-language pedagogy and cross-cultural communication. She currently lives and works in Hyderabad, where she leads a communication training programme for a multinational professional services firm.

Kandaswamy Bharathan is currently executive director and producer, Kavithalayaa Productions, which produced, among many acclaimed media productions, the film *Roja*. Bharathan was instrumental in tapping Japanese and Far Eastern markets through the film *Muthu: The Dancing Maharaja*, which became a phenomenal success in Japan. He also serves as a spokesperson for the Indian entertainment industry in the United States, Europe and Japan through active participation in film festivals, international conferences and events. Currently, he is a visiting faculty member at the Indian Institute of Management, Ahmedabad.

Tej K. Bhatia is a professor in the linguistics and cognitive sciences programmes at Syracuse University, New York. He also served as director of the linguistic sciences programme and acting director of the cognitive sciences programme at Syracuse. He is a visiting research professor at the Research Institute for Languages and Cultures of Asia and Africa, TUFS. He has published works on a wide range of topics, including intercultural and global communication; language acquisition (child and adult language); the bilingual brain; global advertising; Indian diaspora; and the languages of India and Pakistan, particularly Hindi, Urdu and Punjabi. His publications include three handbooks with William C. Ritchie: *Handbook of Bilingualism*, *Handbook of Child Language Acquisition* and *Handbook of Second Language Acquisition*. His authored books include *Advertising and Marketing in Rural India*; *Advertising in Rural India: Language, Marketing Communication, and Consumerism*; *Colloquial Urdu*; *Colloquial Hindi*; *Negation in South Asian Languages*; *Punjabi: A Cognitive-Descriptive Grammar*; and *A History of the Hindi Grammatical Tradition*. With Professor K. Machida, he has co-authored *Kosurebe Hanaseru CD Hindi-go* (Let us talk in Hindi; includes a book and a CD) in Japanese.

Mahesh Bhatt is a renowned film-maker. His film *Saransh* won him the Special Jury Award at the Moscow Film Festival in 1985. Bhatt became famous with films like *Arth*, *Janam* and *Naam*. In 1987 he turned producer, when he set up his own banner, Vishesh Films, with his brother Mukesh Bhatt. He went on to become one of the most recognized figures of the Indian film industry, directing both critically acclaimed films (such as *Daddy* and *Swayam*) and commercial, romantic hits (such as *Awaargi*, *Aashiqui* and *Dil Hai Ki Manta Nahin*).

Cyrus Broacha is an MTV India VJ and stand-up comedian. Starting with a campus show, *MTV-U*, he has now gained national recognition, consolidated by his show *MTV Bakra*. Broacha is MTV International's 'Ambassador for AIDS Awareness'.

Urvashi Butalia is co-founder of India's first feminist publishing house, Kali for Women, and now runs Zubaan, an imprint of Kali. She has long been involved in the women's movement and writes on a wide range of issues. Among her publications are *Women and the Hindu Right: A Collection of Essays* (co-edited with Tanika Sarkar); *Speaking Peace: Women's Voices from Kashmir* (edited) and the award-winning history of Partition, *The Other Side of Silence: Voices from the Partition of India*. She is a recipient of the Padma Shri.

Gurcharan Das is the author of *India Unbound* and *The Difficulty of Being Good: On the Subtle Art of Dharma*. He writes regular columns for the *Times of India*, *Dainik Bhaskar*, *Eenadu*, *Sakal* and other papers, and periodically for the *Wall Street Journal*, *Financial Times*, *Foreign Affairs* and *Newsweek*. His other literary works include a novel, *A Fine Family*; a book of essays, *The Elephant Paradigm*; and an anthology, *Three English Plays*. He was CEO of Procter & Gamble before he took early retirement to become a full-time writer.

Nandita Das has acted in over thirty feature films in ten different languages with many eminent directors. *Firaaq*, her directorial debut, has travelled to many festivals, winning appreciation from both critics and audiences. It has won ten international awards in addition to ten national awards. She was a member of the main jury at the Cannes Film Festival in 2005, among others. She has done her master's in social work from the University of Delhi. Currently, she is chairperson of the Children's Film Society.

Santosh Desai is the author of *Mother Pious Lady: Making Sense of Everyday India*. He is a columnist, media critic and social commentator. Desai is the MD and CEO of Futurebrands, a branding services and advisory company, and serves on the boards of ING Vysya Bank and the Mumbai Business School.

Rahul Dev is editor-in-chief, *Aaj Samaj*, a Delhi-based Hindi daily. A bilingual journalist for over thirty years, he has worked in and headed newspapers as well TV news channels.

Prasoon Joshi is a poet, songwriter and a communication professional who is considered to have led an Indian culture revolution in the westernized world of advertising. He has won more than 400 national and international awards, including the National Film Award for best lyrics for his work in *Taare Zameen Par*. Joshi's lyrics in *Rang De Basanti* and *Taare Zameen Par* have established him among the leading lyricists in the film industry. He was chairman of the jury at Cannes Festival in 2008. Apart from three books of poetry, he has also published works of prose. His first book, *Main Aur Woh,* was published when he was seventeen years old. He is currently working on his fourth book, a collection of his poetry.

Rahul Kansal is director of the *Times of India*. In 1979 he graduated from the Indian Institute of Management, Kolkata, and started his career doing market research with IMRB. After spending some time with McDowell's, when they were launching a new soft drink, Kansal began his fifteen-year stint in advertising. He then worked with Ulka, Ogilvy & Mather, Mudra and Leo Burnett, which he left as deputy MD to join his current assignment with the *Times of India*.

Rita Kothari is the author of *Translating India: The Cultural Politics of English* and *The Burden of Refuge: The Sindhi Hindus of Gujarat*. A well-known translation studies scholar and practitioner, her publications of note include *Angaliyat: The Stepchild*; *Speech and Silence: Literary Journeys by Gujarati Women*; and *Unbordered Memories: Partition Stories from Sindh*. She co-edited *Decentring Translation Studies: India and Beyond* and co-translated *Modern Gujarati Poetry: A Selection*. Kothari heads the media and communications department at the Mudra Institute of Communications, Ahmedabad. She is currently completing a manuscript about the border villages in Kutch, Gujarat.

Shuchi Kothari is a screenplay writer and academic. She writes and produces shorts and features in the media industries in New Zealand, India and the United States. Her film credits include critically acclaimed films such as *Firaaq*, *Apron Strings* and *Coffee & Allah*, and the television series *A Thousand Apologies*. She is a senior lecturer in the film, television, and media studies department at the University of Auckland in New Zealand.

Mathangi Krishnamurthy is an Andrew Mellon postdoctoral fellow at the Institute for Research in the humanities and the anthropology department at the University of Wisconsin, Madison. She completed her doctoral work from the University of Texas at Austin and is currently working on her manuscript focusing on the experiences of young call-centre workers. She has also published and reviewed for the journals *Anthropology of Work Review* and *South Asian Diaspora*.

Siddharth Mishra is an advertising professional based in Mumbai. Originally from Patna, Siddharth grew up in a middle-class, academically oriented family. He moved to Jalandhar to study engineering and then to Ludhiana and Delhi for work. He completed his postgraduate studies at the Mudra Institute of Communications, Ahmedabad, and is now trying to make his mark in the advertising world in Mumbai. Mishra is actively involved in theatre and writing. His other interests lie in cinema, literature, music and quizzing.

Rohini Mokashi-Punekar is associate professor in the humanities and social sciences department, Indian Institute of Technology,

Guwahati. Besides several papers in books and journals, she is the author of *On the Threshold: Songs of Chokhamela*; *Untouchable Saints: An Indian Phenomenon*, which she co-edited with Eleanor Zelliot; and *Vikram Seth: An Introduction*. She is currently translating medieval Varkari poetry from the Marathi, an anthology of which will be published by Penguin in its Black Classics series.

Pramod K. Nayar teaches in the English department, University of Hyderabad. His recent publications include *An Introduction to New Media and Cybercultures*; *Postcolonialism: A Guide for the Perplexed*; *Packaging Life: Cultures of the Everyday*; *Seeing Stars: Spectacle, Society and Celebrity Culture*; and *English Writing and India, 1600–1920: Colonizing Aesthetics*. Among his forthcoming books is *States of Sentiment: The Cultural Politics of Emotions*.

Soumik Pal was born and brought up in Durgapur, a town in West Bengal. He completed his higher studies in Kolkata and then at the Mudra Institute of Communications, Ahmedabad. Though currently employed as an advertising professional in Gurgaon, his real passion lies in the world of cinema. He was a student of film studies at Jadavpur University, Kolkata. Pal has dabbled in short film-making and writing, and is also interested in world cinema and film theory.

Prashant Panday is executive director and CEO of Radio Mirchi. In 2008 Radio Mirchi was ranked the No. 1 media brand in India by an IMRB survey—ahead of the *Times of India* (the biggest newspaper by revenues) and Star Plus (the No. 1 TV channel in India).

G.J.V. Prasad discusses life and literature at Jawaharlal Nehru University, where he is professor of English, the chairperson of the Centre for English Studies and the coordinator of their UGC Special Assistance Programme. His major research interests are Indian English literature, contemporary theatre, Dalit writing, Australian literature and translation theory. Prasad is also a well-known Indian English poet and novelist. His novel *A Clean Breast* was shortlisted for the Commonwealth Prize for best first book from the Eurasia region in 1994 and his collection of poems, *In Delhi without a Visa* (1996), is considered a path-breaking volume. He is a recipient of the Katha award for translation from Tamil. He has co-edited with Sara Rai a collection of stories from Indian languages, *Imaging the Other*. His academic publications include *Continuities in Indian English Poetry: Nation Language Form* and three edited volumes of critical essays—

Vikram Seth: An Anthology of Recent Criticism, The Lost Temper: Essays on Look Back in Anger and the recently published *Translation and Culture: Indian Perspectives.* He has also co-edited *Indian English and Vernacular India.* He is the editor of the Penguin (now Longman) study editions of Samuel Beckett's *Waiting for Godot* and John Osborne's *Look Back in Anger.* His forthcoming publication is *Writing India, Writing English.* He has also written a book of recipes, *South Indian Vegetarian Kitchen,* published by Roli Books. He is the current editor of *JSL,* the journal of the School of Language, Literature and Culture Studies, JNU, and vice-president of the Indian Association for Commonwealth Literature and Language Studies.

R. Raj Rao's latest book is *Hostel Room 131,* a novel. He is a professor in the English department, University of Pune, where he teaches Indian writing in English and creative writing, among other things. He is the author of *Slide Show,* a collection of poems; *One Day I Locked My Flat in Soul City,* a collection of short stories; *The Wisest Fool on Earth and Other Plays*; and *Nissim Ezekiel: The Authorized Biography.* He has edited *Ten Indian Writers in Interview* and co-edited *Image of India in the Indian Novel in English (1960–1980).* Rao is also one of India's leading gay-rights activists.

Devyani Sharma is a lecturer in linguistics at Queen Mary, University of London. She has published extensively in the areas of postcolonial Englishes, bilingualism, sociolinguistics, second-language acquisition and discourse analysis. She is currently completing a book on the formation of new dialects in bilingual communities.

Rupert Snell is a professor at the University of Texas, Austin. He has written numerous Hindi course-books, while working primarily on pre-modern poetry in the Braj dialect. His 1990 paper *The Hidden Hand: English Lexis, Syntax and Idiom as Determinants of Modern Hindi Usage* addresses an aspect of the subject of this volume. His translations from modern Hindi include Harivansh Rai Bachchan's autobiography, *In the Afternoon of Time.* Snell's current projects include an expanded edition of his 1991 book *The Hindi Classical Tradition: A Braj Bhasa Reader*; a study of the poetics of the *Satsai* of Biharilal as well as an English novel supplying a back story to Biharilal's life; and *A Ramcharitmanas Reader.* He is a co-collaborator for this conference.

Atul Tandan has worked as marketing manager at Hindustan Lever Ltd, as GM (Sales) at Cadbury (India) Ltd, as vice-president (marketing) at Bajaj Electricals Ltd and as MD at JL Morison (India) Ltd. He was director, Mudra Institute of Communications, Ahmedabad, from March 2001 to June 2009. His current responsibilities include advisory and consulting with Cadila Pharmaceuticals Ltd and JL Morison (India) Ltd.

Harish Trivedi is professor of English at the University of Delhi and has been visiting professor at the universities of Chicago and London. He is the author of *Colonial Transactions: English Literature and India*, and has co-edited *The Nation across the World: Postcolonial Literary Representations*; *Literature and Nation: Britain and India 1800–1990*; *Post-colonial Translation: Theory and Practice*; and *Interrogating Post-colonialism: Theory, Text and Context*. He has translated a biography of Premchand from Hindi into English (*Premchand: His Life and Times*) and contributed a chapter on 'Hindi and the nation' to *Literary Cultures in History*, edited by Sheldon Pollock. Now and then, he also writes in Hindi.

Daya Kishan Thussu is professor of international communication and co-director of India Media Centre at the University of Westminster in London. Among his recent publications are *Internationalizing Media Studies* and *News as Entertainment: The Rise of Global Infotainment*. He is the founder and managing editor of the Sage journal *Global Media and Communication*.